T0211118

Communications
in Computer and Information Science   **2098**

Rationale

The CCIS series is devoted to the publication of proceedings of computer science conferences. Its aim is to efficiently disseminate original research results in informatics in printed and electronic form. While the focus is on publication of peer-reviewed full papers presenting mature work, inclusion of reviewed short papers reporting on work in progress is welcome, too. Besides globally relevant meetings with internationally representative program committees guaranteeing a strict peer-reviewing and paper selection process, conferences run by societies or of high regional or national relevance are also considered for publication.

Topics

The topical scope of CCIS spans the entire spectrum of informatics ranging from foundational topics in the theory of computing to information and communications science and technology and a broad variety of interdisciplinary application fields.

Information for Volume Editors and Authors

Publication in CCIS is free of charge. No royalties are paid, however, we offer registered conference participants temporary free access to the online version of the conference proceedings on SpringerLink (http://link.springer.com) by means of an http referrer from the conference website and/or a number of complimentary printed copies, as specified in the official acceptance email of the event.

CCIS proceedings can be published in time for distribution at conferences or as postproceedings, and delivered in the form of printed books and/or electronically as USBs and/or e-content licenses for accessing proceedings at SpringerLink. Furthermore, CCIS proceedings are included in the CCIS electronic book series hosted in the SpringerLink digital library at http://link.springer.com/bookseries/7899. Conferences publishing in CCIS are allowed to use Online Conference Service (OCS) for managing the whole proceedings lifecycle (from submission and reviewing to preparing for publication) free of charge.

Publication process

The language of publication is exclusively English. Authors publishing in CCIS have to sign the Springer CCIS copyright transfer form, however, they are free to use their material published in CCIS for substantially changed, more elaborate subsequent publications elsewhere. For the preparation of the camera-ready papers/files, authors have to strictly adhere to the Springer CCIS Authors' Instructions and are strongly encouraged to use the CCIS LaTeX style files or templates.

Abstracting/Indexing

CCIS is abstracted/indexed in DBLP, Google Scholar, EI-Compendex, Mathematical Reviews, SCImago, Scopus. CCIS volumes are also submitted for the inclusion in ISI Proceedings.

How to start

To start the evaluation of your proposal for inclusion in the CCIS series, please send an e-mail to ccis@springer.com.

Jianming Zhu · Qianhong Wu · Yong Ding ·
Xianhua Song · Zeguang Lu
Editors

Blockchain Technology and Application

6th CCF China Blockchain Summit, CBCS 2023
Haikou, China, December 15–18, 2023
Revised Selected Papers

 Springer

Editors
Jianming Zhu
Central University of Finance and Economics
Beijing, China

Yong Ding
Guilin University of Electronic Technology
Guilin, China

Zeguang Lu
National Academy of Guo Ding Institute
of Data Science
Beijing, China

Qianhong Wu
Beihang University
Beijing, China

Xianhua Song
Harbin University of Science and Technology
Harbin, China

ISSN 1865-0929   ISSN 1865-0937 (electronic)
Communications in Computer and Information Science
ISBN 978-981-97-3202-9   ISBN 978-981-97-3203-6 (eBook)
https://doi.org/10.1007/978-981-97-3203-6

Preface

As the program chairs of the 2023 CCF China Blockchain Summit (CCF CBCS 2023), it is our great pleasure to welcome you to the conference proceedings. CBCS 2023 (https://conf.ccf.org.cn/cbcs2023) was held in Haikou, China, during December 15–18, 2023, hosted by the China Computer Federation, the Blockchain Committee of the China Computer Federation, and the National Academy of Sea of Clouds Intelligent Technology Laboratory. The goal of the CBCS conference is to provide a forum for blockchain scientists and engineers.

This year's conference attracted 72 paper submissions. After the hard work of the Program Committee, with each paper receiving at least 3 reviews in a double-blind process, 13 papers were accepted to appear in the conference proceedings, giving an acceptance rate of 18.1%. The major topic of this conference was blockchain science and technology.

We would like to thank all the Program Committee members (64 people from 59 different institutes) for their hard work in completing the review tasks. Their collective efforts made it possible to attain quality reviews for all the submissions within a few weeks. Their diverse expertise in different research areas helped us to create an exciting program for the conference. Their comments and advice helped the authors to improve the quality of their papers and gain deeper insights.

Many thanks should also go to the authors and participants for their tremendous support in making the conference a success.

We thank the team at Springer, whose professional assistance was invaluable in the production of the proceedings. A big thanks also goes to the authors and participants for their tremendous support in making the conference a success.

Besides the technical program, this year CBCS 2023 offered different experiences to the participants. We hope you enjoyed the conference.

March 2024

Jianming Zhu
Qianhong Wu

Organization

General Chairs

Xueming Si   Shanghai Jiao Tong University, China
Liehuang Zhu   Beijing Institute of Technology, China

Program Chairs

Jianming Zhu   Central University of Finance and Economics,
         China
Qianhong Wu   Beihang University, China

Organization Chairs

Yi Sun   Chinese Academy of Sciences, China
Chunjie Cao   Hainan University, China

Forum Chairs

Debiao He   Wuhan University, China
Wei Wang   Beijing Jiaotong University, China
Wei Li   Hangzhou Hyperchain Technology Co., Ltd.,
         China

Publication Chairs

Yong Ding   Guilin University of Electronic Technology, China
Zeguang Lu   National Academy of Guo Ding Institute of Data
         Science, China
Xianhua Song   Harbin University of Science and Technology,
         China

Publicity Chairs

Butian Huang	Hangzhou Yunphant Network Technology Co., Ltd., China
Zhe Liu	Nanjing University of Aeronautics and Astronautics, China

Contents

Smart Contracts

SLL: A Method for Constructing and Executing Smart Law Contracts Based on Domain-Specific Languages

Hao Wen[1]([✉]), Jianming Zhu[1], Danfeng Zhong[1], and Yunzhi Chen[2]

[1] Central University of Finance and Economics, Beijing 100081, China
18105622016@163.com
[2] Hangzhou Vocational Technical College, Hangzhou 310018, China

Abstract. Smart legal contracts are an interdisciplinary concept involving law, blockchain, and information technology, and design or development may require close collaboration between experts in different fields. Research on smart law contracts urgently needs broader support in terms of simplicity, ease of understanding, and practical application. Due to the ambiguity of natural language, the application of smart contracts in the legal field is limited. To overcome this challenge, we design a domain-specific language. Based on the design of legal ontology, our language SLL introduces syntax and semantics that are more similar to natural language contracts. Building an object-oriented language approach helps identify and define common behaviors in contracts, reducing the definition of repetitive behaviors. In executing legal contracts, we have further expanded the breach and termination behavior description. We adopted the Event-B model for logical validation to ensure the consistency of syntax and logic between the contract and code. Compared with traditional technological paths, the SLL method has shown significant advantages: SLL can serve as a conversion bridge between code and natural language. Using the Xtext architecture to develop DSL statements and selecting vocabulary and structures that match natural language contracts ensures concise language expression. In addition, SLL implemented an ontology based syntax mapping to measure whether it is logically consistent with natural language, and used the Event-B model to make logical judgments on it, effectively reducing the differences between legal terms and technical semantics. From a functional perspective, SLL provides a more comprehensive choice for contract execution, especially when dealing with various contract breach and termination issues. Our method can effectively assess the quality of grammar generation and guide the writing of more reasonable smart contracts. These significant advantages demonstrate the enormous potential of SLL in comprehensively innovating intelligent legal contract structures.

Keywords: Smart contracts · Law · Generation rules

This work was supported the National Key Research and Development Program of China under Grant 2022YFB2701800.

J. Zhu et al. (Eds.): CBCS 2023, CCIS 2098, pp. 3–28, 2024.
https://doi.org/10.1007/978-981-97-3203-6_1

1   Introduction

A legal contract can be defined as "a promise or a series of promises that the law aims to provide a remedy for the breach of, or in some way makes the performance of an obligation" [1]. Contracts form a core part of all aspects of business. Like many other industries, the trend toward digitization is promising in this space, leading to a new trend toward integration with smart contracts. [2] Nick Szabo first proposed the concept of smart contracts. Contract costs between the parties to a transaction can be significantly reduced by converting all the contract terms into code and automating the operation with software or hardware. Smart legal contracts, a digital tool designed to facilitate, verify, and enforce contract negotiation or implementation, "mark a new era of contracts" [3]. The application field of intelligent contracts varies from one industry to another. Some scholars define "intelligent contract" as a legal contract characterized by direct application. However, some people believe that "smart contracts" are code scripts used to perform a specific task after certain conditions have been met [7].

Currently, smart contract research primarily encompasses three areas: language establishment, code generation, and contracts' management and oversight. This paper focuses on a comprehensive exploration of language design and optimization in smart contracts. Most smart contract languages are designed from the viewpoint of computer programming specialists. The lack of readability and user-friendliness in smart contract codes for interdisciplinary legal users limits their broader application across various collaborative fields. In recent years, Smart Legal Contracts (SLC) have been proposed by multiple scholars to address related issues. For example, in terms of code semantics, literature [27] discusses methods for confirming and validating syntax-semantics in smart contract code, literature [29] discusses from a legal perspective, and literature [31] provides an in-depth analysis of smart contracts from a natural language perspective. Research related to formal language design can be classified based on the language of the design template into fixed language template research and formal language template research. Research on fixed language templates includes the Linux Foundation's Accord project [8], which created an executable contract template, Cicero. However, the disadvantage is that the reusability of the template is low, as its fixed ergo file is inconvenient for non professionals to change. The most commonly used formal language is Domain-Specific language, and DSL template research can be seen as a Domain-Specific language for intelligent legal contracts. Write using existing Domain-Specific languages, such as using existing XML language to write templates [9], but XML is purely a problem that is difficult to understand. Therefore, most studies still tend to redesign language for specific fields, such as SPESC [10–12], CML [13,14], DasControl [15], Symboleo [16,19], ADICO [20], SmaCoNat [21]. However, these domain specific languages use different methods to extract elements, some through ontological methods, and some through the introduction of institutional analysis methods. How to ensure that formal models include necessary contract elements such as participants and assets, and can vividly express auctions, purchases, and other scenarios is currently the focus of research in this field.

In these specific application scenarios, the specific description of smart contracts is already quite clear, but there are still three core issues from the practical use perspective.

(1) Simplicity. In the contract, some behavior descriptions do not change the contract's content, which leads to repeating similar behaviors, thereby causing redundancy issues.

(2) Understandability. The structural order in the contract, the semantics carried by keywords, and the differences between natural languages.

(3) Consistency. The functional description in the contract is only carried out in compliance with relevant regulations and does not involve the possible consequences of violating existing terms. Furthermore, the designed language cannot guarantee logical consistency with natural language contracts.

In response to the above issues, our proposed SLL is a domain language specifically designed for intelligent legal contracts to address the aforementioned issues. In the process of developing the language, we first used ontology to identify various components in the contract, and then constructed the overall framework and ontology diagram of SLL. Next, by sorting out the logic of existing contracts, we can clarify the key behaviors in the contracts and use them to set up models in Event-B. Finally, we constructed a logical description method to accurately articulate the detailed content of these clauses. The main contributions of SLL are as follows: (1) To address the issue of simplicity, this article delves into the structure of the contract module and extracts behaviors that may affect the contract. SLL provides clear definitions for common contract operations, such as payment, delivery, and modifying contract status. These operations can be directly referred to as internal operation methods, making the contract more concise. (2) When addressing comprehensibility issues, there is no significant difference between the core vocabulary of SLL and its natural meaning. Therefore, we have optimized the contract structure by subdividing the contract content into three main parts: service terms, breach of contract terms, and termination terms, making them more closely linked to the expression of natural language. (3) In order to address consistency issues, SLL has added breach and termination clauses to the contract, optimized the contract content, and expanded its scope of application. The following is a structural description of other chapters in this article. In part 2, a brief overview of smart contracts and domain specific languages was provided. The third part provides an in-depth analysis of the basic framework of SLL language and elucidates its grammatical structure and basic principles through case studies of advance payment contracts. In the fourth part, we delved into relevant academic research. The conclusion provides a comprehensive summary and outlook for future research directions.

2 Background

2.1 Smart Contracts and Law

Blockchain-based smart contracts have been the subject of a lot of research work by many scholars in design and construction, such as SchransF and CoblenzM.

CoblenzM confirmed smart contract accuracy using formal languages. In terms of smart contract applications, Goldenfeinetal et al. discuss the possibility and consistency of smart contract applications from a legal perspective. However, there is limited literature on the language translation for implementing smart contracts. Leveraging these observations, Grigg pioneered the concept of Ricardian contracts in early electronic payment systems. Ricardian contracts are text documents, cryptographically signed by a legal issuer, conveying certain values to the holder. Existing research predominantly utilizes DSLs for constructing smart legal contracts. Xiao He and Qin Bohan et al. proposed a high-level smart contract language capable of implementing cross-domain contracts in a natural language format. They express various types of contracts SPESC [12] in reality by designing custom templates. SPESC contract structure comprises four elements: name, parties, terms, and additional attributes. The first three align with a real contract's name, subject, and main content, while attributes record crucial information and changes, leveraging blockchain's immutability. To facilitate smart contracts' application in legal contexts, Smart Legal Contracts (SLC) [2] merge law and computing, aiming for legal recognition of their form and code execution as electronic contracts. Unlike smart contracts, smart legal contracts exhibit stricter legal features, evident in their language, presentation form, and execution. Due to the interdisciplinary nature of smart legal contracts, a smart contract usually requires the cooperation of experts in many different fields to be designed and implemented [22]. However, current smart contract languages, like Solidity and Go, pose comprehension challenges for experts outside the computing field. This necessitates the development of intelligent legal contract languages designed collaboratively by multidisciplinary experts.

2.2 Domain-Specific Language

DSL is a computer programming language tailored for a specific domain, offering focused expression capabilities: (1) Language nature: DSL must have coherent expression skills (2) Limited expressiveness: DSL only supports the most miniature features required for a particular domain. (3) Domain focus: This language with limited capabilities can only be functional in a clear, small area.

The predominant methods for constructing domain-specific languages are categorized into four types: utilizing LLVM or similar compiler toolchains, employing Lex Yacc toolchains, leveraging ANTLR open-source toolchains, and using metamodel-based modeling tools for model-to-model (M2M) transformations.

2.3 Related Work

Recent research on smart legal contracts includes initiatives like the Linux Foundation's Accord project [8]. This project developed a natural language template. Creating a new smart contract simply involves filling basic elements like the trader's name and account into the template. However, if users need to change the logic, they need to change the ergo logical file. For those who are not template creators or programmers, it takes much time and is not easy to change.

Sepehr Sharifi et al. [14,16–19] proposed a language called Symboleo. The author extracted the contract elements through the ontology method and selected the meat sales contract, data transmission agreement, and energy trading agreement as examples. Symboleo effectively conveys contracts' basic information, rights, and obligations. However, its semantic expression differs from natural language, and it has a high level of abstraction. The comprehensibility is relatively weak.

Xiao He et al. proposed SPESC [10–12], a standardized language. Similarly, this language extracts the same elements of a certain type of smart contract for metadata modeling and then designs and writes the language according to the element diagram. In a series of articles of SPESC, the author selected the simple sales contract, the simple auction contract, and the house lease contract, in turn, to describe and express them with SPESC and further expanded the definition of assets in the house lease contract. It is worth mentioning that although SPESC has restrictions on most of the terms and conditions, it does not describe the consequences of violating the restrictions. SLL has improved this point by describing not only the terms and actions under normal circumstances but also the non-termination and termination violations. In addition, the expression meaning of some keywords in SPESC is different from the actual meaning, such as when, while, and where. When and where are literally understood, but what is expressed in SPESC is a precondition, transaction behavior, and post-condition, which will lead to misunderstanding when reading the contract prepared by SPESC. SLL also improves this point and uses preconditions to express preconditions. It is more understandable to use them to express the post-condition than SPESC.

Mizzi et al. [20] introduced ADICO's institutional syntax into the contract structure and used the ADICO model to define the contract, which can simplify the contract into a structure-based language. Wohrer and Zdun [14] introduced the Contract Modeling Language (CML) for legal contract representation. Element extraction in the language relies on legal ontology. Selected examples include purchase and simple auction contracts, though their content is minimal. Only two or three terms of the contract are selected, not including the default and termination terms of the contract. Dwivedi and Norta [9] suggest using existing XML languages for template creation, noting XML's complexity complicates smart contract development, reducing simplicity and comprehensibility compared to other DSLs. SmaCoNat [21] proposed by Regnath et al. does not have a complete definition and can only describe parts of the contract. Mizzi et al. [20] integrated ADICO's institutional syntax into contract structures, employing the ADICO model to simplify contracts into a structured language.

3   Research Methodology

3.1   Design Goals

SLL (Smart Law Language) is an advanced DSL (Domain-Specific Language) designed for legal contracts. Its design objectives include:

High Expressiveness: Grounded in legal ontology, SLL strives for exhaustive coverage of contracts' essential elements and legal act expressions. By integrating crucial elements and legal behaviors, SLL offers a coherent and comprehensive framework to ensure contract completeness and precision.

Clarity and Accessibility: With syntax mirroring natural language, SLL makes contracts more succinct and comprehensible to readers. This syntax, akin to natural language, bridges the gap between technical and legal domains, facilitating contract comprehension for non-technical users.

Improving development efficiency: SLL focuses on contract status influencing behavior, simplifying coding, and thus improving contract drafting efficiency. In addition, by minimizing redundancy and complexity and providing a consistent way of using detection tools logically, SLL also helps to reduce potential errors and omissions.

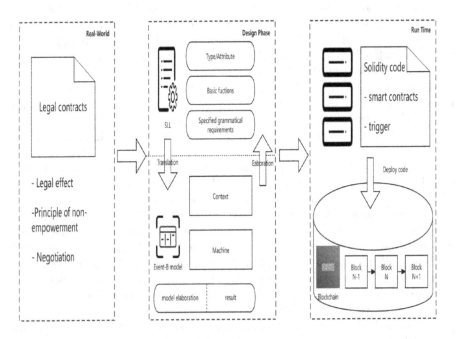

Fig. 1. Overall architecture

SLL utilizes a structural model to represent contract events and logic within the legal domain, enabling its transformation into an executable program. It incorporates state variables and functions for reading and modifying these variables. To mirror natural language syntax, SLL incorporates clauses from actual contracts. This structure guarantees contract execution, consistency, and accuracy. SLL's foundational structure resembles that of a class, rendering contracts actionable and capable of representing legal events and logic as executable programs. Similar to earlier, it includes state variables and functions for managing these variables. Additionally, SLL integrates clauses from real contracts to align closely with natural language syntax, necessitating state designs to instantiate variables and reflect contract statuses. SLL uses clauses to connect grammar elements, where clauses and behaviors are the most relevant. In response to the dynamic nature of natural language that may describe the future behavior of contracts, its composition cannot be clearly defined. Consequently, the model's structural modules are designed to be adaptable, typically comprising at least three components: participants, actions, and the resulting consequences.

3.2   The Advantage of SLL

(1) Semantic richness based on ontology and natural language proximity: The design of SLL adopts an ontology-based approach, which not only accurately captures and defines common behaviors in contracts but also ensures the semantic richness of the language. In addition, SLL adopts structures and keywords close to natural language in its representation, which significantly reduces the complexity of the contract and improves the acceptability of legal experts and non-technical personnel. This combination ensures the logical accuracy of the contract without compromising the intuitive understanding of daily legal language.

(2) Comprehensive Contract Behavior Model and Compliance: SLL not only emphasizes common contractual behaviors but also expands explicitly the description of breach and termination behaviors. This meticulous model design ensures comprehensive contract compliance during execution, reducing legal risks. By comprehensively modeling various possible scenarios throughout the contract lifecycle, SLL provides a solid foundation for the automatic execution of contracts.

(3) Cross-disciplinary integration and wide application: SLL has successfully integrated the concepts of law, blockchain, and information technology into a unified framework. This interdisciplinary approach not only promotes close collaboration among experts in different fields but also ensures the widespread applicability of SLL in various contract and business environments. This approach allows SLL to meet various complex contract requirements while ensuring strict consistency between technology and law.

4   Domain-Specific Language: SLL

SLL is a high-level DSL for legal contracts that use formal rules to component smart contracts. It is designed with several innovative features. Firstly, it is expressive, based on a legal ontology that covers the essential elements of a contract and the expressive elements of an act. The behavior of the contract is summarized and extracted to make the contract more concise. Secondly, its syntax, mirroring natural language via clauses, enhances readability and comprehension, akin to real-world contracts. Thirdly, it improves productivity; SLL abandons the consideration of prioritization of obligations and focuses on behaviors that affect only the state of the contract, simplifying complex code. Lastly, it standardizes the path of action of contract clauses, with clause-triggered antecedent and consequent keywords separated, which helps DSL writers sort out the cause-and-effect relationships of contract clauses.

4.1 Design Baseline

Contracts consolidate the obligations and rights of involved parties. Within the legal framework, contracts undergo a lifecycle that begins with proposal and negotiation, requiring offer, acceptance, and substantial consideration. Contract execution begins with its formal signing or establishment. Execution can encounter interruptions, terminations (successful or not), renegotiations, or updates. SLL's foundational structure resembles a class. SLL encapsulates contract events and logic as an executable program within the legal domain. It includes state variables and functions to read and modify these variables. Furthermore, SLL incorporates clauses akin to those in real contracts, requiring states for variable instantiation and contract status capture, closely mirroring natural language syntax. Ontology captures essential concepts at multiple abstraction levels within a domain. We developed a contract domain ontology, extending the Unified Foundation Ontology (UFO) [8], as illustrated in Fig. 1. Drawing from the contract ontology, we extracted the following concepts: Role Definition: Contractual roles uniquely integrate both responsibilities and rights. Parties are identified as legal entities (individuals or institutions) holding assets and bearing specific contractual responsibilities. A contract encapsulates the allocation of responsibilities and rights among two or more roles involving two or more assets, with at least one asset linked to all executing parties. Assets are items of value, both tangible and intangible. Assets encompass a range of considerations pertinent to contracts. Other asset types, including contracts for goods transportation, invoices, and bills of lading, ensure contract performance. Contracts often stipulate restrictions on the assets' quantity and quality. Legal Status: This term refers to the legal relationships among roles. From our perspective, the principal relationships are obligation and power. Definition of obligation: An obligation arises when a preceding legal situation occurs, leading the debtor to incur specific legal consequences or liabilities towards the creditor. After contract conclusion, remaining responsibilities persist. A typical instance is the confidentiality obligation persisting for six months post-contract termination. Obligations often pertain to assets and are contingent upon specific conditions (triggers). Legal Status: This term refers to scenarios involving contracts, obligations, or rights instances. A situation captures the current state of an event involving multiple long-term participants alongside other conditions and related factors. This condition unfolds within the time interval T without occurring in any specific sub-intervals. Events are specific occurrences at a defined moment, characterized by their immutability. Each event is defined by particular conditions preceding and succeeding its occurrence. For instance, product delivery encompasses a process from the initial "in transit" stage to the final "at the destination" phase. Rights allow a party to establish, modify, suspend, or abolish their legal status. Power is activated by triggers and becomes effective only when certain prerequisites, like legal conditions, are fulfilled.

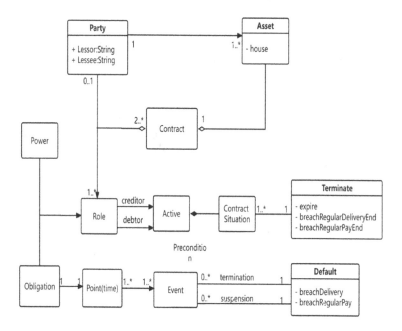

Fig. 2. Law Ontology

This smart contract model can be represented as a formal rule-based model. That is, the actions are defined as a collection of possible events. This suggests that the realistic scenario in which the action occurs integrates the various dimensions that impact the implementation of the action. So, we need to illustrate this type of action in terms of several basic concepts. A party's rights or responsibilities for performing a particular action are specified in the most concise clause language.

4.2   SLL Structure

Contract Module. According to the above analysis, the contract consists of the parties, assets, current status of the contract, various terms, and data types. In the structure of our SLL, we will use four parts for concatenation, including Basic contract information, Contract, Breach, and Termination. The first two are the basic elements that make up the contract, and users can participate in writing it. The latter two are used to control the lifecycle of the contract and determine the lifespan of the smart contract program. For their respective introductions, we will define all the elements in Basic contract information. They are instantiation of terms and elements in real-life scenarios. Contract represents all parties involved in the contract and interacts with Active. According to their respective roles, they have interrelated responsibilities and rights. For example, when a clause clearly stipulates that the rights of one party are active, the corresponding specific events and contract conditions will be adjusted accordingly. Once an event occurs, the contract conditions will also change accordingly, which will be accompanied by the obligations of the other party. As the event is completed, the rights and obligations of both parties will also terminate at some point. In this regard, the Breach and Termination that control the contract lifecycle will be triggered at some point.

1. Basic contract information: (e.g. participants, duration of contract, etc.)When Active reaches the activation status, it usually indicates that the signing of the housing lease contract or handling the abnormal situation is completed, and the contract is officially effective.
2. Contract: According to the classification of contracts, contract design in specific cases is carried out here . For example, in advance payment contract-sterms of advance payment (e.g. terms, amount, time of payment, etc.). When Active needs to fulfill the relevant obligations, it will trigger the corresponding event execution.
3. Breach: (e.g. delivery of goods or services, quality standards, etc.)When an abnormal event occurs, it will trigger Active to refuse to perform the corresponding operation and terminate the contract's life.
4. Termination:(e.g. consequences of late payment, terms of release, etc.) In some cases the contract is in breach of the relevant agreement and the contract goes into termination mode. This is triggered if the contractual status is modified and the contract continues to be valid as required.

Clause Structure. SLL uses clauses to connect syntactic elements that are highly correlated with real-life behavior. In formal models, clauses can be seen as entities, elements can be seen as attributes, and events are the key to connecting them. Due to the dynamic nature of natural language, legal contracts typically specify potential future contractual actions, but their specific composition cannot carry the ambiguity and ambiguity of natural language. Therefore, the structural modules of the model must adapt to real-world conditions and take into account real-world semantics in syntax. The clauses we design for this typically include participants, actions, and the resulting consequences. In the table below, we demonstrate how to use clause syntax to organize elements in common scenarios and express real-life situations in a reasonable manner. In addition, other urgent actions can be proposed to explain in detail the changes in the status of obligations in the contract and the potential impact on the contract situation. We will use Axioms to express this part.

Table 1. Clause syntax and element definitions

Element	Syntax	Description

BasicSpec	`'Basic' name=ID`
	`(dConcepts += DConcept`
	`';')+ 'endBasic'`
		Defines a basic specification with a name and multiple domain concepts.

DConcept	`name=ID ('isA'`
	`conceptTypes+=CType)`
	`('with')?`
	`(attributes+=Att ',')*`
		A domain concept with an identifier, an optional type, and a list of attributes.

Contract	`'Contract' name=ID '('`
	`'PrePayment' ')' ...`
	`'endContract'`
		Defines the structure of a prepayment contract, including various terms and conditions.

Clause	`'Clause' name=ID 'Type'`
	`type=ClauseType`
	`'Condition'`
	`condition=STRING`
		Describes a clause in the contract with a type and condition.

Obligation	`'Obli' name=ID ... 'O'`
	`'(' role1=[Party] ','`
	`role2=[Party] ',' ...`
		Defines an obligation in the contract, specifying roles and associated antecedent and consequent propositions.

Power	`'Powe' name=ID ... 'P'`
	`'(' role1=[Party] ','`
	`role2=[Party] ',' ...`
		Defines a power within the contract, including descriptions, trigger conditions, and roles involved.

Breach	`'Breach' name=ID`
	`'Condition'`
	`condition=STRING`
	`'Penalty' penalty+=REAL`
		Defines a breach condition in the contract and the associated financial penalties.

Termination	`'Termination' name=ID`
	`'Condition'`
	`condition=STRING ...`
		Describes the conditions for contract termination and the notice period required

In practice, SLL uses EBNF based clause syntax to connect syntax elements. Figure 3 illustrates the operational steps involved in executing a contract in the prepayment scenario. It can be observed that the occurrence of events in the contract is often accompanied by changes in entity attributes, attempting to predict all possible events, using a fixed template for realistic fitting does not meet practical needs. Given the dynamism of contract language, we use logic to express future events and compile clauses with special structures, with the aim of generating, triggering, and terminating smart contracts. These types of clauses typically consist of three main components: participants, actions, and action patterns. A contract typically involves two specific parties, the seller and the buyer, with a fixed sales target. In the same type of contract, it is necessary to flexibly adjust and design the normative parameters of the contract due to possible differences in the provisions of the goods between the two parties. In addition, personnel responsible for formulating norms must balance the formality and informality of normative language, and consider whether there are key implicit constraints in normative texts. Language ambiguity may lead to normative misunderstandings, while overly concise contractual expressions may compromise expected clarity. For example, is contract execution completed within a specific time frame, or is it still valid after regular payments? Do the attributes of the product need to meet specific standards? Solving these issues tested the flexibility and security of the contract. To address these challenges, the flexibility of clauses needs to be further improved. Therefore, the behavior expression of the clause after instantiation of basic information is composed of the syntax of the following clauses.

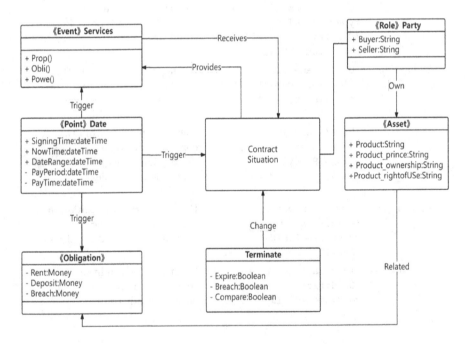

Fig. 3. model of event

Syntax and Semantics. In Xtext, the syntax details of SLL are clearly defined, while Xtext is responsible for generating the basic structure of the language and further deriving the corresponding meta model. After processing the SLL text input file, the parser will generate a meta model instance in its memory, which is named the Abstract Grammar Tree (AST). Next, the Xtend programming generator will traverse this representation to generate more Solidity code based on static and dynamically built support libraries. We use clause syntax based on the EBNF paradigm to connect syntax elements, which are based on the conventions discussed in the previous article. In the context of the contract, in order to trigger the code for the smart contract, DSL needs to include prerequisites and subsequent results, including triggering events, conditions, and the objects involved. Trigger events outline situations that require long-term consideration, distinguishing between internal and external events. Internal events, such as completed actions or fulfilled terms, are within the control of the contracting parties. On the contrary, external events, such as contract termination, are beyond the control of both parties. The premise of this clause sets time and state constraints, which establish the obligations (post conditions) of all parties when the triggering event occurs. The dependency relationship and lifecycle of rights and obligations in contracts are defined through formal semantics. Here, we refer to the approach of Symboleo's paper [14] and propose three axioms that can cover real-life scenarios in summarizing the work of real contracts. After SLL starts running, in some cases, feedback from triggers will affect the execution of obligations. As a formal expression, we allow events to be represented as time and scenes as triggering mechanisms in event expression. For example, the three axioms shown below represent different scenarios that trigger different rights and obligations:

Axiom 1: Activate obligation when conditions are met For example, in the context of prepayment contracts, the fulfillment of prepayment conditions is a key catalyst for activating corresponding obligations. This axiom stipulates that for each obligation within the scope of the contract, its activation depends on the satisfaction of predefined conditions related to advance payment. Specifically, this axiom asserts that if a situation arises where contractual obligations arise in advance, such as the repayment conditions being met and the prepayment amount being positive, it will trigger the relevant obligations.

$$\forall o \in \text{Obligations}, \forall p \in \text{PrePayments},$$
$$(p.\text{PaymentCondition} = \text{true}) \land (p.\text{Amount} > 0) \rightarrow \text{initiates}(p, o)$$

Axiom 2: Termination of Contract for Breach of Terms This axiom addresses the meaning of violating clauses in payment contracts. It believes that any violation or non-compliance with the contractual terms will result in immediate termination of the contract. This axiom emphasizes the principle that contract terms are binding; Therefore, any unfulfilled conditions in these clauses will trigger termination procedures, highlighting the binding force of the contract and its consequences for breach of contract.

$$\forall c \in \text{Clauses}, \forall t \in \text{Terminations},$$
$$(c.\text{Condition} = \text{false}) \rightarrow \text{initiates}(c, t)$$

Axiom 3: Power activation after obligation fulfillment Within the framework of the contract, the completion of obligations not only signifies their fulfillment, but also activates certain rights stipulated in the contract. This axiom establishes a direct relationship between fulfilling obligations and activating relevant powers. It claims that once the obligation is successfully fulfilled, it will activate the power dependent on performance, thereby establishing a connection between contractual obligations and subsequent rights.

$$\forall o \in \text{Obligations}, \forall p \in \text{Powers},$$
$$\text{fulfilled}(o) \rightarrow \text{activates}(o, p)$$

These axioms are elaborated around the context of contracts, providing a fundamental structure for understanding the dynamics of obligations and rights in contractual agreements. They reflect the inherent logical and legal complexity of contractual commitments and their execution.

Detail Expression

(1) Logical expressions connect the relationship between two or more conditional expression statements. SLL defines common logical expressions, that is, and, or, not.

(2) Relationship expressions express the size equality relationship between multiple constants and variables. SLL defines common relationship expressions, namely $<, >, \leq, \geq, \neq, =$.

(3) The operation expression expresses the relationship between multiple constants and variables. SLL defines common operation expressions, namely $+$, $-, *, /, +=, -=, **$.

(4) The main function of a time expression is to describe the time constraints within the expression. Time constraints are commonly used to describe the time span over which events occur and the order in which they progress. In terms of time dimension, the definition of SLL can be divided into two different categories, Firstly, this is to determine the fixed duration required for the event. Taking the num day of Event A as an example, this indicates that the duration of Event A is num days. We use the word within to describe the longest time span of an event, while before and after are used to indicate the order in which events occur. Secondly, we use Term to describe the time range. In order to solve the problem of unstable prepayment time, in the Contract section, we will first clarify the time range used and determine the specific date of each event. We have the ability to clearly distinguish between pre - and post conditions in the time dimension, and establish sequential relationships between various actions based on these conditions. Of course, triggers determined by time expressions can also be used as "oracle machines" to trigger the execution of smart contracts

(5) Parameter expression is used to express the parameter types involved in the expression. This contract mainly includes numerous liability clauses. Obligation is clearly defined as Obli: O, covering debtors, creditors, pioneers, and consequences. Debtors and creditors have a unique position in the law, and their prerequisites and legal outcomes are determined by a

specific proposition. The "pre proposition" and "post proposition" provide a detailed explanation of the specific contexts in which it is necessary to continue to exist in order to fulfill its responsibilities. The relevant obligations will only begin to be implemented when the underlying reasons are transformed into actual conditions. In order to end debt, it is necessary to establish an effective triggering mechanism. A trigger is defined as a scenario based on propositional description, and it is located in a symbolic position of "→". If the trigger is not mentioned in the document, this responsibility will become not clear, but it will take effect when its condition becomes actual. The corresponding relationship between rights and obligations is also described structurally as Powe: P (including creditors, debtors, causes and consequences). In this structure, both creditors and debtors play specific roles, the former describing specific legal situations, while the latter presents propositions about possible legal situations that may arise.

4.3   Event-B: Formal Verification

This article adopts formal methods to ensure the logical consistency of smart legal contracts. The core idea of these methods is to use mathematical logic to describe and verify smart legal contracts, thereby helping to identify potential errors in DSL. In the XText compiler, syntax errors will be prompted accordingly. In order to ensure consistency in event description between legal contracts and smart legal contracts, and to eliminate ambiguity in contract language, we need to use formal verification tools in the model detection process. This article adopts the Event-B method, which is a semi-automatic but effective verification method.

The Event-B method adopts type set theory as its symbolic language, based on propositional logic and predicate logic. Usually, the Event-B model consists of two main parts: one is used to describe the context of the static part of the model, and the other is an abstract machine used to represent the dynamic part. Regarding the specific method of mapping, this study specifies the translation (Tr) function for mapping between SLL and Event-B. This function can convert the Event-B model based on SLL syntax, while clearly explaining the SLL logic and preserving the original semantic information.

Table 2. Transformation Function

SLL	Event-B	Transformation
Type	Set, Axiom	Tr_1
Property	Variable, Invariant	Tr_2
Constructor	Initialization	Tr_3
Basic Function	Event, Constant	$Axiom$

(1) Tr1: In SLL code, type declarations are converted to collections and axioms in Context. If we use data formats such as unsigned integers in SLL, we will construct a representation set in Event-B. For example, in the context of a lease agreement, if we define product information and store it by creating a "product" collection. In the refinement process of C0 and Cn, we will create a product _XXX invariant to represent all information related to the house. Here, we adopt the BNF paradigm and define the rules for mapping to sets based on unsigned integers, further elucidating the Context rules for mapping to Event-B. As shown in the figure, the correspondence between SLL content and Context in Event-B has been clearly defined.

```
1    <DSL_model> ::= <type_section>
2
3    <type_section> ::= "Type" <type_definitions>
4    <type_definitions> ::= <type_definition> |
         ↪ <type_definition> <type_definitions>
5    <type_definition> ::= <simple_type> | <custom_type>
6    <simple_type> ::= "Unsigned Integer" "mapped to"
         ↪ <eventb_set>
7    <custom_type> ::= <name> "mapped to"
         ↪ <eventb_context>
8
9    <eventb_set> ::= "Set" <name>
10   <eventb_context> ::= "Context" <context_definitions>
11   <context_definitions> ::= <set_definition>
         ↪ <axiom_definition>
12   <set_definition> ::= "Set" <name>
13   <axiom_definition> ::= "Axiom" <name> "represents"
         ↪ <description>
14
15   <name> ::= /* A valid identifier, such as
         ↪ ''Product'' */
16   <description> ::= /* A statement describing
         ↪ invariants, such as ''product_XXX represents
         ↪ information related to the Product'' */
```

Listing 1. Tr1 transformation

(2) Tr2: Attribute declaration converts variables and invariants in Machine in Event-B. The basic specific attributes that may need to be described using DSL in Context, such as state, currency, stakeholders, etc., are abstract descriptions of item features. In this section, Tr2 is used to map attributes to the "variables" and "invariants" of Event-B in the present invention. for example

```
1    "Property" house_status: string
```

Listing 2. Tr2 transformation preparation 1

This indicates that the product has a name called product_status The attribute of status, which is of type string. Possible values in the prop keyword include "vacant", "rental", etc.

```
1  "variable" product_status
2  "invariant" product_status_invariant: product_status
       ↪  in {"Vacant", "Rented"}
```

Listing 3. Tr2 transformation preparation 2

When we map it to the Event-B model, we create a corresponding variable and define an invariant to constrain or describe the meaning and possible states of this variable. The mapping result is as follows: The rules for syntax mapping are defined as follows:

```
1  <DSL_model> ::= <attribute_section>
2
3  <attribute_section> ::= "Attributes" <
       ↪  attribute_definitions>
4  <attribute_definitions> ::= <attribute_definition> |
       ↪  <attribute_definition> <
       ↪  attribute_definitions>
5  <attribute_definition> ::= <name> ":" <type> "mapped
       ↪  to" <eventb_attribute>
6
7  <type> ::= /* Supported data types in DSL, such as "
       ↪  integer", "string", etc. */
8
9  <eventb_attribute> ::= "Variable" <var_definition> "
       ↪  Invariant" <invariant_definition>
10 <var_definition> ::= <name>
11 <invariant_definition> ::= <name> "represents" <
       ↪  description>
12
13 <name> ::= /* A valid identifier */
14 <description> ::= /* A statement describing the
       ↪  invariant, such as "product_status_XXX
       ↪  represents the current status of the house"
       ↪  */
```

Listing 4. Tr2 transformation

(3) Tr3: Function declaration transforms events, initialization, etc. in the abstract machine in Event-B, Assuming in DSL, we have the following function description

```
1  event rentProductEvent
2  guard guard_rent: product_status = "Vacant"
3  action act_rent: product_status := "Rented"
```

Listing 5. Tr3 transformation preparation 1

Here, rent guard_rent The purpose of rent is to ensure that goods can only be rented out when they are in an "empty" state. Once the conditions for guarding are met, the action of "act_rent" will be activated, causing the product status to change to "rental" status.

```
1   <DSL_model> ::= <function_section>
2
3   <function_section> ::= "Function" <
        ↪ function_definitions>
4   <function_definitions> ::= <function_definition> | <
        ↪ function_definition> <function_definitions>
5   <function_definition> ::= <name> "(" <parameters> ")"
        ↪ "mapped to" <eventb_event>
6
7   <parameters> ::= <parameter> | <parameter> "," <
        ↪ parameters>
8   <parameter> ::= <name> ":" <type>
9
10  <eventb_event> ::= "Event" <event_definition> "Guard"
        ↪ <guard_definition> "Action" <action_definition>
11  <event_definition> ::= <name>
12  <guard_definition> ::= <name> "represents" <
        ↪ description>
13  <action_definition> ::= <name> "represents" <
        ↪ description>
14
15  <name> ::= /* A valid identifier */
16  <type> ::= /* Supported data types in DSL, such as "
        ↪ integer", "string", etc. */
17  <description> ::= /* A statement describing the guard
        ↪ or action, for example, "guard_XXX represents
        ↪ that the current status of the house is vacant"
        ↪ */
```

Listing 6. DSL Model Code

By using the syntax mapping described by the BNF paradigm, we can directly transform function definitions in DSL into events in the Event-B model, thereby achieving the transformation between DSL descriptions and formal models. The following is a summary of specific cases of mapping transformation. It can be seen that after defining the three transformation functions, DSL elements have achieved one-to-one correspondence with the Event-B model.

In order to comprehensively verify the practicality and flexibility of SLL language, this study comprehensively applied the previously defined SLL syntax norms and selected "prepayment contract" as an empirical case. This case demonstrates the effectiveness of SLL grammar in the field of legal contract preparation, particularly in enhancing the convenience, usability, and readability of contract preparation. The specific contract content and its execution process are presented in detail in Fig. 3, respectively. In the DSL architecture, contracts are divided into two main parts: "Basic" and "Contract", further covering four core clause areas. In the "Basic" section, the contract involves basic information about the payer and receiver, while the "Contract" section is further divided into three sub parts: advance payment terms (defining payment conditions, amounts, and time arrangements), performance obligations (detailing delivery and quality standards of goods or services), and breach of contract clauses (specifying the consequences of delayed payment and termination conditions). The prerequisite conditions set in this contract case include a detailed description of the service or product, a predetermined payment schedule, and the assumption that each payment cycle defaults to one month. In addition, this study conducted an in-depth analysis of the application of SLL language in the preparation of advance payment contracts, further demonstrating its applicability and effectiveness in the field of legal contract automation.

Prepayment Agreement

Buyer: Person, Seller: Company

Prepayment for services from March 1, 2021, to September 1, 2021.

Ownership of the service remains with Alice, Bob has the right of use.

Prepayment amount: 10000, paid upfront.

Additional deposit: 1000, penalty for breach: 2000.

In case of default, the penalty is proportional.

Agreement date: February 9, 2021.

Terms of Service:

Lessee pays the deposit and upfront prepayment.

Lessor provides the specified services.

Lessee pays as per the prepayment schedule; lessor confirms services provided.

At the end of the service period, lessee ceases to use services.

Contract Execution and Consequences:

Service delivery and payment fulfilment are confirmed per agreed schedule.

Failure to deliver services or make timely payments incurs penalties.

• Undelivered services lead to a refund of the corresponding prepayment.

• Delayed payments attract a daily penalty of 1% of the overdue amount

• Continuous service non-delivery for 7 d or payment delay over 30 days may result in contract termination.

The Structured Language for Legality (SLL) demonstrates a comprehensive expression capability for contractual terms, enhancing the precision and automation of legal contract assembly. This section applies SLL to the domain of prepayment contracts, showcasing its efficacy.

(1) Definition of Essential Information: The foundational elements of a prepayment contract, including the identities of the involved parties and pertinent transactional details, are defined within the SLL's Basic Information model. The contract allows for external input of basic information by the contracting parties, ensuring that all primary details are captured as outlined in the Basic Information section.

```
1  // Definition of Basic Information for Prepayment
     ↪ Contract
2  Basic PrePaymentContractExampleA
3     // Definition of the Buyer
4     Buyer "isA"
5         "Type" Person; // Buyer is defined as a
             ↪ Person
6
7     // Definition of the Seller
8     Seller "isA"
9         "Type" Company; // Seller is defined as a
             ↪ Company
10
11    // Definition of the Currency
12    Currency "isA"
13        "Type" USD; // Currency used in the contract
14
15    // Definition of the Product
16    Product "isA"
17        "Type" toy; // Product involved in the
             ↪ contract
18 endBasic
19
20 // Additional notes or definitions can be added here
     ↪ to extend the listing
```

Listing 7. Basic Information In Xtext Definition

(2) Definition of Service Terms: SLL meticulously delineates service terms, including initial payment, service delivery, and ongoing payment obligations, enabling a clear contractual framework.

```
1  Term 01-01-2023 to 12-12-2023
2
3     PaymentDetails
4         Amount 10000.00
5         Condition "Payment upon delivery"
6         DueDate 15-06-2023
7
8     Preconditions
9         Prop legalCompliance Condition "Both parties
             ↪ comply with relevant laws";
10        Prop productQuality Condition "Goods must be
             ↪ of agreed quality";
11        Prop legalCompliance Condition "Both parties
             ↪ comply with relevant laws";
12
13    Postconditions
14        Prop paymentCompletion Condition "Buyer
             ↪ completes the payment";
```

```
15      Prop deliveryCompletion Condition "Seller
            ↪ completes the delivery";
16
17  Clauses
18      Clause deliveryObligation
19      Type Obligation
20      Condition "Seller must deliver goods by
            ↪ agreed date"
```

Listing 8. Service Terms Definition

```
1  Obligations
2      Obli delivery
3      Description "Delivery of goods in agreed
            ↪ condition"
4      : productQuality -> O (Seller, Buyer,
            ↪ productQuality, deliveryCompletion),
5
6      Obli payment
7      Description "Payment in full by due date"
8      : paymentCompletion -> O (Buyer, Seller,
            ↪ paymentCompletion, legalCompliance);
9
10     Powers
11     Powe contractTermination
12     Description "Right to terminate contract on
            ↪ breach"
13     : breachBySeller -> P (Buyer, Seller,
            ↪ breachBySeller, legalCompliance)
14     : breachByBuyer -> P (Seller, Buyer,
            ↪ breachByBuyer, legalCompliance);
```

Listing 9. Obligation & Power

(3) Definition of Breach Clause: Default clauses are articulated to address potential failures in service delivery or payment, with SLL providing mechanisms for default management.

```
1  Breach
2      Breach lateDelivery
3      Condition "Seller fails to deliver on time"
4      Penalty 500.00
5      Resolution "Penalty payable to Buyer",
```

Listing 10. Default Clause Definition

(4) Definition of Termination Clauses: Termination clauses within the contract are defined to specify conditions under which the contract may be dissolved, highlighting the contract's lifecycle.

```
1  Termination
2          Termination mutualAgreement
3          Condition "Both parties agree to terminate"
4          NoticePeriod 30;
```

Listing 11. Termination Clause Definition

It can be seen that SLL terms have strong and concise expression ability of contract terms, including service terms, default terms, and termination terms. We will combine the conversion function specified in Sect. 4 to see if it can be converted into the Event-B model as expected. The converted demonstration is as follows:

CONTEXT PrepaymentContractContext
SETS

– STATUS = {pending, paid, delivered, breached, terminated}

CONSTANTS

– validPaymentAmount, initialDeposit, penaltyAmount

AXIOMS

$$axm1 : validPaymentAmount \in \mathbb{N}$$
$$axm2 : initialDeposit \in \mathbb{N}$$
$$axm3 : penaltyAmount \in \mathbb{N}$$
$$axm4 : validPaymentAmount > 0$$
$$axm5 : initialDeposit > 0$$
$$axm6 : penaltyAmount > 0$$

MACHINE PrepaymentContractMachine
SEES PrepaymentContractContext
VARIABLES

– contractStatus, paymentMade, paymentAmount, depositPaid, serviceDelivered

INVARIANTS

$inv1 : contractStatus \in \{pending, paid, delivered, breached, terminated\}$

$inv2 : paymentMade \in \{TRUE, FALSE\}$

$inv3 : paymentAmount \in \mathbb{N}$

$inv4 : depositPaid \in \{TRUE, FALSE\}$

$inv5 : serviceDelivered \in \{TRUE, FALSE\}$

$inv6 : (contractStatus = paid \Rightarrow paymentMade = TRUE) \wedge$
$\quad (contractStatus = delivered \Rightarrow serviceDelivered = TRUE)$

EVENTS

– Initialisation

$$act1 : contractStatus := pending$$
$$act2 : paymentMade := FALSE$$
$$act3 : paymentAmount := 0$$
$$act4 : depositPaid := FALSE$$
$$act5 : serviceDelivered := FALSE$$

– MakePayment

$$grd1 : contractStatus = pending$$
$$grd2 : paymentAmount = validPaymentAmount$$
$$act1 : paymentMade := TRUE$$
$$act2 : contractStatus := paid$$

– DeliverService

$$grd1 : paymentMade = TRUE$$
$$grd2 : contractStatus = paid$$
$$act1 : serviceDelivered := TRUE$$
$$act2 : contractStatus := delivered$$

– BreachContract

$$grd1 : serviceDelivered = FALSE \land contractStatus \neq terminated$$
$$act1 : contractStatus := breached$$

– TerminateContract

$$grd1 : contractStatus = breached \lor contractStatus = delivered$$
$$act1 : contractStatus := terminated$$

The ability to transform abstract requirements into precise Event-B models implies a profound understanding of logical consistency and formal validation methods. By utilizing the strict framework of Event-B, it is possible to ensure the integrity of system specifications relative to a range of comprehensive attributes, including security, activity, and invariance. This skill set is crucial for making progress in the field of formal methods and has made a significant contribution to the reliability and robustness of software and systems engineering projects, emphasizing a commitment to high-quality, error free development practices. Here, we integrate the Event-B model into our formal meeting, providing a powerful tool for consistency assessment between DSL and legal contracts. Compared to the DSL statements of other smart legal contracts, we have simplified the complexity of expression and achieved consistency with the original natural language logic while implementing rich semantics. The following table includes the basic evaluation indicators of DSL language, and our SLL has performed well in all indicators.

Table 3. Evaluation of DSLs for Smart Legal Contracts

DSL	E[1]	C[2]	Eff[3]	Comp[4]	I[5]	C[6]
SLL	+	+	+	+	+	−
Solidity	+	−	−	+	−	−
Symboleo	+	−	−	+	−	−
SPESC	+	−	+	−	−	−
ADICO	−	+	−	+	−	−
CML	+	−	−	+	−	−
Scilla	−	+	+	+	−	−
SmaCoNat	−	−	−	−	−	−

[1] Expressiveness
[2] Clarity
[3] Efficiency
[4] Compliance
[5] Interdisciplinary
[6] Consistency

5   Conclusion and Future Work

The fundamental components of SLL, the official language for contract specification, and its prerequisites have been delineated by us. Embracing the essence of software engineering, our dedication lies in delivering comprehensive and operational legal contract expression features through a cutting-edge contract execution platform. The foundation of our language lies in conceptual frameworks, encompassing expandable ontologies, scalable state machine models [22], and axiomatic logic guidelines for managing contract-based behavior procedures. Going forward, our aim is to (a) create a tool-assisted method for transforming contract details into smart contract coding, for instance, the automated creation of novel contract templates in the BPMN process [23], like lorikeet [24]. Utilizing the finite state machine method is also feasible [25]. (b) Formulate specifications for contracts, potentially utilizing formal analysis methods for SMT interpretation; (c) enhance grammatical usability; (d) automate the transformation of legal contract documents into formal specifications, such as analyzing current contracts; (e) broaden SLL to bolster sophisticated subcontracting skills, and (f) execute case studies.

References

1. Willis, H.E.: Restatement of the law of contracts of the American Law Institute. Ind. LJ **7**, 429 (1931)
2. Szabo, N.: Formalizing and securing relationships on public networks. First Monday **2**(9) (1997)
3. Woebbeking, M.K.: The impact of smart contracts on traditional concepts of contract law. J. Intell. Prop. Info. Tech. Elec. Com. L. **10**, 105 (2019)

4. Prisacariu, C., Schneider, G.: A formal language for electronic contracts. In: Bonsangue, M.M., Johnsen, E.B. (eds.) Formal Methods for Open Object-Based Distributed Systems, vol. 4468, pp. 174–189. Springer, Heidelberg (2007). https://doi.org/10.1007/978-3-540-72952-5-11

5. Sharifi, S.S.: Smart contracts: from formal specification to blockchain code. Dissertation, Université d'Ottawa/University of Ottawa (2020)

6. Clack, C.D.: Smart contract templates: legal semantics and code validation. J. Digit. Bank. **2**(4), 338–352 (2018)

7. Stark, J.: Making sense of blockchain smart contracts. CoinDesk (2016)

8. Coblenz, M.: Obsidian: a safer blockchain programming language. In: 2017 IEEE/ACM 39th International Conference on Software Engineering Companion (ICSE-C). IEEE (2017)

9. Bhargavan, K., et al.: Formal verification of smart contracts: short paper. In: Proceedings of the 2016 ACM Workshop on Programming Languages and Analysis for Security (2016)

10. He, X., et al.: SPESC: a specification language for smart contracts. In: 2018 IEEE 42nd Annual Computer Software and Applications Conference (COMPSAC), vol. 1. IEEE (2018). https://doi.org/10.1109/COMPSAC.2018.00025

11. Zhu, Y., et al.: TA-SPESC: toward asset-driven smart contract language supporting ownership transaction and rule-based generation on blockchain. IEEE Trans. Reliab. **70**(3), 1255–1270 (2021). https://doi.org/10.1109/TR.2021.3054617

12. Chen, E., et al.: SPESC-translator: towards automatically smart legal contract conversion for blockchain-based auction services. IEEE Trans. Serv. Comput. **15**(5), 3061–3076 (2021). https://doi.org/10.1109/TSC.2021.3077291

13. Wöhrer, M., Zdun, U.: Domain-specific language for smart contract development. In: 2020 IEEE International Conference on Blockchain and Cryptocurrency (ICBC). IEEE (2020). https://doi.org/10.1109/ICBC48266.2020.9169399

14. Rasti, A.: From symboleo to smart contracts: a code generator. Dissertation, Université d'Ottawa/University of Ottawa (2022). https://doi.org/10.1109/MS.2020.2993470.

15. Skotnica, M., Klicpera, J., Pergl, R.: Towards model-driven smart contract systems-code generation and improving expressivity of smart contract modeling. In: Proceedings of the EEWC 2020 (2020)

16. Skotnica, M., Klicpera, J., Pergl, Robert, R.: Towards model-driven smart contract systems-code generation and improving expressivity of smart contract modeling. In: Proceedings of the EEWC 2020 (2020). https://doi.org/10.1109/RE48521.2020.00049

17. Rasti, A., et al.: Symboleo2SC: from legal contract specifications to smart contracts. In: Proceedings of the 25th International Conference on Model Driven Engineering Languages and Systems (2022). https://doi.org/10.1145/3550355.3552407

18. Parvizimosaed, A., et al.: Specification and analysis of legal contracts with symboleo. Softw. Syst. Model. **21**(6), 2395–2427 (2022). https://doi.org/10.1007/s10270-022-01053-6

19. Parvizimosaed, A., et al.: Subcontracting, assignment, and substitution for legal contracts in symboleo. ‑In: International Conference on Conceptual Modeling. Springer, Cham (2020). https://doi.org/10.1007/978-3-030-62522-1-20

20. Frantz, C.K., Nowostawski, M.: From institutions to code: towards automated generation of smart contracts. In: 2016 IEEE 1st International Workshops on Foundations and Applications of Self* Systems (FAS* W). IEEE (2016). https://doi.org/10.1109/FAS-W.2016.53

21. Regnath, E., Steinhorst, S.: SmaCoNat: smart contracts in natural language. In: 2018 Forum on Specification and Design Languages (FDL). IEEE (2018). https://doi.org/10.1109/FDL.2018.8524068

22. Griffo, C., Almeida, J.P.A., Guizzardi, G.: Towards a legal core ontology based on Alexy's theory of fundamental rights. In: Multilingual Workshop on Artificial Intelligence and Law, ICAIL (2015)

23. Le, D.M., Dang, D.-H., Nguyen, V.-H.: On domain driven design using annotation-based domain-specific language. Comput. Lang. Syst. Struct. **54**, 199–235 (2018). https://doi.org/10.1016/j.cl.2018.05.001

24. Tran, A.B., Lu, Q., Weber, I.: Lorikeet: a model-driven engineering tool for blockchain-based business process execution and asset management. BPM (Dissertation/Demos/Industry) (2018)

25. Mavridou, A., Laszka, A.: Designing secure ethereum smart contracts: a finite state machine based approach. In: Meiklejohn, S., Sako, K. (eds.) FC 2018. LNCS, vol. 10957, pp. 523–540. Springer, Heidelberg (2018). https://doi.org/10.1007/978-3-662-58387-6_28

26. Prisacariu, C., Schneider, G.: A formal language for electronic contracts. In: Bonsangue, M.M., Johnsen, E.B. (eds.) FMOODS 2007. LNCS, vol. 4468, pp. 174–189. Springer, Heidelberg (2007). https://doi.org/10.1007/978-3-540-72952-5_11

27. Hirai, Y.: Defining the ethereum virtual machine for interactive theorem provers. In: Brenner, M., et al. (eds.) FC 2017. LNCS, vol. 10323, pp. 520–535. Springer, Cham (2017). https://doi.org/10.1007/978-3-319-70278-0_33

28. Kasprzyk, K.: The concept of smart contracts from the legal perspective. Rev. Eur. Comp. L. **34**, 101 (2018)

29. Goldenfein, J., Leiter, A.: Legal engineering on the blockchain:'smart contracts' as legal conduct. Law Critique **29**, 141–149 (2018)

30. Gomes, S.S.: Smart contracts: legal frontiers and insertion into the creative economy. Brazil. J. Oper. Prod. Manag. **15**(3), 376385 (2018)

31. Allen, J.G.: Wrapped and stacked:'smart contracts' and the interaction of natural and formal language. Eur. Rev. Contract Law **14**(4), 307–343 (2018)

Blockchain Encryption

Optimizing the SM4 Encryption Algorithm for Blockchain Security

Xiaomeng Hu[1,2], Haibo Yi[2(✉)], Wenyu Zhang[1], and Yaning Du[1,2]

[1] University of Science and Technology Liaoning, Anshan 114051, China
[2] Institute of Applied Artificial Intelligence of the Guangdong-Hong Kong-Macao Greater Bay Area, Shenzhen Polytechnic University, Shenzhen 518055, China
haiboyi@szpu.edu.cn

Abstract. Encryption algorithms play a critical role in ensuring data security. However, challenges such as slow operation and suboptimal efficiency arise during the encryption and decryption processes. Improving encryption efficiency has emerged as a critical objective. In this paper, we investigate the intricacies of the SM4 encryption algorithm, identifying complex iterations and computations. Through adopting a more efficient mathematical approach and streamlining processes, we achieve significant improvements in encryption efficiency. Through extensive research in GPU parallel computing, we propose an efficient encryption algorithm based on CUDA streams. This approach carefully considers the characteristics of both the CPU and the GPU, enabling the parallelization of the SM4 block encryption process. It also optimizes byte substitution and left shift operations, resulting in an optimal solution. The integration of fundamental method optimization with GPU parallel computing consistently improves encryption efficiency. Our encryption algorithm consistently outperforms the CUDA-based SM4 algorithm for large volumes of data, especially beyond 30 MB. With a data volume of 1 KB, our improved CUDA stream-based SM4 algorithm consistently outperforms the CUDA-based SM4 algorithm by 0.24μs. With a data volume of 30 MB, our algorithm is nearly 400μs faster. We leverage the security and privacy benefits of the optimized SM4 encryption algorithm by integrating it with blockchain technology. This ensures the security of sensitive information and strengthens the integrity and security of the blockchain system. This approach not only secures data, but also promotes broader adoption of blockchain technology across industries, enhancing its reliability and trustworthiness.

Keywords: SM4 Encryption Algorithm · Blockchain · GPU · CUDA

1 Introduction

In this era of rapidly advancing Internet technology, the widespread sharing of information is a global phenomenon, exerting a profound influence on numerous fields. As Internet information systems continue to expand, the importance of information security is growing more pronounced. There exists an urgent need to develop and implement effective solutions to guarantee the security of information. Modern cryptography assumes a pivotal role in assuring data confidentiality and integrity.

J. Zhu et al. (Eds.): CBCS 2023, CCIS 2098, pp. 31–45, 2024.
https://doi.org/10.1007/978-981-97-3203-6_2

As the volume of data continues to surge, the importance of rapid and efficient cryptographic algorithms for safeguarding information cannot be overstated. The sequential nature of traditional national encryption algorithms leads to slowdowns when processing large amounts of data, resulting in potential inefficiencies. In addition, traditional national secrets algorithms may experience memory limitations or performance bottlenecks, limiting their ability to handle voluminous amounts of data.

To address this challenge, we implement a number of enhancements aimed at improving the efficiency of national encryption algorithms. This initiative serves as a solution for effectively encrypting big data. The specific improvements encompass: 1) We optimize the SM4 encryption algorithm and reduce the number of iterations from 32 to 8 to improve efficiency. 2) We combine the national secret algorithm with GPU parallel computing technology, taking full advantage of the characteristics of CUDA. This enables us to implement parallel processing for each group of SM4 block encryption, as well as byte substitution and byte left shift within the encryption process. 3) We take advantage of the characteristics of CUDA streams to further improve the performance of the SM4 encryption algorithm. 4) We utilize the constant storage Sbox method to increase access speed and decrease memory bandwidth requirements. Through the integration of the optimized SM4 algorithm with powerful GPU hardware computation units, we simultaneously process multiple encryption tasks. This enables high-speed encryption operations on voluminous data.

The integration of blockchain technology with national secret algorithms provides efficient information protection and reliable verification. The national secret algorithm provides robust techniques for the encryption and decryption of data, ensuring both confidentiality and integrity. In addition, the tamper-proof and decentralized nature of the blockchain ensures the true validity and security of the data. This integration not only ensures comprehensive information security, but also provides a reliable foundation for open and transparent information exchange. It serves as a secure and reliable technical cornerstone for development and innovation across various fields. In conclusion, the fusion of national secret algorithms and blockchain technology provides a robust guarantee of information security and establishes a secure and reliable technological foundation for the advancement of various fields.

The remainder of the paper is structured as follows. Section 2 provides an overview of recent research and advances in the field, accompanied by a discussion of relevant work. In Sect. 3, we explain the encryption principles of the standard SM4 algorithm. Section 4 describes our proposed efficient SM4 encryption algorithm, which is based on mathematical principles. Section 5 explores the application of the efficient encryption algorithm to blockchain technology. Section 6 presents the experimental results and an efficiency benefit analysis. Finally, Sect. 7 summarises the conclusions drawn from the entire discourse.

2   Related Work

Our research focuses on two crucial aspects of related work: one is to optimise the efficient SM4 encryption algorithm, and the other is to investigate the application of the national secret algorithm in the context of blockchain technology.

2.1 Efficient SM4 Encryption Algorithm

In 2016, Lv et al. [1] introduce a novel scheme that produces the round key for each of the 32 key expansion rounds. This innovative approach involves incorporating additional memory to compare both old and new keys. In instances where the keys match, the key expansion operation is omitted. Simultaneously, two dedicated modules are crafted for encryption and decryption processes. To enhance overall system performance, this solution undergoes optimization and is currently implemented on an FPGA platform. In 2018, Cheng et al. [2] further improved the performance of the symmetric encryption server. They achieved optimized efficiency in data transfer between CPU and GPU by leveraging the GPU to schedule the SM4 algorithm. In 2021, researchers including Abed [3] identified the optimal design for implementing the SM4 algorithm on an FPGA. They emphasized that with increasing complexity, the number of rounds required for an optimal scalar design also increases. In 2022, Chen et al. [4] use the SM4-CCM as a hardware architecture in IoT applications to achieve the highest level of encryption efficiency. Chen proposes a design space exploration method that decomposes the SM4-CCM algorithm into five layers and provides three candidate architectures for each layer. By constructing and comparing 63 design schemes, they identify the most efficient one through a series of batch comparisons and analyses. At the same time, researchers including Kwon [5] have extensively optimized the SM4 algorithm on AVR, RISC-V, and ARM platforms, resulting in significant improvements in speed, memory usage, and code size. This has led to a significant increase in the computational speed of SM4. In 2022, Jiang et al. [6] successfully implemented the SM4 encryption algorithm on the FPGA. They ingeniously used a pseudo-random sequence generated by a discrete chaotic system to randomly hide the intermediate values during the SM4 encryption process. This further improved the security and efficiency of the encryption algorithm.

FPGAs excel at improving efficiency, but are difficult to implement due to their high cost and complexity. However, its high cost and complex implementation pose certain challenges. Therefore, we advocate the utilization of CUDA technology to optimize the SM4 encryption algorithm. This approach significantly reduces costs and is relatively straightforward to implement, providing a more economical, practical, and efficient solution for SM4 algorithm applications. CUDA optimization not only increases the encryption efficiency of the SM4 algorithm, but also provides robust support for its flexibility and scalability in various application scenarios.

2.2 Application of National Secret Algorithm in Blockchain

In recent years, there has been a notable increase in the integration of national secret algorithms into blockchain design. This underscores the increasing importance and potential application of national secret algorithms in the field of information security. In 2021, Zhang et al. [7] introduced a system based on SM2, SM3, and SM4 algorithms along with a certificate issuance verification mechanism. This greatly improved the data transmission security performance of systems based on SM2 and SM3. In addition, the system intelligently incorporates the SM4 algorithm and uses homomorphic encryption technology to ensure data accuracy verification. Furthermore, in 2022, Ma et al. [8] introduced a traceable supply chain monitoring solution that relies on a private chain and proof-of-work (PoW) consensus mechanism. They integrated the SM3 cryptographic hash algorithm to ensure data integrity, while implementing the SM9 identity-based cryptographic algorithm to ensure data authenticity and confidentiality. In 2023, Fu [9] and other researchers decided to use the SM2 algorithm as a replacement for the traditional ECDSA algorithm, resulting in significant performance improvements in the blockchain design built on this structural platform. The signature and verification efficiency of the algorithm is improved by reducing the inverse operation in the SM2 algorithm.

The national secret algorithm is preferred because of its exceptional level of security, reliability, and efficiency. The integration of the national secret algorithm into the blockchain design enhances security and performance. This assures the confidentiality and integrity of data, effectively thwarting malicious attacks and data tampering. The application of the improved SM4 algorithm to blockchain technology significantly increases the efficiency of encryption algorithms, providing a robust assurance of blockchain security and credibility.

3 SM4 Encryption Algorithm

The SM4 algorithm operates as a symmetric encryption algorithm, where the decryption process closely reflects the encryption process. The only difference is the order of the round keys used. During encryption, the round keys are used in the order rk_0, rk_1,..., rk_{31}, whereas during decryption they follow the reverse order of the encryption round keys: rk_{31}, rk_{30},..., rk_0. After 32 iterations and the application of the reverse transformation, the plaintext is finally obtained as ciphertext. It is assumed that the plaintext (X_0, X_1, X_2, X_3) is encrypted into ciphertext (Y_0, Y_1, Y_2, Y_3) using the round key rk_i, where $i \in \{0, 1,2,3,...,31\}$. The $<<<i$ denotes a left shift of i bits within the loop. The $\oplus$ denotes an XOR operation. F denotes a wheel function and T denotes a synthetic permutation.

In the SM4 encryption algorithm, the round function F plays a pivotal role in both encryption and decryption processes, demanding 32 rounds of iterations Eq. 1.

$$X_{i+4} = X_i \oplus T(X_{i+1} \oplus X_{i+2} \oplus X_{i+3} \oplus rk_i) \qquad (1)$$

T is a synthetic permutation function consisting of a linear transform L and a nonlinear transform τ, as shown in Eq. 2

$$T(\cdot) = L(\tau(\cdot)) \qquad (2)$$

The nonlinear transformation τ consists of four parallel Sboxes. Assuming the input as $A = (a_0, a_1, a_2, a_3)$ and the output as $B = (b_0, b_1, b_2, b_3)$, the representation of the non-linear transformation is shown in Eq. 3

$$B = \tau(X_i) = (Sbox(X_0), Sbox(X_1), Sbox(X_2), Sbox(X_3)) \qquad (3)$$

The input to the linear transformation L is the output of the non-linear transformation τ. The formulation of the linear transformation is shown in Eq. 4

$$L(B) = B \oplus (B <<< 2) \oplus (B <<< 10) \oplus (B <<< 18) \oplus (B <<< 24) \qquad (4)$$

4   An Efficient Encryption Algorithm Based on SM4

In the fields of computer science and cryptography, the existence of efficient algorithms for data processing is crucial. It is imperative to thoroughly examine the iterative aspects of the algorithm and conduct a comprehensive analysis of its structure, calculation methods, and performance characteristics. It is important to acknowledge that multiple iterations can impact computational efficiency. Reducing the number of iterations implies that the algorithm operates more swiftly, as there are fewer steps in the calculation process. This optimization substantially enhances the algorithm's efficiency, which is particularly beneficial when there is a need to process large volumes of data rapidly. Therefore, the optimization of iterative processes stands out as one of the paramount methods to enhance algorithm performance.

To reduce the number of iterations and increase computational efficiency, it is essential to first comprehend the intricate characteristics of a particular computational method. Only through a thorough understanding of the calculation method can we make targeted modifications to reduce the number of iterations and increase the speed of operation. The crux of this process lies in the comprehension of the fundamental mechanics of the computations. This allows us to optimize with precision, ensuring not only a reduction in the number of iterations, but also an increase in efficiency, all while maintaining the correctness and reliability of the algorithm. Therefore, in order to optimize the iterative process, a thorough understanding of how computations are performed is essential.

To minimize the number of iterations, it is critical to have a profound understanding of the iterative algorithm. This allows us to optimize the code by reducing memory access and computational overhead. In the comprehensive analysis of the original iteration process, it is essential to understand the computation of each step and its significance within the overall algorithm. To achieve this, we revise the original 32 iterations and streamline it to a process of 8 iterations. Each iteration now processes four neighboring elements. In contrast to the original loop, which incremented 'i' by 1 per iteration, we now increment 'i' by 4 per iteration. The updated mathematical expression is shown in Eq. 5. (where $i = 0, 4, 8, 12, 16, 20, 24, 28$):

$$
\begin{aligned}
X_0 &= X_0{}^\wedge\ T\!\left(X_1{}^\wedge X_2{}^\wedge X_3{}^\wedge rk_i\right) \\
X_1 &= X_1{}^\wedge\ T\!\left(X_2{}^\wedge X_3{}^\wedge X_0{}^\wedge rk_{i+1}\right) \\
X_2 &= X_2{}^\wedge\ T\!\left(X_3{}^\wedge X_0{}^\wedge X_1{}^\wedge rk_{i+2}\right) \\
X_3 &= X_3{}^\wedge\ T\!\left(X_0{}^\wedge X_1{}^\wedge X_2{}^\wedge rk_{i+3}\right)
\end{aligned}
\tag{5}
$$

Breaking the adapted iterative process into four distinct steps, each responsible for updating X_0, X_1, X_2, and X_3, helps avoid the need to consolidate all updates into a single step. This significantly reduces dependencies and allows computations to proceed more rapidly without waiting for the results of the previous iteration. This finer granularity makes it easier to understand and analyze the behavior of the algorithm, as well as to optimize and parallelize the code. In general, both iterative processes execute the same operations, but the modified iterative process is more granular and easier to manage and comprehend. For voluminous data operations, this decomposition approach proves to be more suitable. The efficient design of the iterative encryption process results in the flowchart shown in Fig. 1.

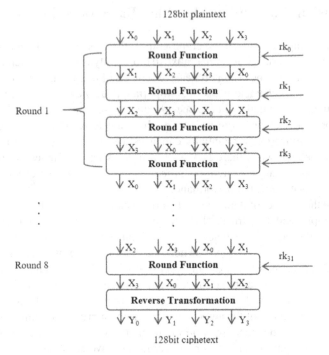

Fig. 1. Improved encryption process.

By breaking an iteration into four independent steps, we improve the readability and maintainability of the code and reduce its overall complexity. This modular design also increases the reliability of the code, since each step can be unit-tested individually. It is important to emphasize that these modifications do not modify the fundamental nature of the algorithm. Instead, they break it down into more refined operations. As a result, encryption performance and the security of national secrets are not affected. These improvements continue to be implemented while preserving the intrinsic properties of the algorithm. This ensures that optimizations are possible that are tailored to specific implementation scenarios.

At the same time, our goal is to improve algorithm execution efficiency by leveraging the full potential of modern parallel computing architectures. This approach ensures the delivery of faster data processing services while maintaining security standards.

The national secret SM4 algorithm includes two key stages: nonlinear transformation and linear transformation. The nonlinear transformation stage involves four byte substitution operations, while the linear transformation stage $(L(B))$ involves four left shift operations. The optimization of these two stages is the focus of our research, which aims to improve the computational efficiency and overall performance of the algorithm. Our goal is to improve the computational efficiency of both B and $L(B)$, thereby facilitating the efficient execution of the national secret encryption algorithm. To achieve this goal, we employ a parallel computing strategy to calculate in parallel $Sbox(X_0)$, $Sbox(X_1)$,

$Sbox(X_2)$, $Sbox(X_3)$, and the left shift operation of B, which includes $(B < < < 2)$, $(B < < < 10)$, $(B < < < 18)$, and $(B < < < 24)$.

We optimize the algorithm by using CUDA to simultaneously process 4 Sboxes replacements and 4 row shifts. This approach significantly optimizes the efficiency of the encryption algorithm. By executing Sboxes operations and left-shift operations in parallel, we effectively reduce the computation time and fully exploit the parallel computing capabilities of modern architectures. The simultaneous execution of corresponding partial operations in both the nonlinear and linear transformations results in an overall improvement in computational speed. This significant efficiency gain is achieved while maintaining the correctness of the algorithm. This optimization strategy is instrumental in speeding up the data encryption process without compromising security.

We improve the national secret SM4 algorithm using CUDA streams. This involves assigning the task of blocking plaintext data to the CPU, while entrusting the encryption operation to the GPU. In addition, we use 'fseek' to guarantee that the contents of encrypted files can be fully read. At the same time, we employ dynamic memory allocation to ensure that the data can be completely loaded into memory. The national secret SM4 algorithm requires that the length of the data to be encrypted must be a multiple of the block size. In cases where the data length doesn't meet this criterion, we require to perform appropriate padding operations. This ensures that the data length complies with the requirement and ultimately guarantees the correctness and reliability of the encryption process.

In the national encryption algorithm using CUDA streams, the encryption operations of each group are independent of each other and lack interdependence. This provides us with the opportunity for parallelization. With each thread assigned to a specific group, we maximize the utilization of the GPU's processing capacity, thereby improving the overall performance of the algorithm.

In the national secret encryption algorithm, there is often a need to access the S-box for byte substitution operations. In CUDA programming, we optimize access to read-only data by making full use of constant memory and texture memory. Constants provide faster access speeds and reduce memory bandwidth requirements compared to global memory.

Texture memory is another form of read-only memory commonly employed in applications such as image processing and pattern matching. It requires special configuration, but provides efficient data caching and access. However, the encryption algorithm relies on random access to plaintext, so the memory access advantages of texture memory cannot be fully leveraged. Therefore, we choose constant memory to store S-boxes in order to maximize the efficiency of the block encryption algorithm. This strategic use of constant memory allows us to optimize algorithm performance while ensuring that the data remains read-only.

In block encryption, efficient use of the Sbox is critical. At the same time, efficient data transfer on the device side is a crucial task. To achieve this, we use the 'cudaMemcpyToSymbol' instruction, which allows efficient transfer of S-boxes. These optimizations significantly improve the performance of block cipher algorithms.

In CUDA, threads naturally aggregate into thread warps, which organize themselves into groups of 32. This is the smallest scheduling unit in CUDA, which means that threads within the same warp execute computations simultaneously. However, the flexibility of CUDA allows the thread block size to be any integer between 1 and 1024. This can lead to scenarios where the thread block size is not a perfect multiple of 32. In such cases, the final thread warp contains fewer than 32 threads, but still occupies the compute unit of an entire thread warp, resulting in a waste of GPU resources.

Therefore, we select a 512-thread configuration for the national secret encryption algorithm. In addition, the lattice size is the plaintext size divided by the product of the number of threads per block and the plaintext group size. By implementing these optimization measures, we effectively avoid a waste of resources and ultimately improve the execution efficiency of the algorithm.

In the design of the national encryption algorithm based on CUDA stream, optimizing data transfer is a pivotal aspect. In this algorithm, both the plaintext and the key are transferred from the CPU using page-locked memory to the video memory of the GPU, replacing the use of pageable memory. This approach provides several advantages. First, it allows data transfer and kernel execution to occur concurrently, improving overall computational efficiency. Second, the page-locked memory can be mapped directly to the device memory, minimizing the frequency and associated overhead of data transfers between the device and the host. Finally, the use of page-locked memory facilitates faster data exchange, further accelerating algorithm execution speed.

By leveraging the scheduling capabilities of CUDA streams, we achieve the overlap of data transfer and kernel operations. This significantly improves the encryption efficiency of the grouping algorithm. The process of executing these overlapping streams is illustrated in Fig. 2. Each stream operates independently without affecting the others. To optimize the GPU's computational efficiency, we partition the data and employ CUDAmemcpyasync() to execute the computation in one stream while simultaneously performing the data transfer in another stream. This strategy enables parallel processing. This approach not only maximizes the GPU's computational capabilities, but also efficiently exploits memory transfer speeds, ultimately improving the overall efficiency of the algorithm.

Fig. 2. Overlapping stream execution

5   Efficient Encryption Algorithm for Blockchain Security

Efficient encryption algorithms play a vital role in ensuring blockchain security. The introduction of the SM4 encryption algorithm provides a reliable guarantee of data security and adds powerful protection to blockchain technology. The improved SM4 algorithm achieves excellent performance in terms of encryption and decryption speed, which provides clear advantages in key scenarios such as processing high volumes of data and real-time transactions. As a result, the SM4 algorithm is capable of processing large amounts of data while providing reliable security for real-time transactions. In addition, the high security of SM4 effectively protects against various malicious attacks, providing a solid guarantee for the stable operation of the blockchain system. Figure 3 clearly shows the seamless integration of the national secret SM4 algorithm and blockchain technology. This not only substantially enhances the security of the blockchain, but also provides opportunities for its application in scenarios such as large-scale data processing and real-time transactions, and provides robust technical support. The highly efficient SM4 encryption algorithm provides a reliable option for protecting sensitive information and important transactions, further ensuring privacy and integrity during data transmission.

Storing encrypted data on the blockchain offers several significant advantages. Firstly, the blockchain is a decentralized, distributed ledger. Once data is recorded, it cannot be tampered with or deleted. This feature guarantees the integrity of the data, and anyone can verify its authenticity, thus establishing trust. Secondly, the distributed nature of the blockchain allows data to be backed up on multiple nodes, which improves the reliability and security of the data. Finally, because the encryption algorithm protects the privacy of the data, even on a public blockchain, only those with the key can decrypt and access the data, thus protecting the privacy of the user.

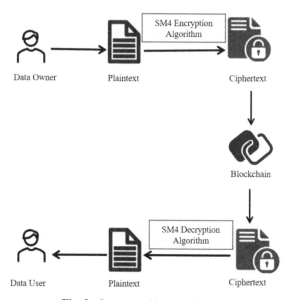

Fig. 3. System architecture diagram

This integration actively and significantly enhances security guarantees in various fields, especially those involving confidential data and important transactions. By combining efficient encryption algorithms with blockchain technology, we not only ensure privacy and integrity during data transmission, but also provide a solid security foundation for blockchain applications.

6 Experimental Results and Analysis

The significant performance advantages of our enhanced SM4 algorithm are empirically validated. We perform SM4 encryption and decryption verification on data ranging from 1 KB to 100 KB and from 1 MB to 100 MB. We conduct a comprehensive comparison between our improved and efficient SM4 algorithm, which is based on underlying operations, and the CUDA-based SM4 encryption algorithm. Through the application of CUDA programming, we conduct experiments on the standard SM4 algorithm to obtain experimental data related to CUDA-based SM4. Detailed measurements and records of the SM4 encryption and decryption process for various data sizes are shown in Table 1. These records not only provide an objective evaluation of the performance of the SM4 algorithm over various data sizes, but also serve as a critical reference for future optimizations and enhancements aimed at improving encryption speed.

Table 1. SM4 encryption and decryption time comparison

	our Encryption(ms)	our Decryption(ms)	Encryption (ms)	Decryption (ms)
1KB	0.0178	0.0177	0.018048	0.017952
5KB	0.058	0.057	0.058177	0.057697
10KB	0.091	0.091	0.091837	0.091573
15KB	0.0918	0.0918	0.091873	0.091681
20KB	0.09194	0.09191	0.092096	0.091892
25KB	0.0928	0.0928	0.092848	0.092672
30KB	0.09286	0.09283	0.093045	0.092872
35KB	0.0927	0.0926	0.093056	0.092352
40KB	0.092705	0.09265	0.093089	0.092617
45KB	0.09271	0.09272	0.093149	0.092857
50KB	0.09273	0.09275	0.093184	0.092895
55KB	0.09276	0.09277	0.093312	0.092948
60KB	0.09276	0.09278	0.093372	0.09301
65KB	0.09278	0.092782	0.093412	0.09317
70KB	0.0927785	0.092785	0.093497	0.093358
75KB	0.09278	0.09279	0.093555	0.093457
80KB	0.092783	0.092795	0.093659	0.093544

(*continued*)

Table 1. (*continued*)

	our Encryption(ms)	our Decryption(ms)	Encryption (ms)	Decryption (ms)
85KB	0.0928	0.0928	0.093795	0.093641
90KB	0.09286	0.09285	0.093683	0.093451
95KB	0.09289	0.09288	0.093784	0.093636
100KB	0.093	0.093	0.093874	0.093734
1MB	0.3572	0.356	0.35739	0.35697
5MB	1.5808	1.5808	1.5817	1.5816
10MB	2.989	2.98	3.0125	2.9932
15MB	4.47	4.46	4.5104	4.4615
20MB	5.943	5.94	6.0112	5.9479
25MB	7.4	7.42	7.4482	7.3716
30MB	8.92	8.91	9.3181	9.2212
35MB	10.386	10.386	11.267	11.114
40MB	11.8	11.814	12.879	12.56
45MB	13.32	13.33	14.593	14.419
50MB	14.78	14.788	16.172	16.107
55MB	16.26	16.269	17.438	17.24
60MB	17.68	17.69	18.917	18.682
65MB	19.216	19.22	21.7	21.667
70MB	20.65	20.63	23.949	23.359
75MB	22.16	22.15	26.058	25.774
80MB	23.61	23.7	27.87	27.504
85MB	25.08	25.088	29.561	29.262
90MB	26.573	26.565	31.296	30.721
95MB	28.04	28.04	33.147	32.086
100MB	29.5	29.51	34.17	33.714

This section presents a detailed analysis of the encryption times for various plaintext and ciphertext data sizes, comparing the CUDA-based SM4 algorithm with the CUDA stream and high-iteration SM4 algorithms. Experimental results are shown in Fig. 4(a), which compares SM4 algorithm encryption times for plaintext data sizes ranging from 1 to 100 MB, and Fig. 4(b), which compares decryption times for ciphertext data sizes in the same range. The comparison in Fig. 4 shows that high-iteration improvements to the SM4 algorithm effectively increase the efficiency of encryption operations. In particular, the SM4 algorithm based on CUDA streaming and high iteration shows the shortest times for both encryption and decryption. This demonstrates that the SM4 algorithm using

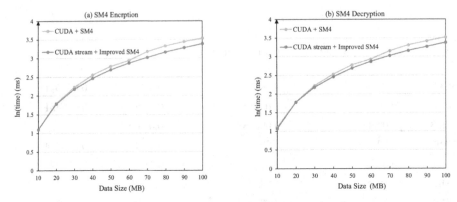

Fig. 4. 1-100MB SM4 encryption and decryption time

CUDA stream and high iteration excels in data processing, providing users with faster encryption and decryption speeds. By utilising the parallel computing capabilities of the GPU, the characteristics of CUDA streams and the highly iterative enhancements to the SM4 algorithm, the efficiency of encryption and decryption operations is significantly improved. Such performance improvements provide a robust reference solution for real-world data application scenarios.

We compare our method to the approach described in reference [10]. In reference [10], the SM4 algorithm is used to encrypt 20,000 K of data on the blockchain, which takes 750 ms. In our case, it takes 5.94 ms to encrypt 20 MB of data.

We securely store and upload encrypted data to the blockchain, ensuring its security. Specifically, it only takes 0.1 ms to upload 3 KB of data to the blockchain. Meanwhile, for a 100 KB file, the encryption process requires about 0.093 ms. This shows that the encryption process requires significantly less time compared to uploading data to the blockchain. Therefore, we can conclude that uploading data to the blockchain after encryption, while slightly more time consuming, significantly increases the security of the data. This signifies that privacy and integrity can be maintained throughout the data transmission process.

This level of security is paramount in many application scenarios, especially those involving sensitive information or critical transactions. As a result, the combination of encryption and blockchain technology not only guarantees data security, but also provides a reliable foundation for future applications.

7   Conclusion

This paper presents the foundational design of the National Secret SM4 encryption algorithm, integrating principles of GPU programming to achieve parallel optimization. This includes the effective utilization of memory, the reduction of memory consumption, and the implementation of more efficient algorithms to enhance program memory utilization efficiency. At the same time, by breaking the algorithm into multiple tasks that can be executed concurrently, the parallel computing capabilities of the GPU are fully exploited, allowing each task to run independently on separate processing units, thereby augmenting the overall computational speed. In addition, the adoption of CUDA stream technology facilitates the concurrent execution of multiple computational tasks, further enhancing the performance of the program. This optimization approach is particularly important in scenarios involving extensive data processing or the need for efficient encryption and decryption, as it maximizes the GPU's parallel computing capabilities.

In addition, we seamlessly integrate the efficient national secret SM4 encryption algorithm into blockchain technology, thereby enhancing data security and privacy protection while achieving greater operational efficiency. The use of the SM4 algorithm guarantees robust protection of information during both data transmission and storage, strengthening the overall security of the blockchain system. Its exceptional efficiency ensures that it never significantly affects system performance, while maintaining security. This integration not only provides users with more dependable privacy and data security guarantees, but also provides a solid technical foundation for the widespread adoption of blockchain applications and the expansion of practical application areas. Our endeavors introduce new opportunities for the development of blockchain technology in the future. At the same time, they provide users and enterprises with more trustworthy data protection solutions in the digital era.

Acknowledgement. The authors acknowledge National Natural Science Foundation of China (No. 62202316), Characteristic Innovation Projects in Guangdong Provincial Universities (No. 2022KTSCX308), Supporting Project of National Natural Science Foundation of China (No. 6022310037K), Scientific Research Startup Fund for Shenzhen High-Caliber Personnel of Shenzhen Polytechnic (No.6021310026K).

References

1. Qian, L., Li, L., et al. High-speed encryption and decryption system based on SM4 algorithm. Int. J. Secur. Appl. **10**(9): 1–8 (2016)
2. Cheng, W., Zheng, F., Pan, W., Lin, J., Li, H., Li, B.: High-Performance Symmetric Cryptography Server with GPU Acceleration. In: Qing, S., Mitchell, C., Chen, L., Liu, D. (eds.) Information and Communications Security: 19th International Conference, ICICS 2017, Beijing, China, December 6-8, 2017, Proceedings, pp. 529–540. Springer International Publishing, Cham (2018). https://doi.org/10.1007/978-3-319-89500-0_46
3. Abed, S.: Performance evaluation of the SM4 cipher based on field-programmable gate array implementation. IET Circ., Devices Syst. **15**(2): 121-135 (2021)
4. Chen, R., Li, B.: Exploration of the high-efficiency hardware architecture of SM4-CCM for IoT applications. Electronics **11**(6), 935 (2022). https://doi.org/10.3390/electronics11060935
5. Kwon, H., et al.: Optimized Implementation of SM4 on AVR microcontrollers, RISC-V Processors, and ARM Processors. IEEE Access **10**, 80225–80233 (2022). https://doi.org/10.1109/ACCESS.2022.3195217
6. Jiang, Z., Yan, W., Ding, W., Yue, L., Ding, Q.: SM4 Chaotic masking scheme against power analysis based on FPGA. Int. J. Bifurcation a Chaos **32**(08), 2250110 (2022)
7. Zhang, S., Meng, H., Li, X., et al. Hunion traceability: a new type of blockchain traceability system based on SM2, SM3 and SM4[C]//Proceedings of the 2021 4th International Conference on Blockchain Technology and Applications, pp. 107–115 (2021)
8. Zijian, M., et al. research on monitoring technology of industrial cannabis based on blockchain and SM series cryptographic algorithm. Int. J. Network Secur. **24**(1), pp.36–48 (2022)

9. Jinhua, F., Zhou, W., Zhang, S.: Fabric blockchain design based on improved SM2 algorithm. Int. J. Seman. Web Inf. Syst. **19**(1), 1–13 (2023). https://doi.org/10.4018/IJSWIS.322403

10. Deng, L., Liu, S., Xu, H., et al.: Blockchain-based charitable donation privacy protection scheme (2022)

11. Sun, J., Yao, X., Wang, S., Ying, W.: Blockchain-based secure storage and access scheme for electronic medical records in IPFS. IEEE Access **8**, 59389–59401 (2020). https://doi.org/10.1109/ACCESS.2020.2982964

12. Kumar, S., Bharti, A.K., Amin, R.: Decentralized secure storage of medical records using blockchain and IPFS: a comparative analysis with future directions. Secur. Priv. **4**(5), e162 (2021)

13. Jayapriya, J., Jeyanthi, N.: Scalable blockchain model using off-chain IPFS storage for healthcare data security and privacy. J. Parallel Distrib. Comput. **164**, 152–167 (2022)

14. Sun, Z., Han, D., Li, D., et al.: A blockchain-based secure storage scheme for medical information. J. Wireless. Com. Network. **2022**, 40 (2022)

15. Goyat, S., Kant, S.: Performance evaluation of parallel AES algorithm implementing GPU. Int. J. Innovative Technol. Explor. Eng. (IJITEE) **8**(6s2) (2019).

16. Assafli, H.T., Hashim, I.A., Naser, A.A.: Advanced Encryption Standard (AES) acceleration and analysis using graphical processing unit (GPU). Appl. Nanosci. **13**(2), 1245–1250 (2021). https://doi.org/10.1007/s13204-021-01985-3

17. Fei, X., Li, K., Yang, W., Li, K.: Analysis of energy efficiency of a parallel AES algorithm for CPU-GPU heterogeneous platforms. Parallel Comput. **94–95**, 102621 (2020). https://doi.org/10.1016/j.parco.2020.102621

18. Siva Kumar, A., Godfrey Winster, S., Ramesh, R.: Efficient sensitivity orient blockchain encryption for improved data security in cloud. Concurrent Eng. **29**(3), 249–257 (2021). https://doi.org/10.1177/1063293X211008586

19. Liu, X., Wang, Z., Jin, C., Li, F., Li, G.: A blockchain-based medical data sharing and protection scheme. IEEE Access **7**, 118943–118953 (2019). https://doi.org/10.1109/ACCESS.2019.2937685

20. Yang, K., Yang, B., Zhou, Y., Wang, T., Gong, L.: Privacy protection of task in crowdsourcing: policy-hiding and attribute updating attribute-based access control based on blockchain. Wireless Commun. Mob. Comput. **2022**, 1–12 (2022). https://doi.org/10.1155/2022/7787866

21. Junejo, A.Z., Hashmani, M.A., Memon, M.M.: Empirical evaluation of privacy efficiency in blockchain networks: review and open challenges. Appl. Sci. **11**(15), 7013 (2021). https://doi.org/10.3390/app11157013

22. Tezcan, C.: Optimization of advanced encryption standard on graphics processing units. IEEE Access **9**, 67315–67326 (2021)

23. Kumar, T.M., Balmuri, K.R., Marchewka, A., Divakarachari, P.B., Konda, S.: Implementation of speed-efficient key-scheduling process of AES for secure storage and transmission of data. Sensors **21**(24), 8347 (2021). https://doi.org/10.3390/s21248347

24. Priya, S.S.S., Karthigaikumar, P., Teja, N.R.: FPGA implementation of AES algorithm for high speed applications. Analog Integr. Circ. Sig. Process **112**(1), 115–125 (2022)

25. Siva Balan, N., Murugan, B.S.: Low area FPGA Implementation of AES architecture with EPRNG for IoT application. J. Electron. Test. **38**(2), 181–193 (2022). https://doi.org/10.1007/s10836-022-05997-x

26. An, S., Seo, S.C.: Designing a new XTS-AES parallel optimization implementation technique for fast file encryption. IEEE Access **10**, 25349–25357 (2022)

27. Ahmad, R., et al.: Performance analysis of enhanced AES-128 and blowfish algorithms through parallel-pipelined-memory techniques. Wirel. Pers. Commun. **127**(4), 3615–3635 (2022). https://doi.org/10.1007/s11277-022-09933-2

28. Puneeth, R., et al.: Security and data privacy of medical information in blockchain using lightweight cryptographic system. Int. J. Eng. **36**(5), 925–933 (2023)

29. Sathya, A., et al.: A Comprehensive study of blockchain services: future of cryptography. Int. J. Adv. Comput. Sci. Appl. **11**(10) (2020)
30. Zhang, T., et al.: Covert channels in blockchain and blockchain based covert communication: Overview, state-of-the-art, and future directions. Comput. Commun. **11**(10), 279–288 (2023). 205, 136–146.NS0, (2020)
31. Guo, H., Li, W., Nejad, M., Shen, C.C.: A hybrid blockchain-edge architecture for electronic health record management with attribute-based cryptographic mechanisms. IEEE Trans. Network Ser. Manage. **20**(2), 1759–1774 (2023). https://doi.org/10.1109/TNSM.2022.318 6006

Blockchain Architecture

Practical Private Intersection-Sum Protocols with Good Scalability

Yuanyuan Li[1], Hanyue Xiao[1(✉)], Peng Han[2], and Zhihao Zhou[3]

[1] College of Computer Science and Technology, Chongqing University of Posts and Telecommunications, Chongqing, China
s220233053@stu.cqupt.edu.cn
[2] Chongqing Academy of Science and Technology, Chongqing, China
[3] School of Automation, Chongqing University of Posts and Telecommunications, Chongqing, China

Abstract. Private intersection-sum (PI-Sum) enables participants to compute the sum of data associated with the intersection without revealing any personal information. It has been a research focus of secure multi-party computation, particularly valuable for a business application: attributing aggregate ad conversions. Most PI-Sum research based on Decisional Diffie-Hellman (DDH) assumptions and techniques such as garbled circuits. They rely on modular exponentiation operations and frequent interactions between participants, resulting in high computational overhead and lack of scalability within practical applications. In this paper, we design two practical PI-Sum protocols with different set domains. Specifically, we convert private sets into the bit-set representation and bloom filters. Then, we encrypt them with elliptic curves (ECC) Threshold ElGamal and Paillier algorithms. Through simulation paradigms and theoretical analysis, it is proved that the efficiency of our protocols are higher than those of the available protocols. Finally, we demonstrate the scalability of our PI-Sum protocols to multi-party private intersection-sum (MPI-Sum).

Keywords: Private intersection-sum · Bit-set · Bloom filter · Homomorphic encryption

1 Introduction

Nowadays, the cooperative computation between different organizations or individuals becomes extremely important while sharing information. Owners who hold various data would like to obtain more valuable information without leaking their own personal data. Secure multi-party computation (SMPC) can solve problems about cooperative computation among multiple participants in a secure fashion, which greatly improves data utilization. As a specific SMPC research, private set intersection (PSI) is designed to compute the intersection of private sets without disclosing any other information. It has been applied in applications such as location sharing [1], genetic sequence matching [2] and ad

J. Zhu et al. (Eds.): CBCS 2023, CCIS 2098, pp. 49–63, 2024.
https://doi.org/10.1007/978-981-97-3203-6_3

conversion [3]. Several efficient traditional PSI protocols based on public-key encryption schemes [4,5], garbled circuits [6] and oblivious transfer extension protocols [7,8] already exist. However, in practical scenarios, simple intersection operations about private sets can no longer satisfy actual requirements. It is necessary to make further computations about the intersection, including cardinality, average and sum, etc. Based on PSI, PI-Sum additionally computes the sum of data related to the intersection. Also, they provide new possibilities for research and applications of secure multi-party computation.

1.1 Related Work

Research about secure computations of basic function operations based on PSI includes [3,9–15]. Mixed computations of intersection and union based on ElGamal algorithm and re-randomization of ciphertexts are proposed in [9]. However, this method is only applicable to small set domains. Ying in [10] proposed secure computations of statistical functions, which reduce monetary costs and communication overhead. Different private set intersection cardinality (PSI-CA) protocols, which utilize polynomial interpolation and hybrid circuit technologies are proposed in [11] for an untrustworthy malicious third party. Similar work is done by Lv *et al.* [12], which reduced communication overhead and improved deviation by limiting the number of 1-bit in the Bloom filter (BF). However, both these two protocols only output the cardinality of the intersection without further computation.

PI-Sum is more practical than PSI-CA. One of the earliest works proposed applying PI-Sum to attributing aggregate ad conversions is by Ion *et al.* [3]. PI-Sum protocols in [13] which use Pohlig-Hellman algorithm (based on DDH assumptions), oblivious pseudo-random function and bloom filters are more efficient than the garbled circuit-based PSI. Another work in [14] presented PI-Sum under a malicious model. However, these three solutions mentioned above require multiple interactions between participants, and it is difficult to extend them to MPI-Sum because of high communication and computation costs. Furthermore, the cryptosystem based on DDH assumptions and operations of large primes need longer keys to ensure system security. This results in slower computations. A private membership testing protocol is designed by Liu *et al.* [15], which utilizes the computational result as an arithmetic shared value to reduce the execution time of statistical computing protocols for PSI. Nevertheless, the computation costs of this protocol were not analyzed specifically, thus restricting the efficiency of this protocol in practical applications.

1.2 Contribution

As mentioned in [13], an advertising conversion occurs when users look through an online advertisement and then make a purchase from the advertised company. The advertised provider knows user data related to ad views, while the company possesses specific user information about purchases, including the precise spend. Both parties are unwilling to expose their private data but still hope to learn the aggregate statistical information about specific users. This scenario can be abstracted as a practical problem: a party owns personal data about users, and another one holds different personal information about some particular users. Both of them want to obtain aggregate statistic for these particular users. Private intersection-sum (PI-Sum) protocols can provide a better solution for such practical applications. Therefore, it is of significant value for us to study PI-Sum protocols.

In this paper, we designed two PI-Sum protocols within different private set sizes for both small and large set domains. Concretely, we take use of different data structures to process the private elements before the execution of protocols, and simplify the interactions between participants to improve the scalability of PI- Sum to MPI-Sum. At a result, our protocols exhibit the following characteristics:

- We present two PI-Sum protocols according to the size of private sets, and convert the set into bit-set representation and BF respectively, which can effectively reduce the computation overhead. Through prototype implementation of our protocols, we compare both computation and communication costs with existing schemes. Experiments show that our protocols are more practical.
- Our protocols based on a variant of the ECC Threshold ElGamal algorithm, which generally requires shorter keys to achieve the same level of security. This makes these two protocols more efficient with practical applications.
- We reduced the number of communication rounds to $O(1)$ without frequent interactions between participants. As a result, our protocols exhibit good scalability.

1.3   Organization

Section 2 mainly introduces fundamental methods and security models. And Sect. 3 elaborates on specific details of two PI-Sum protocols and provides concrete security proofs for our protocols. Then Sect. 4 focuses on the performance of our protocols through theoretical analysis and experimental comparisons. And then we show the scalability of our protocols to MPI-Sum. Finally, we make a conclusion about our study and explain the future research directions in Sect. 5

.

2   Preliminaries

Notations. There are two participants denoted as P_1 and P_2, each holds private set X, Y with the same set size n respectively. Specifically, $X = \{x_i\}_{i=1}^{n}$ and $Y = \{(y_i, t_i)\}_{i=1}^{n}$, where t_i represents integer values associated with y_i. We extract a set from Y and denoted it as $Y' = \{y_i\}_{i=1}^{n}$. After the execution of PI-Sum, P_1 only obtains the private intersection cardinality $|J|(J = X \cap Y')$, while P_2 only obtains the sum of data related to J: $Sum = \sum_{i \in J} t_i$. Then we convert private sets into bit-vectors as B_x for set X and B_y for set Y'. Additionally, we employ a bloom filter $BF(n, m, k)$ where m denotes the size of BF, and k represents the number of hash functions H_k. Specific configurations about these parameters will be detailed in Sect. 2.2.

2.1 Semi-honest Security Model

In this model, we assume that all participants are semi-honest, which follow the protocol strictly but attempt to get more additional information from the protocol. According to [16], we present the security definition of semi-honest model. Let $f(f_1, f_2) : \{0,1\}^* \times \{0,1\}^* \to \{0,1\}^* \times \{0,1\}^*$ be a probabilistic functionality, which is computed by the protocol π. And X,Y represent the private input of P_1, P_2 respectively. Moreover, the view of $P_j(j \in \{1,2\})$ is $view_j^\pi(X,Y) = (X, r_j, m_1^j, m_2^j, ..., m_s^j)$, and r_j is the random value chosen internally by P_j, and m_s^j represents the s-th message received by P_j. $Output_j^\pi(X,Y)$ represents the output of P_j. The protocol π is considered secure if each participant computes information only from its input. We give the following definition about this secure model:

Definition 1. f and π are defined as above. If there exist probabilistic algorithms simulators Sim_1, Sim_2, the protocol π can securely compute f under the presence of semi-honest adversaries:

$$\{(Sim_1(1^\kappa, X, f_1(X,Y)), f(X,Y))\}_{X,Y,\kappa} \overset{C}{\equiv} \{(view_1^\pi(\kappa, X, Y), output_2^\pi(\kappa, X, Y))\}_{X,Y,\kappa} \tag{1}$$

$$\{(Sim_2(1^\kappa, Y, f_2(X,Y)), f(X,Y))\}_{X,Y,\kappa} \overset{C}{\equiv} \{(view_2^\pi(\kappa, X, Y), output_1^\pi(\kappa, X, Y))\}_{X,Y,\kappa} \tag{2}$$

Where $X,Y \in \{0,1\}^*$, κ denotes as the security parameter ($\kappa \in N$).

2.2 Methods for Set Convertion

Bit-Set Representation. We convert private sets into bit vectors based on the representation of bit-set [17]. Let $\mathcal{U} = \{u_1, u_2, ..., u_d\}$ denote the universe. A subset of $\mathcal{U}$ can be represented as $B = \{b_1, b_2, ..., b_d\}$. If $u_i \in \mathcal{U}$, $b_i = 0$, otherwise $b_i = 1 (1 \le i \le d)$. The size of B is always d and independent of the size of a subset, which effectively concealing the size of the subset. For small set domain, we designate the private sets of two parties as X and Y, and both two sets are subsets of $\mathcal{U}$. Then we can convert them into bit vectors: $B_x = \{b_x^1, b_x^2, ..., b_x^d\}$ and $B_y = \{b_y^1, b_y^2, ..., b_y^d\}$. if $u_i \in J$, it indicates that $b_x^i = b_y^i = 0, 1 \le i \le d$.

Bloom Filter. The bloom filter (BF) was introduced in 1970 [18], it is used to compress a set into a fixed-size bit vector, allowing for efficient querying. In this paper, we initialize all bits of a bloom filter $BF(n, m, k)$ to 1. We use k independent hash functions $H_k = \{h_0(x), ..., h_k(x)\}$ to map x to k random positions within the range $[1, m]$ and set bits at corresponding positions to 0. To improve the accuracy of our protocol, it is necessary to consider the false positive rate p generated by BF. This rate refers to the probability that an element is incorrectly identified as being in the set, and p is determined by the formula: $p = 1 - (1 - 1/m)^{nk}$ according to [19]. The value of p decreases as m and n increase. The upper bound of p is given by $\epsilon = p^k \times (1 + \mathcal{O}(\frac{k}{p}\sqrt{\frac{\ln m - k \ln p}{m}}))$. By setting k and m, ϵ can be effectively minimized. When $m \geq n \log_2 e \cdot \log_2 \dfrac{1}{\epsilon}$, BF exhibits optimal performance. By minimizing m, we can found that $k = \log_2 \dfrac{1}{\epsilon}$. Bloom filters used in our protocol all follow these optimal parameters.

2.3 Homomorphic Encryption

Elliptic Curve Threshold ElGamal. Threshold ElGamal algorithm enables secret sharing among multiple participants in [20]. Each participant encrypts data with a shared key and collaborates on decryption with their private keys. Our protocols based on a variant of the Threshold ElGamal algorithm implemented with elliptic curves, and the security of this algorithm depends on elliptic curve discrete logarithm problem (ECDLP) [21]:

Definition 2. *ECDLP: Given an elliptic curve E over F_q, the base point G, and two points $P, Q \in E_{(F_q)}$ to find a integer a, such that $Q = aP$. If a exists, it is computationally difficult.*

Threshold ElGamal algorithm based on Ecc among participants $P_1, P_2, \ldots, P_t$ can be described as follows:

- KeyGen(par)$\rightarrow$ (pk, sk, h): Each participant $P_j (1 \leq j \leq t)$ chooses a private key sk_j and computes their public key $pk_j = sk_j G$ independently. A trusted authority generates the shared public key $h = \sum_{j=1}^{t} pk_j = \sum_{j=1}^{t} sk_j G$ with the private key pairs (pk_j, sk_j) of participants. No participant knows the value of h due to ECDLP.
- Enc(m, r, h) $\rightarrow$ Enc$_h(m)$: Every participant encrypts the plaintext m with public key h and computes a ciphertext tuple Enc$_h(m) = (C_1, C_2) = (rG, rh + mG)$ where $r < q$.
- Dec(Enc$_h(m), \{sk_j\}_{j=1}^{t}$) $\rightarrow$ (mG): Each participant receives the ciphertext Enc$_h(m)$. Then P_j computes $C_1^j = sk_j C_1$ with its private key sk_j. Consequently, all participants decrypt the ciphertext with their private keys collaboratively, and obtain $mG = C_2 - \sum_{j=1}^{t} C_1^j$.

Definition 3. *Elliptic curve Threshold ElGamal algorithm follows additive homomorphism. Given two ciphertexts* Enc$_h(m_1) =$ Enc(m_1, r_1, h), Enc$_h(m_2) =$ Enc(m_2, r_2, h), *they satisfy the following property:*

$$\text{Enc}_h(m_1) + \text{Enc}_h(m_2) = \text{Enc}(m_1 + m_2, r_1 + r_2, h) = \text{Enc}_h(m_1 + m_2) \quad (3)$$

Paillier Cryptosystem. Paillier cryptosystem is a public-key scheme with additive homomorphism and semantic security [22]. It consists of three algorithms as follows:

- KeyGen$\rightarrow$ (pk_p, sk_p): Two primes numbers p, q are randomly selected based on the security parameter, let $N = pq, u = lcm(p - 1, q - 1)$ to compute the least common multiple. $L(x) = \frac{x-1}{N}$, then $s = (L(g^u \bmod N^2))^{-1} \bmod N$ where $g \in \mathbb{Z}_{N^2}^*$. One can obtain a publick key $pk_p = (N, g)$ and a private key $sk_p = (u, s)$.

- $\text{Enc}(pk_p) \to \text{E}_{pk_p}(m')$: m' is the plaintext, a participant can choose a random number $r(r \in \mathbb{Z}_{N^2}^*)$ to compute the ciphertext $\text{E}_{pk_p}(m') = g^{m'} \cdot r^N \text{mod} N^2$.
- $\text{Dec}(sk_p, \text{E}_{pk_p}(m')) \to m'$: The participant can decrypt the cipertext with its own privat key sk_p: $m' = L(\text{E}_{pk_p}(m')^u \text{mod} N^2) \cdot s \text{ mod} N$.

Definition 4. *Given two ciphertexts $E_{pk_p}(m_1)$ and $E_{pk_p}(m_2)$, Paillier cryptosystem satisfies the additive homomorphism of ciphertexts:*

$$E_{pk_p}(m_1) \cdot E_{pk_p}(m_2) = E_{pk_p}(m_1 + m_2) \tag{4}$$

3   PI-Sum Protocols Descriptions

We proposed two PI-Sum protocols for small and large set domains. In both cases, private sets are converted into bit vectors at first. Then we encrypted them with ECC Threshold Elgamal algorithm. After the excution of protocols, the outputs are the sum of associated data and the private intersection cardinality. In this section, we present constructions about PI-Sum protocols.

3.1   PI-Sum Protocol Based Bit-Set

We consider a full set $\mathcal{U} = \{u_1, u_2, ..., u_d\}$. Participants P_1 and P_2 have sets $X = \{x_1, x_2, ..., x_n\}$ and $Y = \{(y_1, t_1), (y_2, t_2), ..., (y_n, t_n)\}$ where $1 < n \le d$ respectively. Both sets X and Y are subsets of $\mathcal{U}$. Specific details of Protocol 1 are illustrated in Fig. 1. Before the excution of Protocol 1, each participant generates a private key sk_j and a public key pk_j, then they obtain the shared public key $h = \sum_{j=1}^{2} pk_j$. Additionally, P_2 generates its key pair (pk_p, sk_p) with Paillier cryptosystem to encrypt t_i. Next P_1 and P_2 convert their sets X and Y' into bit vectors of size d independently: $B_x = \{b_x^1, b_x^2, ..., b_x^d\}$, $B_y = \{b_y^1, b_y^2, ..., b_y^d\}$:

$$\begin{cases} b_x^i = 0, & u_i \in X \\ b_x^i = 1, & u_i \notin X \end{cases} \tag{5}$$

$$\begin{cases} b_y^i = 0, & u_i \in Y' \\ b_y^i = 1, & u_i \notin Y' \end{cases} \tag{6}$$

where $1 \le i \le d$. The protocol is divided into two rounds.

In the first round, P_1 and P_2 encrypt b_x^i and b_y^i with the shared public key h, and P_2 encrypts the associated integer values t_i with pk_p. If $b_y^i = 0$, the encryption can be denoted as $\text{Enc}(pk_p, t_i) \to \text{E}_{pk_p}(t_i)$. Otherwise, P_2 selects a random number r_i and encrypts it as $\text{Enc}(pk_p, r_i) \to \text{E}_{pk_p}(r_i)$. Then P_1 sends ciphertexts $\text{Enc}_h(b_x^i)$ to P_2. After receiving ciphertexts, P_2 executes the homomorphic operation $\text{Enc}_h(b_x^i + b_y^i) = (\overline{C_1^i}, \overline{C_2^i})$, then partially decrypts them with private key sk_2. P_2 computes $sk_2\overline{C_1^i}$ and sends ciphertexts $(\overline{C_i}, sk_2\overline{C_1^i})$ to P_1 in shuffled order. In the second round, P_1 decrypts the ciphertexts received with own private key sk_1 to obtain $b_i' = (b_x^i + b_y^i)G = C_2^i - C_1^i$. Then, P_1 computes $\sum_{i:b_i'=0} E_{pk_p}(t_i)$ and sends it to P_2. After that, P_2 decrypts it with sk_p: $\text{Dec}(sk_p, \text{E}_{pk_p}(t_i)) \to \sum_{i \in J} t_i$.

Correctness. We analyze the correctness of Protocol 1 based on the additive homomorphism of ciphertexts in Sect. 2.3.

- P_1 converts set X into a bit vector B_x, and P_2 converts the set Y' into a bit vector B_y. If $b_x^i = b_y^i = 0$, the element $u_i \in J(1 \le i \le d)$. Conversely, if either $b_x^i = 1$ or $b_y^i = 1$, the corresponding element $u_i \notin J$.
- From Eq. 3, we can know that $\text{Enc}_h(b_x^i) + \text{Enc}_h(b_y^i) = \text{Enc}_h(b_x^i + b_y^i)$. Consequently, $\text{Enc}_h(b_x^i) + \text{Enc}_h(b_y^i) = \text{Enc}_h(0)$ is true only when $b_x^i = b_y^i = 0$. P_1, P_2 decrypt the ciphertexts collaboratively to obtain $b_i' = (b_x^i + b_y^i)G = 0$ (the point at infinity of the elliptic curve E).
- When $b_x^i = b_y^i = 0$, then $b_i' = 0$. P_1 computes the sum of $E_{pk_p}(t_i)$. From Eq. 4, it follows that:

$$\sum_{i:b_i'=0} E_{pk_p}(t_i) = E_{pk_p}\left(\sum_{i \in J} t_i\right)$$

P_2 can decrypt the ciphertext $E_{pk_p}(t_i)$ with own private key sk_p to obtain $\sum_{i \in J} t_i$.

Security Analysis. The security of Protocol 1 relies on the semantic security of ECC Threshold ElGamal algorithm. Referring to the secure proof in [12], we provide the following security analysis:

Theorem 1. *Assume that X, Y are two private sets from a full set. Protocol 1 securely computes a functionality f under the semi-honest model, f can be defined as:*

$$f(X, Y) = (f_1(X, Y), f_2(X, Y)) = (sum, |J|) \tag{7}$$

where $J = |X \cap Y|$, $sum = \sum_{i \in J} t_i$.

Referring to the security model in Sect. 2.1, we use the simulators about P_1, P_2 as subroutines when constructing our simulators. Assuming that P_1 is corrupted, we construct a simulator Sim_1 which obtains both input and output of P_1 and creates the view of P_1 in the protocol:

$$\{Sim_1(P_1, f_1(X, Y))\}_{P_1, P_2} \overset{C}{\equiv} \{view_1^\pi(X, Y)\}_{P_1, P_2} \tag{8}$$

During the setup phase of the protocol, Sim_1 chooses an elliptic curve with the same parameters and obtains the ciphertext $\text{Enc}_h B_x$. Then Sim_1 fills a set Y_s the same size as set Y randomly and converts it to the bit vector B_{y_s}. Next, Sim_1 uses the ECC Threshold ElGamal algorithm to encrypt each element in B_{y_s}. We denote the ciphertexts as $\text{Enc}_h B_{y_s}$. At Last, Sim_1 attempts to learn the sum of data related to the private intersection. From the perspective of P_1, set Y_s generated by Sim_1 is indistinguishable from the execution of actual set Y based on the semantic security of the ECC Threshold ElGamal algorithm.

Assuming that P_2 is corrupted, we construct a simulator Sim_2 with known input Y and output sum. Similarly, for any X and Y, they follows:

$$\{Sim_2(P_2, f_2(X, Y))\}_{P_1, P_2} \overset{C}{\equiv} \{view_2^\pi(X, Y)\}_{P_1, P_2} \tag{9}$$

Protocol 1: PI-Sum Protocol based bit-set

Input:

- A full set $\mathcal{U} = \{u_1, u_2, ..., u_d\}$, and a given public elliptic curve $E(F_q)$ with a base point G.
- P_1: Set $X = \{x_i\}_{i=1}^n (X \subseteq \mathcal{U})$.
- P_2: Set $Y = \{(y_i, t_i)\}_{i=1}^n$, another set $Y' = \{y_i\}_{i=1}^n (Y, Y' \subseteq \mathcal{U})$.

Setup:

- Each participant generates a private key sk_j and computes their public key $pk_j = sk_j G$ independently, then they obtain the shared public key $h = \sum_{j=1}^2 pk_j$.
- P_2 generates a keypair (pk_p, sk_p) based Paillier KeyGen algorithm.
- Both P_1, P_2 excute $X \to B_x$, $Y' \to B_y$ to get two bit vectors of size d respectively.

Protocol steps:

- **Round 1:**

  1. P_1 encrypts b_x^i in B_x with a random number r_x^i in parallel($1 \leq i \leq d$): $\text{Enc}(b_x^i, r_x^i, h) \to \text{Enc}_h(b_x^i)$. Then P_1 sends ciphertexts $\text{Enc}_h(b_x^i)$ to P_2.

  2. P_2 encrypts b_y^i in B_y the same as P_1: $\text{Enc}(b_y^i, r_y^i, h) \to \text{Enc}_h(b_y^i)$. And P_2 computes $\text{E}_{pk_p}(t_i)$ where $b_y^i = 0$. Otherwise P_2 gets $\text{E}_{pk_p}(r_i)$ where $r_i \in \mathbf{Z}_q$.

  3. For each ciphertext P_2 received from P_1, P_2 computes $\text{Enc}_h(b_x^i) + \text{Enc}_h(b_y^i) = (\overline{C_1^i}, \overline{C_2^i})$:

  $$(\overline{C_1^i}, \overline{C_2^i}) = ((r_x^i + r_y^i)G, (r_x^i + r_y^i)h + (b_x^i + b_y^i)G)$$

  the ciphertexts of P_2 can be denoted as $\overline{C_i} = (\overline{C_1^i}, \overline{C_2^i}, \text{E}_{pk_p}(t_i))$.

  4. Then P_2 computes $sk_2\overline{C_1^i}$ and sends $(\overline{C_i}, sk_2\overline{C_1^i})$ to P_1 in shuffled order.

- **Round 2:**

  1. After P_1 receives ciphertexts from P_2, P_1 computes $C_i = (C_1^i, C_2^i) = (\sum_{j=1}^2 sk_j\overline{C_1^i}, \overline{C_2^i})$ with own key sk_1 to get $b_i' = (b_x^i + b_y^i)G$.

  2. Next P_1 computes $\sum_{i:b_i'=0} \text{E}_{pk_p}(t_i)$ and sends it to P_2.

Ouput: P_1 gets $|J|$ and P_2 gets $\sum_{i \in J} t_i$ with own key sk_p, where J is the private set intersection of P_1 and P_2.

Fig. 1. Protocol 1: PI-Sum Protocol based bit-set

In this case, Sim_2 selects an elliptic curve with the same parameters and encrypts B_y. Then, Sim_2 randomly choose several elements from $\mathcal{U}$, which the sum of data associated with these elements is sum. We denote the new set as X_s. Sim_2 encrypts X_s with the shared public key h to obtain $Ench_h B_{x_s}$. Similarly, for P_2, the set X_s is indistinguishable from the execution of real set X. Consequently, we can prove that the simulated view is indistinguishable from the real view. These two parts above constitute the security proof of Protocol 1.

3.2 PI-Sum Protocol Based Bloom Filter

In this part, We propose the PI-Sum protocol based bloom filter for large set domains. Some related notations can be found in Sect. 2. Concrete descriptions about this protocol is shown in Fig. 2. In the pro-process, P_1, P_2 determine a bloom filter $BF(n, m, k)$, where m and k depend on the value of ϵ. All bits in BF are initialized to 1. Then P_1 maps all elements in X to BF with k hash functions, resulting in BF_x. For each $x_i (1 \leq i \leq n)$, the corresponding bit positions $h_1(x_i), h_2(x_i), ..., h_k(x_i)$ in BF are set to 0. The main executions of Protocol 2 can be divided into two rounds as follows.

In the first round, P_1 encrypts BF_x in parallel with the shared public key h, resulting in $Ench_h(b_x^j)$, where $1 \leq j \leq m$. Then P_1 sends the ciphertexts to P_2. For each y_i in Y, P_2 computes $Index_i = \{h_1(y_i), h_2(y_i), ..., h_k(y_i)\}$. If $j \in Indexs_i$, P_2 computes $C_y^i = (\overline{C_1^i}, \overline{C_2^i}) = \sum_{j \in Indexs_i} Ench_h(b_x^j)$. Next, P_2 computes the ciphertexts $(C_y^i, sk_2\overline{C_1^i}, E_{pk_p}(t_i))$ and sends them to P_1 in shuffled order. In the second round, after receiving the ciphertexts, P_1 decrypts them with own private key sk_1 to obtain $\sum_j b_x^j G$ where $j = h_l(y_i), 1 \leq l \leq k$. When $\sum_j b_x^j G = 0$, P_1 computes $\sum_i E_{pk_p}(t_i)$ and sends it to P_2. Then P_2 decrypts ciphertexts with its private key sk_p to obtain $sum = \sum_{i \in J} t_i$.

Correctness. Similarly, we analyze the correctness of Protocol 2 based on the additive homomorphism of ciphertexts in Sect. 2.3. In Protocol 2, We set the false positive rate ϵ of BF to 2^{-20} to make it almost negligible.

- For each x_i in X, P_1 maps them to the corresponding bit positions $b_x^{h_l(x_i)}$ in BF_x with k hash functions. For each y_i in Y, P_2 computes $Indexs_i = \{h_1(y_i), h_2(y_i), ..., h_k(y_i)\}$. If $y_i \in X$, then $b_x^j = 0$ and $j \in Indexs_i$.
- From Eq. 3, we know that $\sum_j Ench_h(b_x^j) = Ench_h(\sum_j b_x^j)$, where $j \in Indexs_i$. $Ench_h(\sum_j b_x^j) = Ench_h(0)$ only when all b_x^j in BF_x are 0. In this case $y_i \in X$, which means $y_i \in J$.
- P_1, P_2 decrypt with their private keys sk_1 and sk_2 together to obtain $\sum_j b_x^j G = C_2^i - C_1^i$. If $\sum_j b_x^j = 0$, then $\sum_j b_x^j G = 0$, and $j = h_l(y_i), y_i \in J$.
- If $\sum_j b_x^j G = 0$, P_1 computes the sum of $E_{pk_p}(t_i)$. From Eq. 4, we know that:

$$\sum_i E_{pk_p}(t_i) = E_{pk_p}(\sum_{i \in J} t_i)$$

P_2 decrypts with its private key sk_p to obtain $\sum_{i \in J} t_i$.

Protocol 2: PI-Sum Protocol based bloom filter

Input:

- A given public elliptic curve $E(F_q)$ with a base point G.
- P_1: Set $X = \{x_i\}_{i=1}^n$.
- P_2: Set $Y = \{(y_i, t_i)\}_{i=1}^n$, another set $Y' = \{y_i\}_{i=1}^n$.

Setup:

- P_1 and P_2 choose a $BF(n, m, k)$, m is the size of BF and k hash functions $H_k = \{h_1, h_2, ..., h_k\}$.
- Each participant generates a private key sk_j and a public key $pk_j = sk_j G$ independently, then they obtain the shared public key $h = \sum_{j=1}^2 pk_j$.
- P_2 generates a keypair (pk_p, sk_p) based Paillier KeyGen algorithm.
- P_1 inserts all elements from X into the BF and obtains BF_x.

Protocol steps:

- **Round 1:**

  1. P_1 chooses a random number r_x^j and encrypts each element $b_x^j (1 \leq j \leq m)$ in BF_x in parallel with the shared public key h: $\text{Enc}(b_x^j, r_x^j, h) \rightarrow \text{Enc}_h(b_x^j)$. Then P_1 sends ciphertexts $\text{Enc}_h(b_x^j)$ to P_2.
  2. P_2 computes Indexs_i $h_l(y_i)$, where $1 \leq l \leq k$ and $C_y^i = (\overline{C_1^i}, \overline{C_2^i}) = \sum_{j \in \text{Indexs}_i} \text{Enc}_h(b_x^j)$. P_2 encrypts t_i as $E_{pk_p}(t_i)$.
  3. P_2 computes $sk_2 \overline{C_1^i}$ and sends $(C_y^i, sk_2\overline{C_1^i}, E_{pk_p}(t_i))$ to P_1 in shuffled order.

- **Round 2:**

  1. P_1 receives ciphertexts from P_2 and computes $C_i = (C_1^i, C_2^i) = (sk_2\overline{C_1^i} + sk_1\overline{C_1^i}, \overline{C_2^i})$ with private key sk_1 to get $\sum_{j \in \text{Indexs}_i} b_x^j G$.
  2. Then P_1 computes $\sum_i E_{pk_p}(t_i)$ where $\sum_{j \in \text{Indexs}_i} b_x^j G = 0$ and sends $\sum_i E_{pk_p}(t_i)$ to P_2.

Ouput: P_1 gets $|J|$ and P_2 gets $\sum_{i \in J} t_i$ with sk_p, where J is the private set intersection of P_1 and P_2.

Fig. 2. Protocol 2: PI-Sum Protocol based Bloom filter

Security Analysis. The secure proof of Protocol 2 also relies on the semantic security of ECC Threshold ElGamal algorithm, which is similar to the proof of the Protocol 1 in Sect. 3.1, so we do not repeat them here.

4   Efficiency Analysis

In this section, we choose two work closely related to our protocols. We analyse the performance of Protocol 1 (3.1) with the protocol in [9], which also utilizes the full set to convert the private set within the small set domain. Additionally, we make comparisons between Protocol 2 (3.2) and the protocol in [13].

4.1   Theoretical Analysis

We analyze both computation and communication complexity based on the entire execution of our protocols and homomorphic encryption. Concretely, we evaluate modular exponentiation, homomorphic operations and communication rounds. In addition, we compare the scalability of these protocols. The specific comparisons are shown in Table 1:

Table 1. $|\mathcal{U}|$ denotes the size of the full set $\mathcal{U}$ and n is the size of private sets. k denotes the number of hash functions of BF

Protocol	Computation		Communication (rounds)	Scalability
	Exponentiations	Homomorphic.		
Protocol 1	$O(2|\mathcal{U}|)$	$O(|\mathcal{U}| + 1)$	2	✓
Protocol 2	$O(2nk)$	$O(n + 1)$	2	✓
[9]	$O(2|\mathcal{U}|)$	$O(2|\mathcal{U}|)$	3	✗
[13]	$O(2nk)$	$O(2n + 1)$	3	✗

The table shows that Protocol 1 has significantly lower computational complexity compared with [9] in the case of full set. While Protocol 2 has lower homomorphic computation overhead than [13]. And the communication rounds of our two protocols are lower, which means that our protocols are more scalable as the participants increase.

4.2   Experimental Analysis

In order to demonstrate the performance of these protocols better, we implemented these four protocols in Java using the IntelliJ IDEA platform. We measured the time of both computation and communication, and also the total execution time of each protocol. The experiments were conducted on a system with the following configurations: Windows 11 Home, 64-bit operating system, Intel(R) Core(TM) i7-12700H @ 2.30 GHz processor, and 16 GB RAM.

Execution Time of Different Steps in Protocol 1(3.1). In the case of small set domain, we let the full set size as $|\mathcal{U}|$, and both private sets are subsets of $\mathcal{U}$. We compared both computation and communication time of Protocol 1 with [9] in different sizes of the full set. Specific results can be shown in Table 2. As the full set size increases, Protocol 1 exhibits significantly lower communication and computation time. We can clearly found that when $|\mathcal{U}|$ is 2^6, the communication time in [9] is approximately 2 times than Protocol 1, while the computation time is 7 times more than Protocol 1. Additionally, the growth trend about total execution time of Protocol 1 is smoother than [9].

Table 2. Comparison of computation time and communication time between Protocol 1 and [9]

Protocol	Time (s)	Full set size					
		2^4	2^5	2^6	2^7	2^8	2^9
protocol 1	Communication	0.098	0.129	0.225	0.269	0.348	0.725
	Computation	**0.082**	**0.101**	**0.155**	**0.201**	**0.292**	**0.408**
[9]	Communication	0.169	0.318	0.471	0.637	0.856	1.547
	Computation	**0.224**	**0.418**	**1.051**	**1.943**	**3.307**	**5.018**

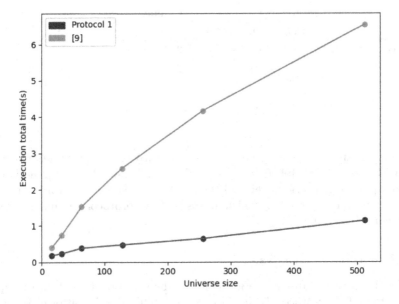

Fig. 3. The comparison of execution total time between Protocol 1 and [9]

Execution Time of Different Steps in Protocol 2 (3.2). When the private sets of participants belong to large set domains, we utilize BF to convert them. In our experiment, we set the false positive rate ϵ of BF to 2^{-20} to make it almost negligible. In Table 3, we make comparisons between Protocol 2 and [13] within different private set size. Both communication and computation time of Protocol 2 are greatly lower than the protocol in [13]. Especially when the set size is 2^{11}, the computation time of the protocol in [13] is 3 times more than Protocol 2. As shown in Fig. 4, when the set size increases, the growth rate about the execution total time of [13] is much larger than protocol 2.

Table 3. Comparison of computation time and communication time between Protocol 2 and [13]

Protocol	Time (s)	Set size					
		2^9	2^{10}	2^{11}	2^{12}	2^{13}	2^{14}
protocol 2	Communication	1.257	3.453	6.684	13.088	29.379	50.912
	Computation	**1.034**	**1.551**	**2.708**	**5.294**	**10.826**	**23.396**
[13]	Communication	2.315	6.827	16.228	28.422	69.529	135.343
	Computation	**2.084**	**2.968**	**7.03**	**14.84**	**39.874**	**63.784**

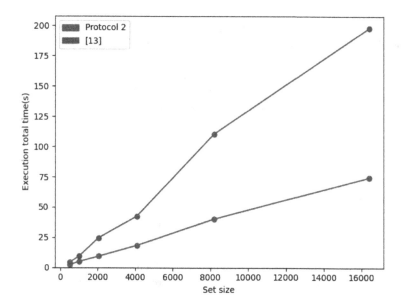

Fig. 4. The comparison of execution total time between Protocol 2 and [13]

Overall, the protocols we designed are greatly performed in both large and small set domains, which also means they are more practical in actual situations.

4.3 Extension to MPI-Sum

Both our protocols involve only two rounds interactions between participants, which is easy to be extended to MPI-Sum. A central party can be selected in the case of multiple participants. Before the execution, each participant converts their private sets into bit-vectors first and encrypts bit-vectors with ECC Threshold ElGamal algorithm independently. Then, they send the ciphertexts to the central party. After receiving the ciphertexts, the central party makes homomorphic computations with them and sends the final result to other participants. After that, each party decrypts the ciphertexts with its private key together. At last, the central party computes the private intersection cardinality based on collaborative decryption results and sends the encrypted sum of associated data to other parties. Thus the other parties can get the sum of the private intersection. Moreover, the central party can be replaced by cloud server to reduce its computation overhead.

5   Conclusion

In general, we propose two PI-Sum protocols for two cases involving both small and large set domains. Our two protocols present good performance through theoretical and experimental analysis. Additionally, our protocols can be extended to MPI-Sum with a good scalability. However, we only provide theoretical explanations of MPI-Sum in this work. In the future, we will conduct further research to explore the practical implementation of MPI-Sum. At the same time, we can combine PSI with the blockchain, which will provide a more secure scheme for practical applications. Also, we can utilize cloud servers to reduce communication and computation overhead for each participant.

References

1. Narayanan, A., Thiagarajan, N., Lakhani, M., Hamburg, M., Boneh, D., et al.: Location privacy via private proximity testing. In: NDSS, vol. 11 (2011)
2. Baldi, P., Baronio, R., De Cristofaro, E., Gasti, P., Tsudik, G.: Countering gattaca: efficient and secure testing of fully-sequenced human genomes. In: Proceedings of the 18th ACM Conference on Computer and Communications Security, pp. 691–702 (2011)
3. Ion, M., et al.: Private intersection-sum protocol with applications to attributing aggregate ad conversions. Cryptology ePrint Archive (2017). https://eprint.iacr.org/2017/738
4. Meadows, C.: A more efficient cryptographic matchmaking protocol for use in the absence of a continuously available third party. In: 1986 IEEE Symposium on Security and Privacy, pp. 134–134. IEEE (1986)
5. De Cristofaro, E., Tsudik, G.: Practical private set intersection protocols with linear complexity. In: Financial Cryptography and Data Security, FC 2010. LNCS, vol. 6052, pp. 143–159. Springer, Heidelberg (2010). https://doi.org/10.1007/978-3-642-14577-3_13
6. Pinkas, B., Schneider, T., Tkachenko, O., Yanai, A.: Efficient circuit-based PSI with linear communication. In: Ishai, Y., Rijmen, V. (eds.) Advances in Cryptology. EUROCRYPT 2019. LNCS, vol. 11478, pp. 122–153. Springer, Cham (2019). https://doi.org/10.1007/978-3-030-17659-4_5

7. Kolesnikov, V., Kumaresan, R., Rosulek, M., Trieu, N.: Efficient batched oblivious PRF with applications to private set intersection. In: Proceedings of the 2016 ACM SIGSAC Conference on Computer and Communications Security, pp. 818–829 (2016)

8. Pinkas, B., Rosulek, M., Trieu, N., Yanai, A.: SpOT-light: lightweight private set intersection from sparse OT extension. In: Boldyreva, A., Micciancio, D. (eds.) Advances in Cryptology. CRYPTO 2019. LNCS, vol. 11694, pp. 401–431. Springer, Cham (2019). https://doi.org/10.1007/978-3-030-26954-8_13

9. Wang, W., Li, S., Dou, J., Du, R.: Privacy-preserving mixed set operations. Inf. Sci.**525**, 67–81 (2020)

10. Ying, J.H.M., Cao, S., Poh, G.S., Xu, J., Lim, H.W.: PSI-stats: private set intersection protocols supporting secure statistical functions. In: Ateniese, G., Venturi, D. (eds.) Applied Cryptography and Network Security, ACNS 2022. LNCS, pp. 585–604. Springer, Cham (2022). https://doi.org/10.1007/978-3-031-09234-3_29

11. Le, P.H., Ranellucci, S., Gordon, S.D.: Two-party private set intersection with an untrusted third party. In: Proceedings of the 2019 ACM SIGSAC Conference on Computer and Communications Security, pp. 2403–2420 (2019)

12. Lv, S., et al.: Unbalanced private set intersection cardinality protocol with low communication cost. Futur. Gener. Comput. Syst. **102**, 1054–1061 (2020)

13. Ion, M., et al.: On deploying secure computing: Private intersection-sum-with-cardinality. In: 2020 IEEE European Symposium on Security and Privacy (EuroS&P), pp. 370–389. IEEE (2020)

14. Miao, P., Patel, S., Raykova, M., Seth, K., Yung, M.: Two-sided malicious security for private intersection-sum with cardinality. In: Micciancio, D., Ristenpart, T. (eds.) Advances in Cryptology. CRYPTO 2020. LNCS, vol. 12172, pp. 3–33. Springer, Cham (2020). https://doi.org/10.1007/978-3-030-56877-1_1

15. Niu, Z., Wang, H., Li, Z., Song, X.: Privacy-preserving statistical computing protocols for private set intersection. Int. J. Intell. Syst. **37**(12), 10118–10139 (2022)

16. Lindell, Y.: How to simulate it–a tutorial on the simulation proof technique. In: Tutorials on the Foundations of Cryptography: Dedicated to Oded Goldreich, pp. 277–346 (2017). https://doi.org/10.1007/978-3-319-57048-8_6

17. Ruan, O., Wang, Z., Mi, J., Zhang, M.: New approach to set representation and practical private set-intersection protocols. IEEE Access **7**, 64897–64906 (2019)

18. Bloom, B.H.: Space/time trade-offs in hash coding with allowable errors. Commun. ACM **13**(7), 422–426 (1970)

19. Bose, P., et al.: On the false-positive rate of bloom filters. Inf. Process. Lett. **108**(4), 210–213 (2008)

20. Desmedt, Y.: Threshold cryptosystems. In: Seberry, J., Zheng, Y. (eds.) Advances in Cryptology. AUSCRYPT 1992. LNCS, vol. 718, pp. 1–14. Springer, Heidelberg (1993). https://doi.org/10.1007/3-540-57220-1_47

21. Galbraith, S.D., Gaudry, P.: Recent progress on the elliptic curve discrete logarithm problem. Designs Codes Cryptogr. **78**, 51–72 (2016). https://doi.org/10.1007/s10623-015-0146-7

22. Paillier, P.: Public-key cryptosystem based on discrete logarithm residues. In: EUROCRYPT 1999 (1999)

Blockchain Data and Behavior Analysis

Detecting Rug Pull Scams on Blockchain via Feature Fused Graph Classification

Ye Qiao, Guang Li, Jieying Zhou, and Weigang Wu$^{(\boxtimes)}$

School of Computer Science and Engineering, Sun Yat-sen University,
Guangzhou 510006, China
`wuweig@mail.sysu.edu.cn`

Abstract. The development of decentralized finance (DeFi) is largely motivated by the blockchain technology. As one of the core applications of DeFi, decentralized exchanges (DEXes) have become a popular choice to trade digital assets, but they also suffer from various scams. Rug pull is a fastly increasing scam, which commits fraud by issuing meaningless tokens. To detect rug pull scams, existing methods usually employ machine learning models based on manually extracted features, while they ignore the learning of the topology structure of token transactions, which is crucial for detecting rug pull scams. In our work, we propose a feature fused graph classification model for rug pull scams detection. In addition to manually extracting token features, we consider the implicit structural information of token transactions. After constructing a graph for transactions of each token, we utilize graph pooling to learn the embedding of the graph, and concatenate it with the extracted features so as to form a complete token representation for classification. Moreover, we propose two new temporal features in feature extraction. The experimental results indicate that our detection model outperforms other methods in detection performance.

Keywords: Blockchain · Decentralized exchanges · Rug pull scams detection · Feature extraction · Graph classification

1 Introduction

Blockchain [21] is a public and decentralized distributed ledger technology that ensures transparency and immutability through consensus mechanisms. It serves as the underlying technology for cryptocurrencies like Bitcoin [18] and Ethereum [4]. As blockchain continues to evolve, the use of smart contracts [31] enables users to deploy various decentralized applications, promoting the prosperity of decentralized finance (DeFi) [27] and attracting an increasing number of users. However, as blockchain has received increasing attention, many scams have emerged, such as phishing scams, Ponzi schemes, etc. Existing methods for detecting these scams include machine learning based on extracted features [8,9], network embedding [23] and node classification [6] based on transaction graphs, vulnerability detection [1] and opcode analysis [12,30] based on smart contracts, etc.

J. Zhu et al. (Eds.): CBCS 2023, CCIS 2098, pp. 67–83, 2024.
https://doi.org/10.1007/978-981-97-3203-6_4

Rug pull is a new form of cryptocurrency scams, mainly referring to fraud through rug pull tokens, which is particularly prevalent on decentralized exchanges (DEXes) [15]. DEX is a kind of cryptocurrency exchanges built on blockchain technology and smart contracts and enables users to trade cryptocurrencies and tokens. Rug pull scammers take advantage of DEXes, build what appear to be legitimate projects to attract users to invest, and end up taking investors' cryptocurrencies and disappear. According to the report from *Chainalysis*[1], the value of cryptocurrencies stolen through rug pull scams in 2021 reached $2.8 billion, accounting for 35.90% of the total value. Thus, rug pull scams have caused great harm to users' digital assets, it is urgent and meaningful to study detection methods of rug pull scams.

Unfortunately, very few studies have been conducted on rug pull detection. Studies [16,24] propose different strategies for labeling tokens and train classifiers on statistical features extracted from token transactions to detect rug pull tokens. These features include the price of tokens, the number of accounts, etc. [19] proposes a list of features and uses a hybrid feature selection technique to identify the most pertinent features to detect rug pull scams. These studies only consider extracting features from the patterns of rug pull scams, without considering the topology structure of token transactions from the perspective of graphs.

Figure 1 shows examples of transaction graphs of the two types of tokens respectively. The nodes denote accounts, while edges denote transactions occurring between these accounts. It is noticeable that there are substantial differences in the topology of transaction graphs of different types of tokens. The transaction graph of the rug pull token mainly presents a star-shaped distribution with a central point, while the transaction graph of the normal token has multiple transaction centers. The difference in the transaction graphs of the two tokens reflects the difference in the trading patterns of the two types of tokens. Therefore, by learning the topology structure of token transaction graphs can better distinguish between different categories of tokens.

Motivated by the observation, we propose an effective rug pull scams detection model by incorporating manually extracted features and graph pooling learned embeddings. Specifically, we extract features such as *lifetime* by analyzing different characteristics presented by rug pull tokens and normal tokens. Then we construct a graph for transactions of each token and we utilize graph pooling to aggregate node embeddings of a graph into an embedding of the whole graph. On this basis, we concatenate the graph embedding and the extracted features to train the detection model. We carry out experiments on authentic Blockchain datasets to assess the performance of our model and compare it with other methods. The experimental results indicate that the detection performance can be significantly enhanced by considering the topology structure of graphs and extracted features. In summary, our work provides the following contributions:

---

[1] https://go.chainalysis.com/2022-Crypto-Crime-Report.html.

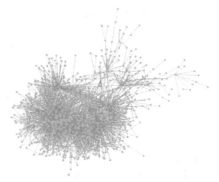

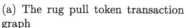

(a) The rug pull token transaction graph

(b) The normal token transaction graph

Fig. 1. Two types of token transaction graphs.

- We propose a feature fused graph classification model to detect rug pull scams, which incorporates manually extracted features and graph pooling learned embeddings.
- We propose two new time-related features, considering the lifetime of tokens and the time interval with the largest decrease in the price of tokens.
- We utilize graph pooling methods to learn the embeddings of token transaction graphs, which allowing automatic learning of implicit information within the graph.

2   Background and Related Work

This section begins with an introduction to the relevant background. Then we illustrate the related work on rug pull scams detection on blockchain and graph classification.

2.1   Ethereum, Tokens and Decentralized Exchanges

Ethereum is a Turing-complete blockchain platform that supports smart contracts, which are pieces of bytecode that automatically executes predefined actions when certain conditions are met. The Ethereum Virtual Machine (EVM) serves as the virtual runtime environment for executing the bytecode of smart contracts. In the course of executing a smart contract, alterations to the contract's state can be recorded on the blockchain by triggering events [17].

Smart contracts can be employed to create tokens, representing a variety of assets, such as digital currencies, real estate, etc. Most of token contracts follow the ERC20 [22] standard, which outlines a set of rules and functions to implement the fundamental functionalities of tokens, enabling different tokens to be compatible within the Ethereum ecosystem. In this paper, the tokens we refer to are ERC20 tokens. Tokens can be transferred between different accounts and a "transfer" event will be emitted to record the details of the transaction.

DEX is a peer-to-peer trading platform, where users can directly manage and trade tokens without trusting any third parties. The two most common design patterns for DEXes are order-book and automated market makers (AMMs). This paper centers its attention on the identification of rug pull scams taking place on the AMMs based DEXes. AMMs based DEXes rely on liquidity pools to offer token pairs and use a mathematical formula to automatically calculate the token price. A liquidity pool is a kind of smart contract designed to reserve two tokens and allow users to trade with it rather than with other individual users. Representative DEXes include Uniswap[2], Pancakeswap[3], etc.

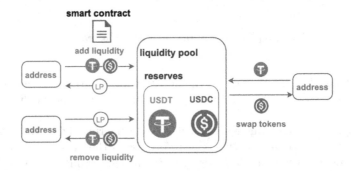

Fig. 2. The interaction with DEXes.

Figure 2 shows the types of operations that users can interact with DEXes, including creating a liquidity pool, adding and removing liquidity, and swapping tokens. Users can create liquidity pools on DEXes for two tokens and add initial liquidity, and the initial ratio is determined by the creators. They can also add liquidity by depositing both tokens into the pool proportionally. These participants are called liquidity providers (LP) and are rewarded with liquidity provider tokens (LP tokens). After that, a "min" event recording the reserves of two tokens will be emitted. Removing liquidity refers to liquidity providers exchanging the two tokens with LP tokens. The LP tokens will be burnt and will trigger a "burn" event. Swapping tokens is to exchange one token for another token through the liquidity pool. Then a "swap" event will be emitted recording the amount of tokens swapped. Moreover, after any operation occurs, a "sync" event will be emitted to record the storage of token pairs in the liquidity pool.

2.2 Rug Pull Scams and Detection

Rug pull is a type of cryptocurrency scams that has become the most prevalent financial scams on DEXes. It is cheap and easy to create new tokens and get

---
[2] https://docs.uniswap.org/.
[3] https://pancakeswap.finance/.

them listed on DEXes without code audits. Scammers create a new token and pair it with another mainstream token to create a liquidity pool. They create fake transactions to increase the token price and promote it through social media or online forums to attract investors. There are two main types of rug pull scams on DEXes. The first is stealing liquidity. The scammers will sell or withdraw all the tokens held in the liquidity pool. The second is dumping tokens. When the token price rises continuously, scammers will quickly sell a large amount of tokens issued by them, causing the token price to plummet.

In order to detect rug pull scams, some methods have been proposed in the existing papers. [24] proposes a heuristic method which marks tokens as scam tokens if the name and symbol of tokens are similar to official tokens. Besides, they use a guilt-by-association method to expand the category of scam tokens, and train a machine learning classifier based on the labeled dataset. [16] analyzes the characteristics of tokens and extracts features to mark tokens and train XGBoost [7] and FT-transformer [11] models to detect rug pull scams. Then they extract the data within 24 h after the liquidity pool has been created to train a classifier, which can detect potential scams in the future. [19] introduces the block-dependent features to improve the feature extraction process in [16]. And they employ a hybrid feature selection technique to discern a list of the most crucial features. Besides, some literature also focuses on comprehensive investigations of token ecosystems. [2] conducts an empirical investigation and analysis of the widespread presence of rug pull scams. [5] researches the ecosystem of tokens and liquidity pools on Ethereum and Binance Smart Chain and analyzing and quantifying the prevalence of one-day rug pull tokens.

In summary, the existing rug pull detection methods focus on extracting features based on the characteristics of tokens. These studies ignore the topology structure of token transactions.

2.3 Graph Classification

Graph classification is a task of assigning a label to an entire graph. It uses a graph pooling to downsample a graph while retaining its important features. There are many researches on graph pooling, which are mainly grouped into the two big branches: global pooling and hierarchical pooling [10]. Global pooling [29] adopts summation operations or neural networks to integrate the embeddings of nodes to a embedding of the graph. Hierarchical pooling aims to learn hierarchical representations for capturing structural information of graphs. It can be categorized into two types: graph coarsening pooling and node selection pooling. Graph coarsening pooling seeks to map nodes into distinct clusters and aggregates the clusters into supernodes to obtain a coarsen graph [3,25,26]. Node selection pooling learns the importance score of each node, sorts the nodes and discards the nodes with lower scores [14,28].

3   Data Collection and Preprocessing

In this section, we provide a detailed account of data collection and data pre-processing.

3.1   Data Collection

In our model, we employ the token dataset labeled in [16]. The dataset contains 27588 tokens, including 26957 rug pull tokens and 631 normal tokens. In addition, we collect reports of rug pull scams on DEXes from Twitter and obtain 45 rug pull tokens to expand the dataset. We take rug pull tokens as positive samples and normal tokens as negative samples.

After obtaining the labeled tokens, we get the liquidity pool contracts corresponding to these tokens on DEXes through https://etherscan.io. In our model, two kinds of data including event data and token transactions are collected. We obtain the transactions of tokens and *Mint, Burn, Swap* and *Sync* events of each liquidity pool from their creation to February 15, 2022 (the date we conducted our experiment) through the APIs provided by etherscan.io[4].

Event data and token transactions represent two different activity trajectories of tokens, namely, the outer circulation and the inner circulation. The event data represents the outer circulation and records the changes in the state of liquidity pool. From event data, we can analyze characteristics of tokens. Token transactions represent the inner circulation and are the transfer process of tokens between different accounts, revealing the topology relationships between accounts.

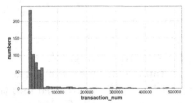   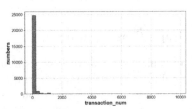

(a) The distribution of the number of trans- (b) The distribution of the number of transactions of normal tokens   actions of rug pull tokens

Fig. 3. The distribution of the number of token transactions.

3.2   Data Preprocessing

The dataset exhibits a positive to negative sample ratio of approximately 42 : 1. In reality, the tokens listed on DEXes exhibit the similar ratio, as most of them are garbage tokens. We tallied the transactions count for the two tokens and

---

[4] https://docs.etherscan.io/api-endpoints/logs.

the distribution of which is shown in Fig. 3. Based on Fig. 3 and statistics, it is obtained that 85% of normal tokens have transactions within 100000, while 95% of rug pull tokens have transactions within 300. Based on our observations, we can distinguish tokens with too few transactions and tokens with huge transaction volumes based on the number of transactions. To mitigate the influence on the graph classification results caused by a significant disparity in the transaction volumes of the two tokens, we filter out tokens with fewer than 300 transactions and greater than 100000 transactions. After filtering we retain 1288 rug pull tokens and 529 normal tokens. We mark this dataset as "Dataset 1" and retain the original dataset, which we refer to as "Dataset 2".

4   Methodology

We propose a feature fused graph classification model to detect rug pull scams. Our model comprises three major parts: pattern feature extraction, graph pooling and feature fusion. The framework of the model is visualized in Fig. 4. First, based on the preprocessed datasets, we extract features from the event data. Second, constructing a transaction graph for each token, and obtain the embedding of the entire graph which represents the topology structure features of token transactions. Finally, the embedding is connected with the original extracted features to obtain the representation of the token for classification. This section provides a detail introduction to each part of our model.

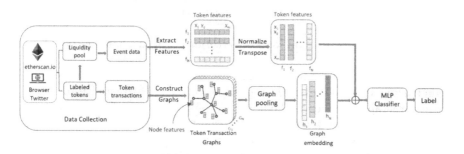

Fig. 4. Framework of our model.

4.1   Pattern Feature Extraction

Pattern feature extraction is a crucial upstream task to extract features based on the different properties of rug pull tokens and normal tokens. Based on the features proposed in [16], we extracted 11 features from event data in total and propose two new time-related features among them on detecting rug pull tokens.

Firstly, the liquidity and the price of the token are important for detecting rug pull tokens as they can lead to abnormal fluctuations in token prices and a shortage of liquidity. Therefore, we define the following four features:

- **price.** The price of the token at the last timestamp. It is calculated by dividing the reserves of another token by the reserves of the token in the liquidity pool.
- **liquidity.** The product of the reserves of the two tokens at the last timestamp.
- **price_max_drop.** The largest drop of the price of tokens from a peak to a trough. It is calculated by $(max\_price - min\_price)/max\_price$.
- **liq_max_drop.** The most significant drop of liquidity from a peak to a trough. It is calculated by $(max\_liquidity - min\_liquidity)/max\_liquidity$.

Secondly, we extract five statistical features to measure the amount of interaction with the liquidity pool and the number of accounts owning tokens. These features reflect the activity of the token and its associated liquidity pool. These features are as followed:

- **num_mint.** The number of *mint* event. It refers to the number of times the liquidity is added.
- **num_burn.** The number of *burn* event. It refers to the number of times the liquidity is removed.
- **num_swap.** The number of *swap* event. This denotes the number of times the user accounts have swapped tokens with the liquidity pool.
- **num_sync.** The number of *sync* event. It refers to the number of operations user accounts interact with the liquidity pool.
- **tx_accounts.** Total number of the unique accounts which trade with the liquidity pool.

Finally, taking into account the difference in the survival periods of two types of tokens and the difference in their price fluctuations over time, we propose two time-related features.

lifetime. The time interval from the creation of token's liquidity pool to the last transaction.

The liquidity pool for a normal token on DEXes is available for user interaction in the long term. However, the rug pull scammer will attract investors to add liquidity or swap tokens for the liquidity pool. As the proportion of tokens in the liquidity pool decreases, the price of the token will rise. Typically, the scammer will withdraw liquidity shortly after the token price reaches their expectations.

max_to_min_time. The time interval between the highest and lowest points of token prices.

The price of a normal token tends to fluctuate within a reasonable range, while a rug pull token often exhibits the phenomenon of rise rapidly and fall within a brief timeframe.

In summary, all the features above are defined on single token. We extract the outer circulation features of all tokens from the event data and incorporate them as pattern features into subsequent training.

4.2 Graph Construction

We construct a graph for the transactions of each token by defining the sending account and the receiving account of a transaction as nodes, while the transactions between two accounts as edges. The graph we have constructed is undirected because the adjacency relationships between nodes in the topology structure of the graph are undirected. If there are multiple transactions between two accounts, we keep only one of them. However, we take all edges into account to calculate the degree of the nodes, which serves as the initial features of the nodes.

We represent a token transaction graph as $G = (A, X)$, where $A \in \{0,1\}^{n*n}$ represents the adjacency matrix, n is the number of nodes, and $X \in \mathbb{R}^{n*f}$ is the node feature matrix and f is the initial feature dimension of the node. We have a collection of graphs $\mathcal{G} = \{G_1, G_2, \ldots\}$ and a set of labels $\mathcal{Y} = \{y_1, y_2, \ldots\}$, where y_i is the label of G_i.

4.3   Graph Pooling

We take the topology structure of token transaction graphs into consideration by learning the embeddings of the graphs. We apply the learning method proposed in [29] to the pooling of token transaction graphs. The framework of the graph pooling part is shown in Fig. 5, The main modules include: Firstly, using graph convolution layers to aggregate node features and learn local structural information of the graph. Subsequently, calculate the importance scores of nodes. Secondly, the graph pooling layer sorts node features based on their importance scores, selecting a subset of nodes and unifying input sizes. Finally, traditional convolution neural networks are employed to learn the graph embedding.

Graph Convolution Layer. Graph convolution network (GCN) [13] is an effective convolution method to aggregate features of neighboring nodes in the spectral domain. We use GCN as the embedding layer, defined as:

$$X^{l+1} = \sigma(\tilde{D}^{-\frac{1}{2}} \tilde{A} \tilde{D}^{-\frac{1}{2}} X^l W^l) \tag{1}$$

where σ is the activation function, $\tilde{A} = A + I$ is the adjacency matrix with self-loop added to each node, I is the identity matrix, $\tilde{D} = \sum_j \tilde{A}_{ij}$ is the degree matrix of $\tilde{A}$, and W^l is the trainable weighted matrix at layer l. X^l is the output of the l-th graph convolution layer. The initial node features are used in the first graph convolution layer, i.e., $X^0 = X$.

In our model, we stack multiple graph convolution layers to aggregate neighboring node features and deeper layers will learn more important features through aggregating higher-order neighboring node features. Next we concatenate the output $X^l, l = 1, \ldots, h$ of each graph convolution layers to create a concatenated output Z, which is defined as:

$$Z = X^{1:h} = [X^1, \ldots, X^h] \tag{2}$$

where $Z \in \mathbb{R}^{n*\sum_h d}$ denotes the node embedding matrix, and h is the number of graph convolution layers, and d is the dimension of the hidden embedding. In the concatenated output Z, each row represents a node embedding, including its multi-scale structural information.

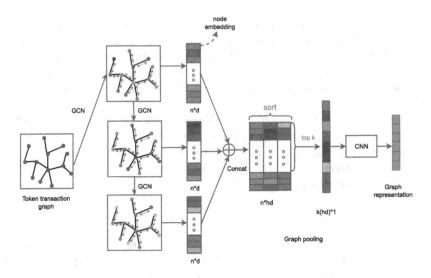

Fig. 5. Framework of graph pooling.

Graph Pooling Layer. The graph pooling layer adopts the idea of node selection pooling, because some token transaction graphs have a large scale of nodes and edges. Therefore, using graph coarsening pooling will result in excessively high computational complexity. In this section, we elaborate on the procedure of learning graph embeddings.

The self-attention score [14] of a node signifies the significance of the node. In other word, the higher the score of a node, the more crucial the node. We use a graph convolution layer to learn the score of each node and form a self-attention score vector S, which is calculated by (1), where $W^l \in \mathbb{R}^{d*1}$, $S = X^{l+1} \in \mathbb{R}^{n*1}$, S_i is the score of i-th node. According to the self-attention score, we can decide which nodes in the graph to reserve.

We calculate the self-attention score after multiple graph convolution layers. Then we adopt the node selection method to retain a portion of nodes and their embedding H according to the self-attention score.

$$idx = topk(S, k) \tag{3}$$

$$H = Z[idx] \tag{4}$$

where $topk$ is the function that sorts nodes based on their scores and returns an index set of the k-largest value in S, and k is a hyperparameter used to calculate the number of nodes to be retained. We compute the number of nodes for each graph and arrange them in ascending order. We select the number of nodes to be retained such that $k*100\%$ of the graphs have the number of nodes less than the number nodes to be retained. And then set k to the number of retained nodes. $H \in \mathbb{R}^{k*\sum_h d}$ is a sorted node embedding matrix of retained nodes. Because the size of the input graph are different, the pooling layer will uniform the sizes of the output tensor. If $n < k$, then $k - n$ zero rows will be added.

After pooling we get a tensor H which contains the node embeddings in a consistent order. Reference [29] has proved that nodes in distinct graphs tend to be assigned similar relative positions when they exhibit similar structural roles. Therefore, traditional convolution neural networks can be trained to read graph nodes in sequence. To train CNNs after the pooling layer, we first reshape the H into a $k(\sum_h d) * 1$ vector. Next we use several 1-D convolution layers and MaxPooling layers to learn local pattern on nodes sequence. Finally we reshape the output of the last CNN layer into a column vector r, which denotes the graph embedding of the input graph.

4.4 Feature Fused Graph Classification

Our feature fused graph classification model combines features learned from extraction and graph pooling. With the above operation, we obtain pattern features matrix $F \in \mathbb{R}^{G_n * m}$ for all tokens and the graph embeddings $R \in \mathbb{R}^{G_n * d}$ of the transaction graphs of tokens, G_n is the number of graphs in a batch of training and $m = 13$ is the pattern features' size. We first use a linear layer to transform pattern features' size into d and then we obtain a combined matrix by concatenating the pattern features F to graph embeddings R. This combined matrix is then utilized as the input for the subsequent *MLP* layer and use a *Log-Softmax* function to obtain the output. Moreover, to train our model, we utilize the loss function $\mathcal{L}$ based on negative log likelihood. They are defined as:

$$\hat{y} = LogSoftmax(MLP(Concatenate[R, F]) \tag{5}$$

$$\mathcal{L} = -\sum_{i=1}^{n} \frac{\hat{y}_{i,y_i}}{n} \tag{6}$$

where $\hat{y}$ is the label predicted by our model, and $\hat{y}_{i,y_i}$ denotes that take the value with index y_i from $\hat{y}_i$.

5   Experiments

We perform experiments using two real datasets on Ethereum to evaluate our model in this section. We validate the effectiveness of our model through comparisons with other baselines.

5.1   Experimental Settings

Dataset. We use the two datasets illustrated in Sect. 3 to evaluate the performance of our model. The statistics of token transactions of the two datasets are summarized in Table 1. We extract pattern features from event data and construct a graph for the token transactions of each token.

Table 1. Statistics of token transactions of datasets.

Dataset	Number of Graphs	Avg. # of Nodes per Graph	Avg. # of Edges per Graph
Dataset 1	1817	1968.47	2739.42
Dataset 2	27588	322.17	452.79

Experimental Settings. Each dataset is randomly divided into three segments: 70% of the data is allocated for training, 20% for validation, and 10% for testing. In our detection model, we use 3 graph convolution layers to aggregate node features, followed by a graph convolution layer to learn the self-attention score. The dimension of node embedding and graph embedding are set to 32. The pooling ratio k is set to 0.4. We use two 1-D convolution layers and an MLP layer. We concatenate the pattern features and graph embeddings before the MLP layer, and use a linear layer for pattern features before concatenate. We employ a log_softmax classifier following the MLP layer. We establish the learning rate at 0.0005 and use Adam optimizer. We encapsulate pattern features into the graph as input, and the model ultimately outputs the predicted graph labels.

Evaluation Metrics. To measure the effectiveness of our model, we adapt four commonly used evaluation metrics: Accuracy, Precision, Recall, and F1score.

$$Accuracy = \frac{TP + TN}{TP + FP + TN + FN} \tag{7}$$

$$Precision = \frac{TP}{TP + FP} \tag{8}$$

$$Recall = \frac{TP}{TP + FN} \tag{9}$$

$$F1score = 2 \times \frac{Precision \times Recall}{Precision + Recall} \tag{10}$$

Baselines. To illustrate the effectiveness of our proposed model, we conduct comparisons with methods that use features only and use token transaction graphs only, respectively. Additionally we explore various graph pooling methods for experiments. The baselines are included as followed:

- **XGBoost** [7]. Only consider the pattern features illustrated in Sect. 4.1 to train a XGBoost classifier.
- **SAGPool** [14]. Based on the self-attention score, hierarchically aggregates neighboring node information and selects nodes to obtain the pooling graph.
- **CGIPool** [20]. Contrastive learning is implemented to maximize the mutual information between the input and the coarsened graphs.
- **SortPool** [29]. Sortpool sorts the node embeddings in ascending order, chooses a subset of nodes, and subsequently concatenates the node embeddings into a graph-level vector.

Table 2. Overall performance comparison.

Model	Datasets							
	Dataset 1				Dataset 2			
	Acc	Recall	Precision	F1score	Acc	Recall	Precision	F1score
XGBoost	0.9769	0.9622	0.9589	0.9604	0.9944	0.8710	0.8065	0.8780
SAGPool	0.9257	0.8588	0.8718	0.8644	0.9955	0.9298	0.8689	0.8983
CGIPool	0.9508	0.9016	0.9483	0.9244	0.9924	0.9692	0.9831	0.9761
SortPool	0.9560	0.9769	0.9621	0.9695	0.9948	0.9956	0.9971	0.9965
Our model$_{SAGPool}$	0.9836	0.9841	0.9688	0.9764	0.9725	0.9855	0.9784	0.9819
Our model$_{CGIPool}$	0.9615	0.9848	0.9630	0.9738	**0.9961**	0.9697	0.9921	0.9846
Our model$_{SortPool}$	**0.9890**	**0.9958**	**0.9857**	**0.9916**	0.9952	**0.9969**	**0.9981**	**0.9975**

5.2 Experimental Results

Table 2 provides a summary of the experimental results when using only pattern features, only graph pooling methods, as well as our proposed model combining pattern features and different graph pooling methods. Generally, it is evident from the results that our proposed model can achieve better results than baselines in two datasets.

First, compared to XGBoost, our model improves the performance by 3.54% points and 11.95% points on F1score on the two datasets, respectively. This is because that XGBoost only uses token features without considering the structure of token transaction graphs. Reference [16] uses more features than our model, and achieves 0.9936 accuracy, 0.9838 precision, 0.9540 recall, and 0.9684 F1score on Dataset 2. In contrast, our model effectively improves the detection performance using less manually extracted features.

Second, our model improves the performance by 2.21 percentage points on F1score on Dataset 1 than that of the best graph pooling method and achieves 0.9975 F1score on Dataset 2. This suggests that combining pattern features and structural information can more accurately detect the rug pull tokens. Besides, we analyze that this is because the graph structural information of the two categories in Dataset 2 is quite different. Therefore, our model has a smaller improvement in the experimental results on Dataset 2 than the results obtained by only using the graph pooling method.

Third, different graph pooling methods also have an impact on the experimental results. SortPool performs better than SAGPool and CGIPool. The main reason is that the transaction graph for rug pull tokens typically has a relatively small number of nodes, using hierarchical pooling may cause overfitting.

Finally, the overall experimental performance on Dataset 2 is better than that on Dataset 1. We can infer that this is because most positive samples have very small transaction volumes, leading to a larger difference between positive and negative samples.

In summary, our model effectively improves the accuracy of detecting rug pull tokens, which is significant for the asset security of Ethereum users, the sustainable development of the decentralized financial ecosystem and the regulation of illicit behaviors on the Ethereum platform.

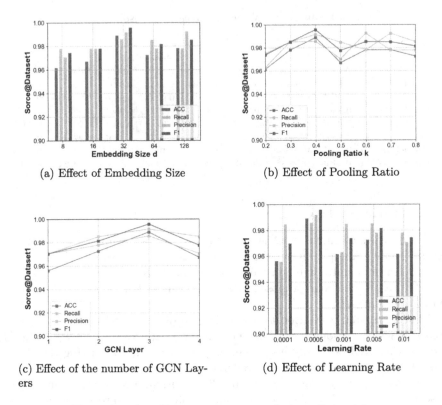

(a) Effect of Embedding Size

(b) Effect of Pooling Ratio

(c) Effect of the number of GCN Layers

(d) Effect of Learning Rate

Fig. 6. Results of hyperparameters analysis on Dataset 1.

5.3 Parameter Sensitivity

As graph convolution layers and graph pooling layers plays crucial roles in our model, we explore their impact on the performance. Figure 6 shows the effect of four hyperparameters on experimental results, including the node embedding size d, the pooling ratio k, the number of GCN layers and the learning rate. We conduct experiments on Dataset 1 to analyze.

Figure 6(a) shows the effect of the embedding size on our model's performance. We can observe that the four evaluation metrics first increase and then decrease. The best performance is achieved at $d = 32$. If the embedding size is too small, it will not learn the node features sufficiently. On the contrary, with the high dimension it will cause overfitting and increase the computational complexity. complexity.

Figure 6(b) shows the effect of pooling ratio k. With the increase of k, the four evaluation metrics fluctuate within a small range and the F1score reaches the peak at $k = 0.4$. The larger k is, the more nodes are reserved in the pooling layer, it will cause greater space consumption. So k takes 0.4 to get the best performance.

Figure 6(c) shows the effect of the number of GCN layers. With an increase in the number of GCN layers, the deep aggregation of neighbor information makes node embeddings indistinguishable, leading to oversmoothing.

Figure 6(d) shows the effect of the learning rate. A smaller learning rate can improve the convergence performance. We can see that the overall performance reaches the best when the learning rate is 0.0005.

5.4   Feature Effectiveness Analysis

To assess the effectiveness of the two time-related features we proposed, We discard these two features separately and conduct experiments again. Table 3 summarizes the experimental results on Dataset 1 after discarding specific features using XGBoost and our model. "Feature1" represents it does not contains these two features, and "Feature2" discards *lifetime* and "Feature3" discards *max_to_min_time.*

It can be observed that both of these two features can individually improve the experimental results, and combining them further enhances the experimental results. Moreover, *lifetime* shows a better improvement. We analyze the distribution of the lifetime of two types of tokens and find that over 80% of rug pull tokens have a lifetime of less than 120 days, while over 80% of normal tokens have a lifetime greater than 300 days. Therefore, the features we proposed are effective.

Table 3. Feature performance comparison.

Datasets	Model							
	XGBoost				Our model$_{SortPool}$			
	Acc	Recall	Precision	F1score	Acc	Recall	Precision	F1score
Feature1	0.9576	0.9435	0.9093	0.9258	0.9780	0.9805	0.9882	0.9843
Feature2	0.9587	0.9417	0.9149	0.9280	0.9835	0.9926	0.9833	0.9874
Feature3	0.9730	0.9582	0.9490	0.9535	0.9863	0.9958	0.9833	0.9895
All Features	**0.9769**	**0.9622**	**0.9589**	**0.9604**	**0.9890**	**0.9958**	**0.9875**	**0.9916**

6   Conclusion and Future Work

In recent years, rug pull scams have become very common on DEXes, significantly impacting the security of users' digital assets. In this work, we propose a rug pull detection model by combining feature extraction and graph pooling. The key of our model lies in employing graph pooling to aggregate the node embeddings of token transaction graphs into an embedding of the graph. This process learns the topology structure of token transaction graphs. We further enhance the training process by incorporating manually extracted pattern features of tokens with graph embedding. Finally, we evaluate the performance of our model and conduct a comparison with baseline models and the experimental results show that our model can more accurately detect rug pull tokens. This contributes to the regulation of illegal behaviors on DEXes.

In the future, we plan to expand the ground truth dataset to enhance the credibility of data. In addition, as our model relies on transaction records, it is difficult to detect rug pull tokens at the time of their creation. Therefore, we can further explore the smart contracts of tokens and liquidity pools, and detect rug pull tokens through the analysis and identification of their smart contracts.

Acknowledgment. This work is partially supported by the Key-Area Research and Development Program of Guangdong Province (No. 2020B0101090005).

References

1. Agarwal, R., Thapliyal, T., Shukla, S.K.: Vulnerability and transaction behavior based detection of malicious smart contracts. In: Meng, W., Conti, M. (eds.) Cyberspace Safety and Security. LNCS, vol. 13172, pp. 79–96. Springer, Cham (2022). https://doi.org/10.1007/978-3-030-94029-4_6
2. Agarwal, S., Atondo Siu, J., Ordekian, M., Hutchings, A., Mariconti, E., Vasek, M.: Defi deception–uncovering the prevalence of rugpulls in cryptocurrency projects (2023)
3. Bianchi, F.M., Grattarola, D., Alippi, C.: Mincut pooling in graph neural networks. arXiv preprint arXiv:1907.00481 (2019)
4. Buterin, V., et al.: A next-generation smart contract and decentralized application platform. White Paper **3**(37), 2-1 (2014)
5. Cernera, F., Morgia, M.L., Mei, A., Sassi, F.: Token spammers, rug pulls, and sniper bots: an analysis of the ecosystem of tokens in ethereum and in the binance smart chain (BNB). In: 32nd USENIX Security Symposium (USENIX Security 23), pp. 3349–3366. USENIX Association (2023)
6. Chen, L., Peng, J., Liu, Y., Li, J., Xie, F., Zheng, Z.: Phishing scams detection in ethereum transaction network. ACM Trans. Internet Technol. **21**(1), 1–16 (2020)
7. Chen, T., Guestrin, C.: Xgboost: a scalable tree boosting system. In: Proceedings of the 22nd ACM SIGKDD International Conference on Knowledge Discovery and Data Mining, pp. 785–794. Association for Computing (2016)
8. Chen, W., Guo, X., Chen, Z., Zheng, Z., Lu, Y.: Phishing scam detection on ethereum: towards financial security for blockchain ecosystem. In: IJCAI, pp. 4456–4462 (2020)
9. Chen, W., Zheng, Z., Cui, J., Ngai, E., Zheng, P., Zhou, Y.: Detecting ponzi schemes on ethereum: towards healthier blockchain technology. In: Proceedings of the 2018 World Wide Web Conference, pp. 1409–1418. International World Wide Web Conferences Steering Committee (2018)
10. Georgousis, S., Kenning, M.P., Xie, X.: Graph deep learning: state of the art and challenges. IEEE Access **9**, 22106–22140 (2021)
11. Gorishniy, Y., Rubachev, I., Khrulkov, V., Babenko, A.: Revisiting deep learning models for tabular data. Adv. Neural. Inf. Process. Syst. **34**, 18932–18943 (2021)
12. Jung, E., Le Tilly, M., Gehani, A., Ge, Y.: Data mining-based ethereum fraud detection. In: 2019 IEEE International Conference on Blockchain (Blockchain), pp. 266–273 (2019)
13. Kipf, T.N., Welling, M.: Semi-supervised classification with graph convolutional networks. arXiv preprint arXiv:1609.02907 (2016)

14. Lee, J., Lee, I., Kang, J.: Self-attention graph pooling. In: International Conference on Machine Learning, pp. 3734–3743. PMLR (2019)
15. Lehar, A., Parlour, C.A.: Decentralized exchanges. Available at SSRN 3905316 (2021)
16. Mazorra, B., Adan, V., Daza, V.: Do not rug on me: leveraging machine learning techniques for automated scam detection. Mathematics **10**(6), 949 (2022)
17. Mohanta, B.K., Panda, S.S., Jena, D.: An overview of smart contract and use cases in blockchain technology. In: 2018 9th International Conference on Computing, Communication and Networking Technologies (ICCCNT), pp. 1–4 (2018)
18. Nakamoto, S.: Bitcoin: a peer-to-peer electronic cash system. In: Decentralized Business Review, p. 21260 (2008)
19. Nguyen, M.H., Huynh, P.D., Dau, S.H., Li, X.: Rug-pull malicious token detection on blockchain using supervised learning with feature engineering. In: 2023 Australasian Computer Science Week, pp. 72–81. Association for Computing Machinery (2023)
20. Pang, Y., Zhao, Y., Li, D.: Graph pooling via coarsened graph infomax. In: Proceedings of the 44th International ACM SIGIR Conference on Research and Development in Information Retrieval, pp. 2177–2181. Association for Computing Machinery (2021)
21. Pilkington, M.: Blockchain technology: principles and applications. In: Research Handbook on Digital Transformations, pp. 225–253. Edward Elgar Publishing (2016)
22. Victor, F., Lüders, B.K.: Measuring ethereum-based ERC20 token networks. In: Goldberg, I., Moore, T. (eds.) Financial Cryptography and Data Security, FC 2019. LNCS, vol. 11598, pp. 113–129. Springer, Cham (2019). https://doi.org/10.1007/978-3-030-32101-7_8
23. Wu, J., et al.: Who are the phishers? phishing scam detection on ethereum via network embedding. IEEE Trans. Syst. Man Cybernet. Syst. **52**(2), 1156–1166 (2020)
24. Xia, P., et al.: Trade or trick? detecting and characterizing scam tokens on uniswap decentralized exchange. Proc. ACM Measur. Anal. Comput. Syst. **5**(3), 1–26 (2021)
25. Ying, Z., You, J., Morris, C., Ren, X., Hamilton, W., Leskovec, J.: Hierarchical graph representation learning with differentiable pooling. Adv. Neural Inf. Process. Syst. **31** (2018)
26. Yuan, H., Ji, S.: Structpool: structured graph pooling via conditional random fields. In: Proceedings of the 8th International Conference on Learning Representations (2020)
27. Zetzsche, D.A., Arner, D.W., Buckley, R.P.: Decentralized finance. J. Financ. Regulat. **6**(2), 172–203 (2020)
28. Zhang, L., et al.: Structure-feature based graph self-adaptive pooling. In: Proceedings of the Web Conference 2020, pp. 3098–3104. Association for Computing Machinery (2020)
29. Zhang, M., Cui, Z., Neumann, M., Chen, Y.: An end-to-end deep learning architecture for graph classification. In: Proceedings of the AAAI Conference on Artificial Intelligence (2018)
30. Zhang, Y., Kang, S., Dai, W., Chen, S., Zhu, J.: Code will speak: early detection of Ponzi smart contracts on ethereum. In: 2021 IEEE International Conference on Services Computing (SCC), pp. 301–308 (2021)
31. Zheng, Z., et al.: An overview on smart contracts: challenges, advances and platforms. Futur. Gener. Comput. Syst. **105**, 475–491 (2020)

Blockchain Consensus Mechanism

An Improved Hashgraph Consensus Algorithm Based on Sharding Technology

Yuanyuan Li[1], Yue Chen[1(✉)], Peng Han[3], Xin Huang[2], and Linzhao Sun[1]

[1] College of Computer Science and Technology, Chongqing University of Posts and Telecommunications, Chongqing, China
liyy@cqupt.edu.cn, {s220231012,s220201080}@stu.cqupt.edu.cn
[2] School of Automation, Chongqing University of Posts and Telecommunications, Chongqing, China
huangxin@cqupt.edu.cn
[3] Chongqing Research Center for Information, Chongqing, China
han.peng@edusign.cn

Abstract. Hashgraph, as one of the most popular DAG-based consensus algorithms, has the potential to overcome the throughput bottleneck of blockchain technology with its efficient consensus mechanism. However, the consensus process of Hashgraph suffers from issues such as multiple steps, complex procedures, poor stability, and duplicate transaction packaging. To address these problems, this paper proposes some solutions.

Firstly, this model integrates sharding concepts to optimize the gossip communication protocol. It divides the network into sub-networks based on the comprehensive reputation evaluation value(CREV) of nodes, reducing the number of neighboring nodes and enhancing the efficiency of event propagation by mitigating blind communication. Secondly, within each sharding, a fair and random election of a leader node is conducted using the comprehensive reputation evaluation value to govern the consensus process. This reduces the steps of the algorithm and improves consensus efficiency while ensuring security. Lastly, a transaction sending mechanism based on Verifiable Random Function(VRF) is proposed to prevent duplicate transactions from entering events and improve the system's effective throughput.

Experimental results demonstrate that this model outperforms Hashgraph in terms of effective throughput, latency, and event propagation efficiency.

Keywords: blockchain · Hashgraph · sharding · gossip · CREV · VRF

1 Introduction

Blockchain is a distributed ledger technology that ensures the security, immutability, transparency, and traceability of data through cryptography, distributed consensus theory, and incentive mechanisms. The core concept of

J. Zhu et al. (Eds.): CBCS 2023, CCIS 2098, pp. 87–104, 2024.
https://doi.org/10.1007/978-981-97-3203-6_5

blockchain is widely recognized to have first appeared in the Bitcoin whitepaper released by Satoshi Nakamoto [1].

The core of blockchain lies in its consensus algorithm, which determines the degree of decentralization, scalability, and security of the blockchain system. According to Vitalik's DSS conjecture [2], a blockchain system cannot simultaneously achieve all three properties, meaning that having two of these properties inevitably weakens the third one. Based on the emphasis of different consensus algorithms, blockchain is categorized into three types: public chains, consortium chains, and private chains. Public chains, represented by PoW and PoS [3] consensus algorithms, prioritize security and scalability by sacrificing system throughput.

Consortium chains achieved good scalability at the cost of partial decentralization. However, consensus protocols centered around PBFT [4] introduce high communication complexity, further hindering the performance development of blockchain systems. Additionally, leader-based mechanisms like Paxos [5] and Raft [6], if subjected to DoS attacks, exhibit single points of failure. Gradually, more people have come to realize that extending and improving a single chain is no longer sufficient to meet the performance and scalability requirements of blockchain systems.

Researchers have shifted their focus to the study of distributed ledgers based on Directed Acyclic Graphs (DAG). DAG-based distributed ledger technology inherently possesses high concurrency. Among these, Hashgraph [7] is a consensus algorithm based on a parallel chain DAG structure, using the gossip protocol [8] for communication. Its promising consensus efficiency is expected to overcome the throughput limitations of blockchain systems. However, experiments have revealed challenges with this algorithm, such as issues related to member node scalability, consensus delay, and transaction duplication.

In this paper, we address the above problems by introducing the idea of sharding, increasing the number of nodes that can be accommodated by Hashgraph, proposing a VRF-based [9] transaction sending mechanism to solve the problem of repetitive packing of transactions, and improving the effective throughput of the system.

The main contributions are summarized as follows:

- We propose a weight-based sharding algorithm to improve the event propagation rate and reduce the communication overhead.
- We use leader nodes within the sharding to participate in the consensus process to improve system throughput and reduce latency.
- To address the problem of difficult deduplication of hashgraph transactions, we propose a VRF-based transaction sending mechanism to avoid duplicate transactions into events and improve the payload of the system.
- The results are validated through simulation experiments, and the experiments showed that in different scenarios (varied numbers of nodes, different shard counts, varying network latencies, and differing transaction duplication rates), the effective throughput, consensus latency, and scalability were superior to Hashgraph.

The remainder of this paper is organized as follows. Section 2 discusses DAG-based consensus algorithms and improvements to Hashgraph, analyzing their strengths and weaknesses. Section 3 presents our system model and consensus algorithm to solve these problems. Section 4 provides a security analysis of the model. Section 5 validates the model's scalability, throughput, and latency. In Sect. 6 we present a conclusion and discuss the future direction of research.

2   Related Work

Existing DAG-based consensus algorithms can be categorized into three categories. These categories are based on different reference structures between nodes. They include the backbone chain, the parallel chain, and the naive chain [10]. GHOST [11], Inclusive Blockchain Protocol(IBP) [12] and Conflux [13] are DAG consensus protocols based on backbone chains, which use the DAG structure for certain improvements in response to the problem of high concurrency in traditional blockchains. GHOST will select a path as the backbone chain based on the current DAG structure, and the other blocks will be discarded, resulting in a waste of resources. Meanwhile, Conflux and IBP, although the block utilization reaches 100%, but there is the problem of repetitive packing, and the effective throughput of the system cannot be increased approximately linearly with the increase of arithmetic power. Dagcoin [14] and IOTA [15] are consensus protocols based on plain-chain DAG. Dagcoin and IOTA are all DAG consensus algorithms based on transactions as the basic unit that constitutes the ledger. Each transaction needs to verify and refer to two transactions in the ledger, and users need to perform a certain amount of PoW when creating transactions to avoid flooding attacks by malicious nodes, but DAG consensus protocols based on plain chains generally have security problems and cannot give strict security proofs, and there are not many studies.

The hashgraph [7], based on a parallel chain DAG consensus protocol, offers stringent security proofs, higher event propagation rates, and efficient consensus mechanisms. To further enhance Hashgraph's consensus efficiency and scalability, researchers from both domestic and international backgrounds have introduced various diverse consensus solutions. Nguyen et al. [16] proposed StakeDAG, utilizing a PoS+DAG approach for cross-validation and post-checking to ensure the integrity and sustainability of the entire network. Fu et al. [17] introduced fixed leader nodes in Jointgraph to lead the consensus process, simplifying consensus steps and accelerating consensus efficiency. Zhou et al. [18] and the team put forth a reputation-based Hashgraph algorithm to address the issue of Jointgraph's excessive reliance on centralized nodes.

To enhance Hashgraph's event propagation rate and scalability, Gong et al. [19] proposed a mobile self-organizing network blockchain model based on Hashgraph. They divided nodes into clusters of varying sizes based on their geographical locations and network conditions. Within clusters, they improved consensus efficiency using cluster heads, and between clusters, they utilized routing nodes to enhance event propagation efficiency. Gao et al. [20] introduced a shard-based

Hashgraph algorithm based on the concept of sharding. They incorporated a comprehensive evaluation mechanism based on node states to dynamically shard a large number of nodes. Within each sharding, they accelerated the consensus process using an enhanced strong visibility rule, ultimately improving scalability.

In general, Hashgraph is suitable for consortium environments, but the increasing number of consortium chain nodes poses a scalability challenge to its protocol. Furthermore, the Hashgraph consensus protocol cannot handle transaction deduplication, further diminishing the effective throughput of the system. To address these challenges, this paper presents an improved model of the Hashgraph consensus algorithm based on sharding technology.

3   System Model

This model, based on Hashgraph's "gossip about gossip" mechanism, ensures all nodes eventually learn an event. However, as the number of nodes increases, its random communication approach becomes inefficient, leading to scalability problems. To enhance the scalability and efficiency of the Hashgraph consensus algorithm, this paper employs a weight-based sharding method, dividing the network into multiple subnetworks, with a leader node elected in each sharding to manage the consensus process. This paper classifies the nodes participating in the consensus into leader nodes and ordinary nodes. Ordinary nodes store and forward events within their shards. The leader node is responsible for liaising with the leader nodes of other shards, forwarding part of the events within each sharding. At the same time, each node can create events. Nodes within a sharding are only responsible for the consensus of events generated within their sharding, but can reference events within other shards that have not reached consensus.

3.1   Node Comprehensive Reputation Evaluation Model

The performance of the nodes in the system determines their reputation value, and the reputation value model combined with the reward mechanism constrains the Byzantine behavior of the nodes to some extent [21]. According to the historical choices of nodes in the consensus process and the network performance, the range of gossip communication is divided to improve the efficiency of event propagation and the efficiency of consensus while reducing the blindness of communication. However, consensus nodes with poor historical performance are more likely to receive low bookkeeping rights and discourage motivation, resulting in a vicious circle and bifurcation. Therefore, in this paper, we divide the network into multiple partitions with reference to the nodes' Credit C, Token T, Geographical position G_p, Network status N_s, and Computer resource C_r. The sum of the weights of all nodes in each partition is basically equal in terms of probability to ensure that each partition generates events at the same rate. Nodes within each partition are geographically similar and have relatively good network status on average, but differ in token holdings and reputation values, preventing the Byzantine nodes of the system from gathering in a particular partition and causing the consensus within the partition to be unavailable.

In order to reasonably evaluate the reputation of a node, the integrated reputation value of a node needs to be recalculated each round relying on the latest consensus results. The proposed formula for assessing the integrated reputation value of node i in this paper is shown in (1).

$$CREV_r^i = \frac{1}{1 + e^{P_r^i - \overline{P_r}}} \tag{1}$$

where $CREV_r^i$ denotes the comprehensive reputation assessment value of node i in the r round, P_r^i denotes the capability value of node i in the r round, and $\overline{P_r}$ denotes the average capability value of all nodes in the r round, and its calculation formula is shown in (2).

$$P_r^i = \alpha \cdot C + \tau \cdot T + \beta \cdot G_p + \gamma \cdot N_s + \delta \cdot C_r \tag{2}$$

where, $\alpha + \tau + \beta + \gamma + \delta = 1$, can be dynamically adjusted according to the operational state of the system. G_p is determined by the virtual central node generated by the distance clustering algorithm, N_s is obtained based on the average delay in communication with other nodes, T represents the percentage of the node to all the system, and C_r references the system performance of the node. These belong to the basic attributes of the nodes and can be obtained directly by the system. The reputation value is used to measure the historical performance of the node, and the proposed reputation formula in this paper is shown in (3).

$$C^i = \varepsilon \cdot Ph + \theta \cdot Ef + \mu \cdot Er \tag{3}$$

The credibility of a node is determined by its historical performance, with higher Ph and Ef representing a greater contribution of the node to the stable operation of the system. The number of error feedbacks received by the system determines the level of Er.

3.2   Consensus Algorithm

Round Division. The Hashgraph algorithm improves consensus efficiency by assigning each new event a round. If subsequent events can strongly see more than 2/3 of the witnesses from the previous round, a new round is assigned. However, the strong visibility condition may affect the speed of round assignment. In this paper, we adopt a leader-led consensus process to simplify the rules for dividing rounds by defining an event to be strongly visible as the sum or number of member node weights on the visible path is greater than 2/3. If a new event is strongly visible over 2/3 of the witnessed events, a new round is divided for the event, and the comprehensive reputation evaluation value is written to the event and broadcasted to other nodes through the cross-reference of the event. If there is a reference relationship between two events A and B, it is said that A can see B (assuming A is higher than B in the hashgraph, otherwise, B can see

A). If event x can see the witness event of the n round through multiple paths, and the nodes contained in these paths exceed 2/3 of all nodes, then x is defined as the witness event of the n+1 round.

In Fig. 1(a), the round division of Hashgraph is shown. Among them, the gray events are witness events, and the white ones are ordinary events. Figure 1(b) shows the round division rules of this paper. Within a sharding, each node has a CREV value. According to the weight of the CREV of the nodes, if event x can see the witness event of the n round through multiple paths, and the total CREV of these nodes exceeds 2/3 of the total, then x is called the witness event of the n+1 round.

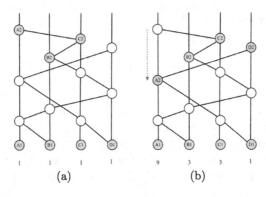

(a)   (b)

Fig. 1. Comparison of round division. Illustration of round division. Assuming that the number of nodes in a given sharding is 4, then according to the round division rule of Hashgraph, each event must be strongly seen for at least 2/3 of the previous witness events before a new round can be divided. As shown in (a), white represents normal events and light gray represents witness events. In (b), we calculate the CREV of each node (weight ratio is A:9, B:3, C:3, D:1, respectively). Based on the number of visible path member nodes, it is known that A2(light blue) is strongly visible to D1, and also based on the sum of weights of the visible path member nodes, it is known that A2 is strongly see to both B1 and C1. (Color figure online)

The improved strong visible rule increases the speed of round division and improves the consensus efficiency of the algorithm. And, based on node reputation statistics we will also introduce new leader election algorithm and event sequencing rules.

Leader Election. In order to accelerate the efficiency of event consensus and manage the nodes in the sharding, we elect the leader nodes within each sharding according to certain rules to dominate the consensus process. Since adding the leader mechanism will decrease the degree of decentralization within the sharding, if the Byzantine node is incorrectly selected as the leader node and misinformation misleading the consensus process occurs, then it will seriously affect the security of the system. To counteract this error, the system needs to incorporate an identity permission access mechanism to supervise the nodes involved in the consensus process, so we assume that the model application scenario is a coalition chain or a private chain.

The model in this paper elects a leader node in each round. The leader node in each round is randomly generated by VRF based on CREV. Specifically, the node performs VRF operation according to the current round and its own private key, and the nodes in the sharding are sorted according to the size of the public key value combined with CREV to divide the Hash interval, so that the Hash interval occupied by its CREV is larger, and finally the result of VRF if it falls in the range of its own division, then the node becomes the leader node in that round. The leader election algorithm ensures that the leader election is fair within a sharding, but the selected node is not necessarily honest and is not guaranteed to be fault-free during its term. Therefore, if a leader node makes a mistake during its term, the leader election algorithm is retriggered, and the faulty node is excluded from the system.

Algorithm 1 Leader Election Algorithm

1: **Input:** candidate public key Vk^c, private key Sk^c, comprehensive reputation evaluation value $CREV^c$, round r
2: **Output:** leader public key Vk, VRF Output $hash$, proof π
3: // STEP1: Get election result
4: let s be the set of sharding nodes' public keys Vk^i
5: let x variable store value of subset of $CREVs$
6: // sort Vk according to the public key values
7: **for each** Vk^i in s *order from smaller to larger* **do**
8:     **if** $Vk^i < Vk^c$ **then**
9:         add the $CREV^i$ corresponding to Vk^i to x
10:     **end if**
11: **end for**
12: // get the VRF hash value boundary range of the candidate node c
13: let $left^c$ and $right^c$ represent the VRF hash range limit value of candidate node c
14: $left^c \leftarrow \frac{x}{the\ sum\ of\ CREVs} \cdot 2^{256}$
15: $right^c \leftarrow \frac{x+CREV^c}{the\ sum\ of\ CREVs} \cdot 2^{256}$
16: // VRF operation
17: $(hash, \pi) \leftarrow VRF(r, Sk^c)$
18: **if** $left^c < hash$ && $hash \leq right^c$ **then**
19:     output $Vk^c, r, hash, \pi$
20: **end if**
21: // STEP2: Verification result
22: **if** $VRFverify(Vk^c, r, hash, \pi) \neq 0$ **then**
23:     output true
24: **else**
25:     output false
26: **end if**

The algorithm implements a fair election of leaders according to CREV size for the nodes within the division without obtaining the private key information of other nodes. However, the result of the election may have various cases, no node is selected, one node is selected and multiple nodes are selected. Therefore, this paper stipulates that if no node is selected or there are multiple candidate nodes selected, the candidate node with the largest CREV is selected to become the leader and the election result and proof are put into the witness event broadcast to other nodes. A point worth stating is that this paper uses the VRF algorithm based on the ECVRF-P256-SHA256-TAI implementation [22], so the value domain of the hash is $(0, 2^{256}]$.

Event Confirmation. In the model of this paper, events need to go through intra-sharding consensus and inter-sharding consensus to determine finality. We rely on leaders to improve the intra-sharding consensus efficiency and use an improved gossip protocol to improve the efficiency of event propagation between shards, thus improving the overall consensus efficiency of the system. Within shards, events have faster round division and faster consensus efficiency, requiring only two stages: election of leaders, and consensus of leaders to confirm events. An event that wants to reach consensus within a sharding can use Hashgraph or this model scheme. Figure 2 shows the differences between these two approaches.

In Fig. 2(a), if the hashgraph needs to confirm B1 in the first round, then the current hashgraph needs to learn to know a certain witness event in the third round. Suppose at this point, the B3 event is learned, so B3 counts the votes of all witness events for B1 in the second round. From the figure, according to the "virtual voting" rules of Hashgraph [7], B1 can see A2, B2, C2, and D2, B3 can collect votes from all events, therefore B1 determines the finality. The model specifies that each node uniquely has a leader node at some determined round, and an event passes 2/3 nodes or the sum of CREVs on the visible path exceeds 2/3, then the event determines finality.

In Fig. 2(b), suppose that the leader of the third round is A3, and A3 can see D2 through parallel chain B and the sum of CREVs in the path exceeds 2/3, then D2 reaches consensus within the sharding. If more than 2/3 of the nodes indirectly or directly refer to D2 at this point, D2 determines finality and all ancestor nodes of D2 also confirm finality. In Fig. 2(b), black, dark green, and dark blue are the events that are consensual under the A3 leader event. The blue events, including light blue and dark blue, are witness events divided by the model in this paper, therefore our consensus is faster than Hashgraph.

CREV Sharding-Based Gossip Communication Protocol. The introduction of sharding presents a challenge to random gossip communication. Since nodes within a sharding only contribute to the consensus of events within the sharding, there is no need to store events from other shards that reach consensus. The original gossip communication mechanism randomly selects the communication object among all nodes and pulls new events from the local hashgraph copy of the communication object, but a particular node does not need to know

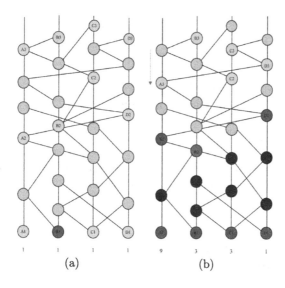

(a)   (b)

Fig. 2. The influence of leader on intra-sharding consensus

all the node addresses after the sharding, so the random gossip communication protocol is improved in this paper.

We divide the nodes into ordinary nodes and leader nodes. Ordinary nodes pull events within the sharding based on random communication, and leader nodes have to communicate with the nodes within the sharding in addition to the leaders of other shards. More, the sum of CREV within each sharding represents the event generation rate as well as the consensus efficiency, so dividing the communication probability for each leader neighbor according to the different CREV can improve the event propagation efficiency.

In the leader perspective, nodes need to participate not only in the intra-sharding consensus but also pull events from other shards. For consensus efficiency consideration, these two tasks should be executed in parallel. Considering that after pulling an unconsensus event within another sharding, probabilistically there will not be more new events generated in the next period than the other sharding, it is necessary to reduce the probability of continuous communication with that node after one communication.

Algorithm 2 Leader Node Running Algorithm

1: let Nb_1 be the set of ordinary neighbor node
2: let Nb_2 be the set of leader neighbor node
3: let S be the set of $CREVs$ of nodes in Nb_2
4: run the following three loop in parallel threads
5: **loop**
6:     send all new events to a ordinary node in Nb_1
7: **end loop**

```
 8: loop
 9:    //Select a leader for communication based on CREV
10:    let x record last selected leader node
11:    for i in Nb₂ do
12:        i.probability ← i.CREV / the sum of S
13:        //reduce communication probability
14:        if i == x then
15:            i.probability ← i.probability · e⁻¹
16:        end if
17:        x ← randomly selected according to i.probability in Nb₂
18:        send all new events without consensus to x
19:    end for
20: end loop
21: loop
22:    receive events from its neighbor node in Nb₁ and Nb₂
23:    verify received events and create a new event
24: end loop
```

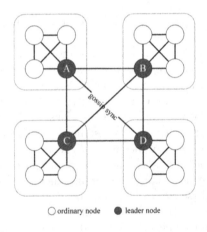

Fig. 3. Gossip communication model

In Fig. 3, there is a leader node within each sharding, which has two functions. First, it participates in the consensus within the sharding, packages transactions, and submits new events. And, as a leader node, it leads the consensus process to speed up the consensus efficiency. Second, as an ordinary node, it verifies and receives events that are not consensused by other shards. Each ordinary node can only communicate with other nodes within the sharding to learn their new events but is not allowed to communicate directly with other nodes within the sharding, which can reduce the communication frequency of the system and increase the amount of information in one communication. Second, each leader node maintains a list of leader neighbors locally and obtains the communication probability of each neighbor node by computing CREV to obtain the final communication object. The gossip communication between leaders broadcasts the events within each sharding that have not yet been agreed upon, allowing ordinary nodes to learn about events within other shards and ensuring consensus security.

3.3 VRF Transaction Sending Mechanism

Since Hashgraph nodes cannot determine whether a transaction has been packaged on the chain when a new event is generated. However, clients often choose to send multiple nodes repeatedly to ensure that transactions are not lost, which leads to repetitive packing of transactions and reduces the effective throughput of the system. Therefore, this paper proposes a transaction sending mechanism based on VRF (Verifiable Random Function). This mechanism ensures that transactions are uniquely and randomly sent to a node in the network for packaging, avoiding the possibility of repetitive packaging. When a client selects a node to send a transaction, it first performs a VRF operation on the content of the transaction and puts the output *hash value* and *proof* into the transaction and sends it to the target node together. The selection of the target node is determined according to its output *hash value*, and according to the initialization setting of the system, the value field of its result is divided into multiple intervals, and each interval maps a node, and as long as the hash value of the transaction falls in the interval range of that node, it is proven that the transaction is unique sent to this node.

In Fig. 4, the verification information structure of the event is shown, and when the consensus node performs gossip synchronization, it can calculate whether the transaction uniquely and legally belongs to the parallel chain, thus preventing duplicate transactions from entering the ledger.

The transaction sending mechanism consists of four main steps. The client generates a pair of public and private key accounts, sets the sender field to the public key of the account when sending a transaction, and signs the content of the transaction with the private key:

$$keygen(r) \rightarrow (VK, Sk) \tag{4}$$

The VRF value is calculated based on the content of the transaction after the signature:

$$VRF\_hash(Sk, Transaction) \rightarrow (value, proof) \tag{5}$$

Quantize the hash obtained through the VRF to (0,1):

$$\frac{value}{2^{bits\_len(value)}} \rightarrow p \tag{6}$$

According to the uniform division rule, the p-taking interval is assigned to the member nodes. Assuming that the system has a total of x consensus nodes,

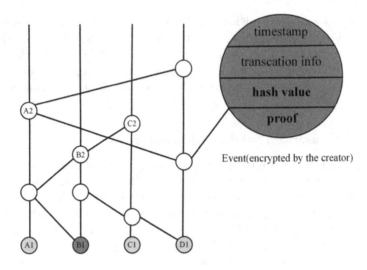

Fig. 4. Event structure with VRF information

and the nodes are sorted according to their public key value size, then the target node n are

$$
n \leftarrow
\begin{cases}
1 & 0 < p \leq \frac{1}{x} \\
2 & \frac{1}{x} < p \leq \frac{2}{x} \\
\vdots & \vdots \\
x & \frac{x-1}{x} < p \leq 1.
\end{cases}
\tag{7}
$$

Considering the case that the receiving node is down or Byzantine, each time the client sends a transaction, it should listen to the response information of the receiving node and the Hashgraph copies of other nodes, and if the receiving node does not return or returns an error message, the transaction timestamp is regenerated and sent to the new receiving node.

4   Security Analysis

This section analyzes the security of the model and specifically how the model protects against several common security attacks on the blockchain, including the double spending attack, the sybil attack and the DoS attack.

System Assumptions: More than 2/3 of the nodes in the system are honest and hold more than 2/3 of the CREV s, and less than 1/3 of the Byzantine nodes. Digital signatures are valid and cannot be broken by brute force. We also assume that the network is asynchronous and that messages between nodes can be delayed, intercepted, and deleted, but are eventually received, regardless of how long the communication lasts.

Double Spending Attack: In this paper's model, nodes only contribute to the event consensus within the sharding, so the double spending attack can occur only within the sharding. Suppose the adversary generates event(x, y) is a fork and the double spending attack is successful, then both events are globally agreed upon. Suppose that a malicious node creates x and y in the R round and the following four cases exist. a)$R+1$ round of leader confirmation x. b)$R+1$ round of leader confirmation y. c)$R+1$ round of leader cannot see x and y. d)x and y are seen by the leaders of $R+1$ rounds at the same time, then the feedback is wrong and the reference is rejected.

Obviously, it's impossible for the double spending attack to succeed in c) or d) conditions can't reach intra-sharding consensus, and only if a) and b) are satisfied at the same time, it is possible to succeed. In the following, I will show that global consensus cannot be reached even under the condition that both a) and b) are satisfied.

Assume that the number of nodes in the system is n, the number of Byzantine nodes is f, and the number of honest nodes is $n - f$. where $h1$ honest nodes can see x, and $h2$ honest nodes can see y. Since honest nodes will not be able to see both x and y, it follows that

$$\begin{cases} h1 + h2 + f \leq n \\ h1 + f > 2/3n \\ h2 + f > 2/3n. \end{cases} \tag{8}$$

From (8), we can get $f > n/3$, which contradicts the assumption of $f < n/3$. Therefore, the fork events x, y cannot reach global consensus at the same time, and the double spending attack fails.

Sybil Attack: The sybil attack refers to an adversary forging multiple identities to achieve a dominant position in terms of number within a sharding. In this paper, the application scenario of the model is assumed to be a permission chain or private chain, where nodes need CA-like certificates to join the network, and an adversary cannot apply for multiple identities to control multiple nodes, thus allowing defense against witch attacks.

DoS Attack: The purpose of DoS attack is to exhaust the network or resources of the target node, so that its services are temporarily interrupted and the clients cannot access normally. In the model of this paper, the leader node is the target of DoS attack, and we avoid the impact of DoS attack by replacing the leader in each round, so that even if the leader in round $R+1$ is unable to make consensus on the events in round R due to the attack, the leader in round $R+2$ is able to make consensus on the events in round R instead of the leader in round $R+1$.

5   Evaluation

In this section, we simulate the system performance, including event propagation rate, throughput, and latency, of the Hashgraph, the Sharding Hashgraph

[20], and the model in this paper. Then we analyze the experimental results to demonstrate the superiority of our model.

5.1 Implementation Details

The experimental hardware environment is an Asus 14-core CPU laptop with 16G of RAM. Java multithreading is used to simulate communication between nodes. Each node has 20 processing threads, the gossip synchronization interval is 0.5 to 0.6 s, and each event is packed with at most 10 transactions. The latency mentioned in this section is the average time from the first write to the local Hashgraph copy to the consensus.

5.2 Throughput and Latency

To verify the superiority of the models in this paper, we set up the performance of two sharding sizes with different number of nodes and compared the throughput of the three models. In Fig. 5, it is clear that our model has better throughput performance than Hashgraph and sharding Hashgraph as the number of nodes increases. By introducing the sharding mechanism, which divides the communication of nodes into a smaller range based on their historical performance, the overall performance of the system can be significantly improved. Figure 6 shows that our model has better system scalability. It can be seen that Hashgraph significantly increases the consensus latency of the system as the throughput increases, while the sharding Hashgraph significantly reduces the consensus latency due to the introduction of the sharding mechanism, where nodes only need to contribute to the consensus of the events within the sharding, citing

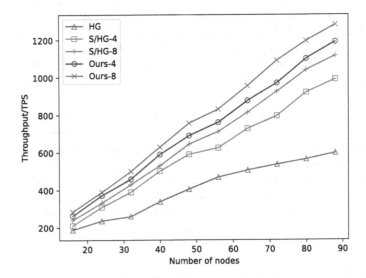

Fig. 5. Our model has better performance than Hashgraph and Sharding Hashgraph

other sharding as the events that have not reached consensus. Additionally, our model introduces the leader mechanism within the sharding to further reduce the time to reach consensus within the sharding.

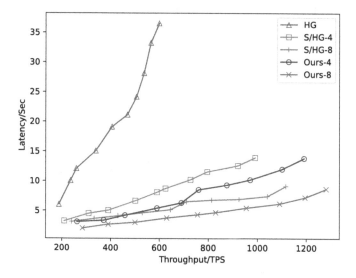

Fig. 6. Our model has better system scalability compared to Hashgraph and Sharding Hashgraph.

5.3   Event Propagation Efficiency and Effective Throughput

To illustrate the superiority of the gossip communication mechanism used in this paper's model and the rationality of CREV-based sharding. We show in Fig. 7 the effect of the Hashgraph system without the introduction of the sharding mechanism and the Hashgraph system with the introduction of the sharding mechanism on the efficiency of event propagation. The vertical coordinates in the figure represent the time when an event is learned by all nodes. To further illustrate the effect of sharding size on event propagation efficiency. We set up two sets of comparisons with sharding sizes of 4 and 8. It can be seen that our model has an overall better event propagation rate than the Hashgraph. additionally, as the number of nodes increases and the percentage of cross-sharding gossip communication increases, the efficiency of event broadcast decreases. Therefore, in designing specific applications, we should consider the impact of sharding size on system performance.

Figure 8 shows the role of the VRF transaction sending mechanism in different repetition rate environments. We set up three sets of comparisons, two of which do not introduce the VRF transaction sending mechanism. To further show the effectiveness of the mechanism, the Hashgraph system without the introduction of the VRF transaction sending mechanism is placed in two network environments with different transaction repetition rates. In this case, it

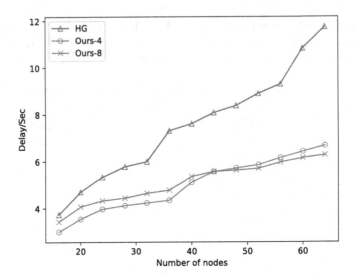

Fig. 7. Influence of sharding size on event propagation efficiency

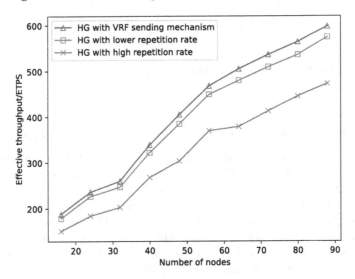

Fig. 8. Impact of VRF transaction sending mechanism on system payload

is assumed that 4%-5% of the transactions in the low repetition rate environment are legitimate duplicate transactions, and 20%-25% in the high repetition rate environment. It can be seen that the value of the VRF transaction sending mechanism is better demonstrated in the high repetition rate environment.

6   Conclusion

In this paper, we propose a sharding Hashgraph consensus algorithm based on the leader mechanism and introduce Node Comprehensive Reputation Evaluation Value to solve the intra-sharding and inter-sharding event consensus problems caused by the split network environment and improve the performance of the system.

Within the sharding, we use the leader mechanism to improve the consensus efficiency of Hashgraph by reducing the original three rounds of event sequencing to two rounds of event sequencing. Second, we use enhanced strongly seeing rule to improve the speed of round division and further improve the consensus efficiency within the sharding. Among the shards, we propose a CREV-based node sharding algorithm to evenly divide nodes with different weights within each sharding to prevent Byzantine node focus. Moreover, according to the different categories of nodes, the appropriate gossip communication range is divided for each node to improve the propagation rate of events. To reach a global consensus on events, we propose the citation rules for most nodes to guarantee the security of events. Finally, to improve the effective throughput of the system, we propose a VRF-based transaction sending mechanism to ensure that the transactions received by nodes are unique across the network. Experimental results show that the model in this paper improves throughput and event broadcast rate and reduces latency while combining security and scalability.

Acknowledgments. We sincerely thank our supervisors and instructors for their careful guidance and valuable suggestions. We thank all anonymous reviewers and experts for their valuable comments and criticisms. Their contributions were crucial to the improvement of this thesis. Finally, thanks to all organizations and individuals who provided data, resources, and support for this study.

References

1. Nakamoto, S.: Bitcoin: A Peer-to-Peer Electronic Cash System (2008). https://bitcoin.org/bitcoin.pdf
2. Buterin, V.:A Guide to 99 Fault Tolerant Consensus (2018). https://vitalik.ca/general/2018/08/07/99_fault_tolerant.html
3. Zheng, Z., Xie, S., Dai, H.-N., Chen, X., Wang, H.: Blockchain challenges and opportunities: a survey. Int. J. Web Grid Serv. **14**, 352–375 (2018). https://doi.org/10.1504/IJWGS.2018.095647
4. Castro, M., Liskov, B.: Practical byzantine fault tolerance. In: Proceeding of the Third USENIX Symposium on Operating Systems Design and Implementation (OSDI), pp. 173–186. USENIX Association, New Orleans, Louisiana, USA (1999)
5. Lamport, L.: The part-time parliament. ACM Trans. Comput. Syst. **16**(2), 133–169 (1998). https://doi.org/10.1145/279227.279229
6. Ongaro, D., Ousterhout, J.: In search of an understandable consensus algorithm. In: Proceeding of the 2014 USENIX Annual Technical Conference(USENIX ATC 14), pp. 305–319. USENIX Association, Philadelphia, PA (2014)

7. Baird, L.: The swirlds hashgraph consensus algorithm: Fair, fast, byzantine fault tolerance. Swirlds Tech Reports SWIRLDS-TR-2016-01, Tech. Rep. 34, 9–11 (2016)

8. Demers, A., Greene, D., Hauser, C., Irish, W., Larson, J.:Epidemic algorithms for replicated database maintenance. In: Proceedings of the Sixth Annual ACM Symposium on Principles of Distributed Computing - PODC '87. (1987). https://doi.org/10.1145/41840.41841

9. Micali, S., Rabin, M., Vadhan, S.: Verifiable random functions. In: 40th Annual Symposium on Foundations of Computer Science (Cat. No.99CB37039), pp. 120–130. IEEE Comput. Soc, New York City, NY, USA (1999). https://doi.org/10.1109/SFFCS.1999.814584.

10. Gao, ZF., et al.: State-of-the-art survey of consensus mechanisms on dag-based distributed ledger. Ruan Jian Xue Bao/J. Softw. **31**(4), 1124–1142 (2020). http://www.jos.org.cn/1000-9825/5982.htm

11. Sompolinsky, Y., Zohar, A.: Secure high-rate transaction processing in bitcoin. In: Böhme, R., Okamoto, T. (eds.) FC 2015. LNCS, vol. 8975, pp. 507–527. Springer, Heidelberg (2015). https://doi.org/10.1007/978-3-662-47854-7_32

12. Lewenberg, Y., Sompolinsky, Y., Zohar, A.: Inclusive block chain protocols. In: Böhme, R., Okamoto, T. (eds.) FC 2015. LNCS, vol. 8975, pp. 528–547. Springer, Heidelberg (2015). https://doi.org/10.1007/978-3-662-47854-7_33

13. Li, C., Li, P., Zhou, D., Xu, W., Long, F., Yao, A.: Scaling Nakamoto consensus to thousands of transactions per second (2018). http://arxiv.org/abs/1805.03870

14. Lerner, S.D.: DagCoin: A cryptocurrency without blocks. https://bitslog.files.wordpress.com/2015/09/dagcoin-v41.pdf

15. Popov, S.: The tangle (2018). https://assets.ctfassets.net/r1dr6vzfxhev/2t4uxvsIqk0EUau6g2sw0g/45eae33637ca92f85dd9f4a3a218e1ec/iota1_4_3.pdf

16. Nguyen, Q., Cronje, A., Kong, M., Kampa, A., Samman, G.: StakeDag: Stake-based Consensus For Scalable Trustless Systems. http://arxiv.org/abs/1907.03655, (2019)

17. Xiang, F., Huaimin, W., Peichang, S., Xue, O., Xunhui, Z.: Jointgraph: A DAG-based efficient consensus algorithm for consortium blockchains. Softw: Pract Exper. **51**, 1987–1999 (2021). https://doi.org/10.1002/spe.2748

18. Zhou, Y., Jia, L., Jia, Y., Yang, Y.: Hashgraph consensus algorithm based on credit. Appl. Res. Comput. **38**, (2021). https://doi.org/10.19734/j.issn.1001--3695.2020.12.0546

19. Blockchain model for mobile Ad hoc networks based on Hashgraph. Appl. Res. Comput. **38** (2021). https://doi.org/10.19734/j.issn.1001-3695.2023.01.0020

20. Gao, N., Huo, R., Wang, S., Huang, T., Liu, Y.: Sharding-Hashgraph: a high-performance blockchain-based framework for industrial internet of things with hashgraph mechanism. IEEE Internet Things J. **9**, 17070–17079 (2022). https://doi.org/10.1109/JIOT.2021.3126895

21. Jiacheng, H., Xinhua, X., Shichun, W.: Improved scheme of delegated proof of stake consensus mechanism (1).pdf. J. Comput. Appl. **39**, 2162–2167 (2019). http://www.joca.cn/EN/10.11772/j.issn.1001-9081.2018122527

22. Pornin, T.: Deterministic Usage of the Digital Signature Algorithm (DSA) and Elliptic Curve Digital Signature Algorithm (ECDSA). https://datatracker.ietf.org/doc/html/rfc6979

Improved Blockchain Sharding Consensus for Cross-Shard Validation

Yuanyuan Li[1], Linzhao Sun[1(✉)], Peng Han[2], Shenhai Zheng[1], and Yue Chen[1]

[1] College of Computer Science and Technology, Chongqing University of Posts and Telecommunications, Chongqing, China
s220201080@stu.cqupt.edu.cn
[2] Chongqing Research Center for Information and Automation Technology, Chongqing, China
han.peng@edusign.cn

Abstract. The consensus algorithm, which serves as the core of blockchain technology, enables the realization of decentralized and secure trusted service delivery environments. To address the complex validation mechanisms for cross-shard transactions in sharding consensus algorithms, this paper proposes a comprehensible four-layer sharding consensus algorithm. It introduces synchronous nodes responsible for storing and updating the global state to ensure the consistency of cross-shard transactions, and routing nodes responsible for forwarding cross-shard transactions to the relevant shards to ensure their atomicity. Furthermore, this paper presents a "relevant reference" approach based on a Distributed Acyclic Graph (DAG) ledger structure of parallel chains to verify cross-shard transactions, thus unifying the validation and consensus of cross-shard transactions and simplifying the validation process. Experimental results demonstrate that the proposed algorithm achieves higher throughput and lower confirmation latency compared to other sharding consensus algorithms.

Keywords: Blockchain · Sharding · Consensus · DAG

1 Introduction

Blockchain technology, with the consensus algorithm at its core [1], provides a new infrastructure that can revolutionize existing service models and offer greater trust and convenience for both service providers and consumers. The consensus algorithm is the mechanism that determines how to validate and add new transactions or blocks in a blockchain network. With the emergence of Bitcoin [2] as a reference point in time, consensus algorithms can be divided into classical distributed consensus algorithms before Bitcoin and blockchain consensus algorithms after it [3]. Lamport [4] first proposed the consensus problem in the field of distributed computing, known as the Byzantine Generals Problem. It primarily studied how non-faulty nodes in a network cluster with possible faulty nodes and peer-to-peer message communication can reach a consensus on a specific value [5]. This laid the foundation for the development of consensus algorithms.

As the number of nodes and the size of the ledger increases, blockchain systems face performance bottlenecks such as low transaction throughput, high transaction latency, and low scalability [6]. To address the performance bottleneck and scalability challenges of blockchain, database partitioning techniques were introduced into blockchain through their development called RSCion [7] by Danezis. The consensus algorithms for blockchain sharding technology have already had preliminary concepts. In the same year, Luu proposed the Elastico [8] consensus mechanism, which was the first Byzantine fault-tolerant secure sharding protocol and introduced the concept of sharding in blockchain systems. When the entire blockchain network is divided into multiple independent network shards, the size of each individual shard is reduced. Multiple shards can process transactions in parallel, thus enhancing the performance of the blockchain system.

However, the introduction of sharding technology has also brought new challenges. For example, how to ensure the consistency and atomicity of cross-shard transactions. Existing research works mostly address the consistency and atomicity of cross-shard transactions through complex validation mechanisms. However, the extensive time spent on cross-shard transaction validation has resulted in a decrease in consensus efficiency [6]. For example, SharPer [9] directly utilizes transactions to form transaction chains, and as the proportion of cross-shard transactions increases, it is prone to transaction conflicts, thereby affecting consensus efficiency. To address this issue, this paper proposes a four-layer sharding consensus algorithm. Based on the ledger of the Distributed Acyclic Graph (DAG) structure of parallel chains, the proposed model employs the "relevant reference" approach for the verification of cross-shard transactions, unifying the validation and consensus of cross-shard transactions, and simplifying the validation process. The main contributions of this paper are as follows.

1. A comprehensible four-layer sharding consensus algorithm was designed, which introduced synchronous nodes to store and update the global state, enabling state sharding and ensuring consistency of cross-shard transactions. Additionally, routing nodes were introduced to forward cross-shard transactions to the relevant shards, ensuring the atomicity of cross-shard transactions.
2. The paper introduces a validation approach called "relevant reference" based on a ledger of the DAG structure of parallel chains to verify cross-shard transactions. This approach simplifies the verification process and improves the consensus efficiency of cross-shard transactions.

The rest of this paper is organized as follows. Section 2 discusses related work. The algorithm proposed in this paper will be presented in Sects. 3 and 4. Section 5 analyzes the security of the proposed algorithm. The performance of the algorithm is evaluated through experiments in Sect. 6, and Sect. 7 concludes the paper.

2   Related Work

In blockchain sharding based on a single-chain ledger structure, such as AHL [10], a two-phase lock and two-phase commit scheme is proposed to achieve data synchronization between shards and address the issue of cross-shard transactions. In blockchain sharding based on DAG ledger structure, such as SharPer [9], the blockchains of individual shards are organized to form a global ledger. Cross-shard transactions are used to connect the blockchain ledgers of different shards through transaction edges, resulting in a DAG ledger structure based on parallel chains [11].

In addition to that, OmniLedger [12] provides a distributed ledger architecture that offers horizontal scalability through parallel processing of cross-shard transactions without sacrificing long-term security and decentralization. ChainSpace [13] simulates the execution of transactions in advance and identifies potential conflicts, which are then executed in different shards. RapidChain [14] utilizes routing nodes for forwarding cross-shard transactions. Developers of Ethereum [15] shard the blockchain, with certain nodes validating transactions only from specific shards, reducing the network load. Channel [16] constructs a public and trusted Channel that all Channel nodes can join, enabling processing of cross-shard transactions. Zero-knowledge proofs are employed in the public and trusted Channel for data synchronization between shards. Monxide [17] introduces the concept of eventual atomicity to address cross-shard data interaction, simplifying the transaction validation process but resulting in asynchronous cross-shard transactions and high confirmation latency. Zilliqa [18] uses Practical Byzantine Fault Tolerance [19] (PBFT) consensus within individual shards at a higher frequency, using a two-round EC-Schnorr multi-signature scheme to replace traditional PBFT consensus, reducing the communication complexity of PBFT consensus to $O(n)$. Luo [1] proposed a Double-Layer (DL) sharding consensus protocol, which uses a two-phase PBFT mechanism to validate cross-shard transactions. It also relies on reputation values and Verifiable Random Functions (VRF) as the foundation for cross-shard communication. Introducing a fresh approach, Yang [20] presented a 2LDAG architecture that combines DAG with a PoP protocol to guarantee the integrity of IoT data. In a separate study, Zhang [21] proposed leveraging the DAG-lattice structure for IoV and implementing PBFT as the consensus algorithm to establish a parallel consensus mechanism. In a parallel extension of the PBFT protocol, Song [22] utilized the L-DAG structure, achieving successful application in consortium blockchain scenarios. Currently, there are relatively few methods that combine sharding technology with DAG technology to enhance the performance of blockchain systems, and most of them merely treat the DAG structure as data storage. If the parallel capability of the DAG structure can be applied to sharded blockchain systems, it will further improve the system's performance. As the proportion of cross-shard transactions increases, cross-shard transactions may become blocked during consensus confirmation between shards. Compared to DL methods, this paper introduces a DAG ledger structure between shards to increase parallelism through references.

To sum up, existing methods often rely on complex cross-shard verification mechanisms to ensure the atomicity and consistency of cross-shard transactions. Therefore, this paper proposes an improved consensus algorithm for blockchain sharding technology. Compared to the state of the art, the approach proposed in this paper forms transaction chains on a block-by-block basis. Furthermore, the "relevant reference" method proposed in this paper simplifies the cross-shard transaction verification process while ensuring throughput and consensus efficiency.

3   Model

3.1   Model Establishment

In this section, we will first introduce some key fundamental assumptions, including network assumptions, sharding assumptions, and node assumptions. These assumptions provide the fundamental framework for our subsequent analysis and design.

Node Configuration. This paper proposes a state-based sharding scheme where nodes within a shard are responsible for storing the transaction states within that shard. Therefore, in order to ensure the atomicity and consistency of CSTs, the nodes are configured as follows.

- **Common node**: Initiating transactions and voting on transactions generated within the shard.
- **Leader node**: Packaging transaction requests initiated within the shard and forwarding CSTs.
- **Routing node**: Forwarding blocks containing CSTs to the relevant shards.
- **Synchronous node**: Storing and updating the global state while providing state query services.

Model Assumptions

1. **Network**: Communication between nodes in the network is asynchronous, meaning that message delivery may have some delay, but this delay is limited and can be completed within a certain time frame. In practical network communications, there may be some inherent latency, but it is generally feasible to complete the communication within a reasonable timeframe. Therefore, this assumption enhances the real-world applicability of the model.
2. **Shards**: Each shard operates independently when processing transactions and maintaining states. The operations within one shard do not directly impact other shards. This ensures the independence and isolation of each shard, treating each shard as a separate, self-contained unit, which aids in problem simplification.

3. **Nodes**: Leader nodes and common nodes may exhibit Byzantine behavior. However, to enhance the security of Cross-Shard Transactions (CSTs), routing nodes and synchronous nodes are presumed to be non-Byzantine nodes, signifying their ability to withstand non-Byzantine faults exclusively. Consequently, in scenarios where there are precisely $3f+1$ leader nodes and common nodes, a maximum of f Byzantine nodes can exist to maintain security. This strategy is implemented to safeguard the integrity of CSTs, and the allocation of distinct roles fortifies the system's resilience.

The model introduced in this paper is constructed on the basis of the assumptions mentioned earlier. The establishment of these assumptions aligns with real-world scenarios and enhances the generality of the model presented in this paper. This generality facilitates the application of this model in a broader range of blockchain environments. In summary, the reasonableness and generality of these assumptions contribute to the construction of a universal sharding consensus model.

Block Structure. Additionally, we will discuss the redesign of the block structure to accommodate the proper forwarding of cross-shard transactions. The new block structure introduces several essential fields to facilitate the handling of cross-shard transactions. The block structure redesigned in this paper is shown in Fig. 1.

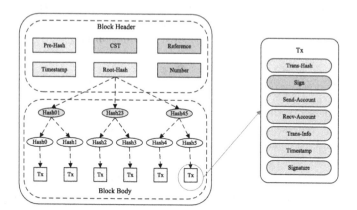

Fig. 1. The redesigned block structure in this paper introduces three new fields: CST, *Reference*, and *Number*. CST represents the identifier of cross-shard transactions, *Reference* denotes the reference to blocks in other shards (using block hash values), and *Number* indicates the shard identification. Additionally, the *Sign* field is added to transactions to differentiate whether a transaction is a cross-shard transaction.

3.2 Shard Generation

Sharding effectively reduces the size of the blockchain, but it also has the potential to diminish security within individual shards, rendering them more susceptible to the aggregation of Byzantine nodes and, in turn, the potential failure of a shard. Consequently, the creation of shards should aim to achieve a delicate equilibrium between unpredictability in shard outcomes and a fair distribution based on node performance.

Therefore, this paper adopts a uniform random partitioning algorithm that combines node reputation values and VRF for shard partitioning. The algorithm evenly distributes the nodes into different shards based on their reputation values, thereby reducing the probability of failure of the shard due to the concentration of Byzantine nodes within a shard. Additionally, the introduction of randomness through VRF during shard partition makes the partitioning results unpredictable, thereby reducing the likelihood of malicious node attacks.

Reputation Value. CPoW [23] is the first blockchain consensus algorithm to use reputation-based consensus. Sun [24] introduced a hybrid consensus scheme that addresses the issues of transaction security and efficiency. By integrating the reputation mechanism into transactions and consensus, this approach effectively handles the identified challenges. In the sharding algorithm proposed in this paper, the reputation values of the nodes are used as a crucial basis for the shard partitioning.

In order to assess the behavior of nodes accurately, it is necessary to quantify the contribution of each node's behavior. The reputation value calculation formula C_i proposed in this paper is shown in equation (1).

$$C_i{}^r = \left(\frac{2 * p_i{}^r}{p_i{}^r + e^{-10*(C_i{}^{r-1}-C_i{}^{r-2})^3}} \right)^3 \tag{1}$$

Here, $C_i{}^r$ represents the reputation value of the ith node in the rth partition round, and $p_i{}^r$ represents the quantified contribution of the ith node in the rth partition round, as calculated by Eq. (2).

$$p_i{}^r = \alpha * d_i + \beta * s_i + \gamma * o_i \tag{2}$$

In the above, α, β, and γ are weight parameters, and $\alpha+\beta+\gamma = 1$. d_i represents the ratio of correctly processed transactions by the ith node, s_i represents the average transaction processing speed of the ith node and o_i represents the ratio of historical online time of the ith node.

VRF. VRF [25] is a cryptographic hash function based on public-private key pairs. Because of its ability to be verified and its randomness, it has found extensive applications in blockchain systems. For example, in the consensus algorithm Algorand [26], VRF is used to randomly select nodes to participate in consensus.

In this paper, VRF is used to introduce randomness during the process of shard generation, making the results of shard partitioning unpredictable. Additionally, due to the verifiability of the VRF by all nodes, it ensures the correctness of the shard partitioning results.

Partitioning of Shards. The evaluation of node reputation levels is based on their respective reputation values, and nodes that exhibit varying levels of reputation are uniformly distributed across shards. This approach diminishes the likelihood of Byzantine node concentration and guarantees the presence of nodes with various reputation levels within each shard, thereby enhancing the overall robustness of the shard. To further ensure equity and unpredictability in the shard partitioning process, each node has the capacity to employ a Verifiable Random Function (VRF) to generate a random number specific to the ongoing partitioning round. This number can be collectively verified by all nodes, and it serves as a determining factor for the allocation of the node to a particular shard. The uniform random partitioning algorithm used in this paper is elucidated in Algorithm 1. The allocation of each node to a specific shard follows a random and unpredictable pattern, and the security of this randomness is upheld through the use of VRF.

3.3   Four-Layer Sharding Model

The four-layer sharding consensus algorithm, as designed in this paper, is illustrated in Fig. 2. The introduction of the DAG ledger structure forms the foundation of the cross-shard transaction validation mechanism in this paper. Within each shard (see layer 3 in Fig. 2), common nodes and leader nodes achieve consensus on a block-by-block basis, where the leader nodes are responsible for packaging the received transaction requests into blocks and forwarding the blocks containing CSTs to routing nodes (see layer 4 in Fig. 2), known as CST requests. Routing nodes receive blocks from various shards and forward them to the respective shards that are relevant to the CSTs, known as CST verification.

Each shard operates independently, maintaining only its own state, which is a chain composed of blocks. The chains of different shards are parallel to each other and form a DAG structure of parallel chains through cross references (see layer 1 in Fig. 2). This DAG structure of parallel chains represents the global state stored in the synchronous nodes. Therefore, when nodes within a shard need to conduct CSTs, they can query the state from synchronous nodes (see layer 2 in Fig. 2) if they do not have access to the states of other shards. Synchronous nodes respond to the query with the state information they possess. Synchronous nodes store and update the global state, and they need to follow a synchronization protocol to update the stored state and maintain consistency among synchronous nodes. The detailed synchronization protocol will be explained in Sect. 4.1. In shard systems that do not adopt the DAG ledger structure, while intra-shard transactions are processed in parallel, the handling of cross-shard transactions is often sequential, resulting in a notable reduction in efficiency. In contrast, the

---

Algorithm 1: Uniform Random Shard Partition Algorithm

---

    input   : Set of Reputation Values $\{C\}$, Set of Random Values of VRF $\{V\}$, Set
              of Proofs of Random Values for VRF $\{P\}$, Number of Nodes N,
              Number of Shards S

    output: Set of Node Shard IDs $\{D\}$

    // Sort each node by reputation value

    // $v_i^* \in \{V^*\}, p_i \in \{P\}$

1 $\{V^*\} \leftarrow \boldsymbol{Rank}(\{C\}, \{V\})$;

    // l is the average number of nodes per shard

    // "|" is used to represent integer division

2 $l \leftarrow S \mid N$;

3 **if** $N \bmod S \neq 0$ **then**

      // r is the number of levels for dividing based on reputation
          values

4      $r \leftarrow S + 1$;

5 **else**

6      $r \leftarrow S$;

7 **end**

8 **for** $i \leftarrow 0$ **to** $N - 1$ **do**

      // $level$ is the grade at which the ith node is classified based on
          its reputation value

9      $level \leftarrow (l \mid i) \bmod r$;

      // Verifying the correctness of the random number for each node

10   **if** $\boldsymbol{Verify}(p_i, v_i^*) = True$ **then**

11         $ind \leftarrow i - level \times l$;

          // D is the shard number

12         $D_i \leftarrow \boldsymbol{Hash}(ind, v_i^*)$;

13   **end**

14 **end**

15 **return** $\{D\}$

DAG ledger structure enables parallel processing of cross-shard transactions, thereby further improving the system's parallel capability.

4   Consensus Process

4.1   State Synchronization Protocol

The DAG ledger structure enhances the concurrency of transactions between shards. Consequently, a state synchronization protocol is introduced among synchronous nodes to store and update the DAG ledger.

Synchronization of states among synchronous nodes is required to ensure the consistency of CSTs. The state synchronization protocol among synchronous nodes in this paper is similar to the Gossip protocol [27]. As shown in Fig. 3, the state synchronization protocol between synchronous nodes in this paper can be divided into four phases.

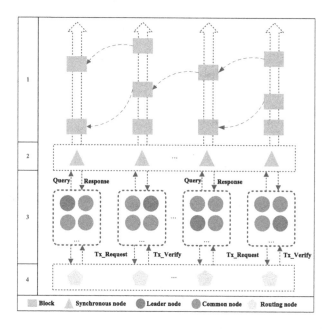

Fig. 2. Four-Layer sharding consensus algorithm

1. **Query phase**: Upon receiving a ⟨*Query*⟩ message, the synchronous node checks if it has the requested state information. If the node possesses the queried state, it directly packages the state information into a ⟨*Response*⟩ message and sends it back to the node that initiated the ⟨*Query*⟩. If the node does not have the requested state, it encapsulates the ⟨*Query*⟩ message along with its own stored state directory information into a ⟨*Sync-Query*⟩ message and randomly sends it to other synchronous nodes.

2. **Sync-Query phase**: Upon receiving a ⟨*Sync-Query*⟩ message, the synchronous node checks if it has the requested state information. If the node possesses the queried state, it directly packages the state information into a ⟨*Response*⟩ message and sends it back to the node that initiated the ⟨*Query*⟩. If the node does not have the requested state, it encapsulates the ⟨*Query*⟩ message along with its own stored state directory information into a ⟨*Sync-Query*⟩ message and randomly sends it to other synchronous nodes. Additionally, based on the received state directory information from the sending node, the node packages its own missing state information and the stored state directory information into a ⟨*Sync*⟩ message and replies to the sending node.

3. **Sync phase**: Upon receiving a ⟨*Sync*⟩ message, the synchronous node examines the state directory information received from the sending node. It packages the state that the sending node lacks but the receiving node possesses into a ⟨*Synced*⟩ message and replies to the sending node. Subsequently, the synchronous node updates its own stored state information based on the state updates received in the ⟨*Sync*⟩ message.

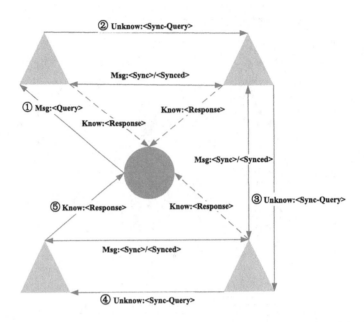

Fig. 3. Assuming solid lines represent a potential flow of messages. Unlike the Gossip protocol, the synchronization protocol among synchronous nodes is not performed periodically but triggered when a synchronous node receives a ⟨*Query*⟩ message.

4. **Synced phase**: Upon receiving a ⟨*Synced*⟩ message, the synchronous node updates its stored state information based on the received state updates.

4.2 Intra-shard Consensus

Within each shard, the PBFT [19] consensus algorithm is utilized to achieve intra-shard consensus. When a node initiates a cross-shard transaction, it first sends a state query request to a specific synchronous node. If the synchronous node has the requested state, it directly returns the query result. Otherwise, after completing the synchronization of synchronous node states, it returns the query result. Based on the returned query result, the node initiates the request for cross-shard transaction. Common nodes are selected as leader nodes in sequence on the basis of the view numbers and node numbers. The leader node is responsible for packing transaction requests, initiating consensus, and sending the consensus results to synchronous nodes for state recording. The process of intra-shard consensus within each shard is illustrated in Fig. 4.

What distinguishes it from PBFT is that, after reaching consensus on a specific block, the leader node directly encapsulates the block into a message ⟨*Record*⟩ and sends it to a designated synchronization node for state recording.

The consensus process within each shard is independent and parallel. The consensus result is added to the ledger within the respective shard and recorded

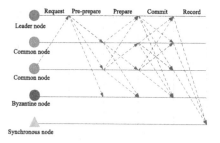

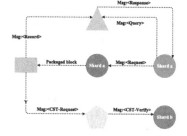

Fig. 4. The process of intra-shard consensus

Fig. 5. Shard state recording and CSTs routing

by a specific synchronous node in the global state. If a block has already reached consensus within a shard that contains CSTs, the block needs to be encapsulated into a message ⟨*CST-Request*⟩ and sent to a routing node. The routing node then encapsulates the ⟨*CST-Request*⟩ message into a ⟨*CST-Verify*⟩ message and forwards it to the shards associated with the CSTs in the block, initiating the cross-shard consensus process for that block. Shard state recording and CST routing are illustrated in Fig. 5.

4.3 Relevant Reference

This paper introduces the concept of "relevant reference" to validate cross-shard transactions, meaning that the confirmation and consensus of a transaction are determined through cross-referenced citations to relevant shards.

Direct Reference. The leader node of a shard, upon receiving the ⟨*CST-Verify*⟩ message containing a block with CSTs, executes the transactions relevant to its own shard and verifies their correctness. Upon successful verification and acceptance of the block, the leader node references this block when packaging the next block by setting the *Reference* field to the hash value of the referenced block. It is important to note that the referenced block must originate from a different shard. Furthermore, the referenced block does not need to be stored within the relevant shard, but instead, the packaged block is encapsulated into a ⟨*Record*⟩ message and sent to a designated synchronous node for state recording. The *Reference* field is set to indicate the reference relationship between blocks. This block referencing method, achieved by setting the *Reference* field, is known as a direct reference.

Indirect Reference. If block *a* directly references block *b*, then block *a* indirectly references the previous block, block *c*, on the shard's blockchain ledger. Similarly, the previous block of block *c* is indirectly referenced relative to block *a*. This method of establishing reference relationships through the referencing of subsequent blocks is known as indirect reference.

As shown in Fig. 6, 2a and 3a have reached the global consensus state. For a block containing CSTs to reach a global consensus state, it must satisfy the following two conditions:

- **Condition 1**: The block is directly or indirectly referenced by a majority (more than 2/3) of the shards.
- **Condition 2**: The block is directly referenced by all relevant shards.

The cross-shard transaction validation process is also a process confirmed by the consensus of other shards. Through direct and indirect references in the DAG ledger structure, the cross-shard transaction validation process is streamlined, thereby improving the efficiency of cross-shard transactions. The inherent parallelism of the DAG ledger structure makes cross-shard transactions less susceptible to blocking. The parallel processing of cross-shard transactions is facilitated by the DAG ledger structure, leading to an additional improvement in the system's parallel capabilities. Assuming that cross-shard transactions persist, they will be eventually confirmed within a certain timeframe [28].

5   Security Analysis

The security of the PBFT [19] algorithm has been proven. When the number of Byzantine nodes within a shard does not exceed one-third of the total number of nodes in the shard, the correctness of the intra-shard consensus result and the security of the shard can be guaranteed. Additionally, this paper employs a uniform random partitioning algorithm for shard partitioning, which reduces the likelihood of Byzantine nodes clustering within the same shard.

5.1   Double-Spending Attacks

To demonstrate the impossibility of "double-spending attacks", let us make the assumption that a Byzantine node initiates two identical CSTs, $tx1$ and $tx2$, targeting different shards in an attempt to launch a "double-spending attacks", there are two possible scenarios:

1. **Scenario 1**: Both transactions, $tx1$ and $tx2$, are included in the same block. If the number of Byzantine nodes in the shard does not exceed 1/3, the security of the PBFT algorithm ensures that only one of $tx1$ and $tx2$ will be confirmed. Otherwise, the shard is malicious and the block may be routed to the relevant shards. When the honest relevant shards validate the block, they will not accept and reference it. Under the assumption that the proportion of Byzantine nodes is at most 1/3, the maximum number of malicious shards is also within 1/3. Therefore, the *condition 2* for achieving global consensus of a block containing CSTs is not satisfied and the block will not be ultimately confirmed.

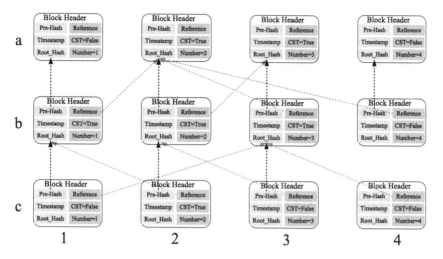

Fig. 6. Assuming that 2*a* and 3*a* have been directly referenced by all relevant shards, satisfying *condition 2* for achieving a global consensus state. 2*a* is directly referenced by 1*b*, 3*b*, and 4*b*, indicating that the majority of shards reference 2*a*, satisfying *condition 1* for achieving a global consensus state. Therefore, 2*a* has reached a global consensus state. Additionally, 3*a* is directly referenced by 2*b* and indirectly referenced by 1*c* and 4*c*, indicating that the majority of shards reference 3*a*, satisfying *condition 1* for achieving a global consensus state. Therefore, 3*a* has also reached a global consensus state.

2. **Scenario 2**: The two transactions, $tx1$ and $tx2$, are included in different blocks, *block1* and *block2*. Malicious shards may accept both blocks, while honest shards will only accept one of the blocks. Let's assume there are a total of k shards, with m malicious shards accepting both *block1* and *block2*, the number of honest shards accepting *block1* is a , and the number of honest shards accepting *block2* is b. For "double-spending attacks" to succeed, it is necessary to satisfy *condition 1* for achieving global consensus of a block containing CST. We can obtain the following inequality Eq. (3). However, this contradicts the assumption that the proportion of Byzantine nodes is at most 1/3. Therefore, the "double-spending attacks" is not possible to succeed with "double-spending attacks ".

$$\left.\begin{array}{c} m + a + b \leq k \\ m + a > \dfrac{2}{3}k \\ m + b > \dfrac{2}{3}k \end{array}\right\} \Rightarrow m > \dfrac{k}{3} \tag{3}$$

5.2   51% Attack

Due to nodes being evenly distributed across shards based on their reputation scores, the probability of malicious nodes controlling each shard is reduced. Furthermore, the shard formation process is difficult to predict and can be verified by any node, increasing the cost of malicious behavior. Based on 6.1, the reputation of the nodes tends to change for the nodes with a significant contribution, and the nodes engaged in continuous malicious activity are quickly detected. In conclusion, a 51% attack is costly and, under certain assumptions, can be considered a highly unlikely event.

6   Experimental Evaluation

This paper implemented the PBFT, Double-Layer (DL) [1], and the algorithm proposed in this paper using the Python threading and Socket libraries. The experimental setup is equipped with a 12th Gen Intel Core i5-12500H processor (clock speed 3.10 GHz), 16 GB RAM (15.7 GB available), running a 64-bit operating system based on an x64 processor. In our implementation, each thread represents an independent node, and realistic communication environments are simulated by setting appropriate random wait times. In the absence of malicious nodes, we tested the throughput and consensus efficiency of each algorithm. We also compared the throughput and consensus efficiency of each algorithm with different numbers of nodes and shards to analyze their variations and stability.

6.1   Change in Reputation Value

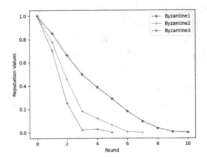 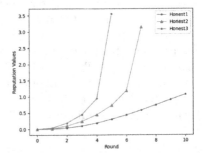

Fig. 7. The variation of Byzantine node reputation values under different degrees of malicious behavior. From top to bottom, the nodes' maliciousness increases in sequence.

Fig. 8. The variation of honest node reputation values under different levels of contribution. From top to bottom, the levels of contribution increase in order.

We represented the extent of malicious activities by malicious nodes and the level of contribution by honest nodes through simulating changes in node reputation values. From Fig. 7 and Fig. 8, it can be observed that the higher the degree of malicious behavior by a node, the faster its reputation score declines. This enables the shards to quickly identify Byzantine nodes and take appropriate actions. During each round of shard partitioning, nodes can be randomly and evenly assigned to different shards, reducing the probability of Byzantine nodes clustering within a shard. Furthermore, the higher the level of contribution of a node, the faster its reputation score increases. This encourages honest nodes to contribute more, swiftly creating a larger gap between them and Byzantine nodes.

6.2   Throughput and Confirmation Latency

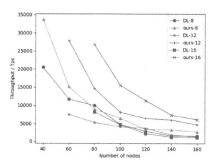
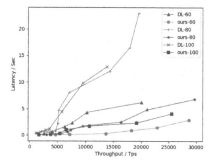

Fig. 9. When the number of shards is 8, 12, and 16, the throughput of DL and the proposed algorithm is compared at different numbers of nodes.

Fig. 10. The block confirmation latency of the DL algorithm and the proposed algorithm is compared at different throughput levels when the number of nodes is 60, 80, and 100.

Assuming that each block contains 1024 transactions, as shown in Fig. 9, with the same waiting time and number of shards, the throughput of the proposed algorithm is higher than that of the DL algorithm. Here, throughput refers to the average number of transactions generated per second. Additionally, as shown in Fig. 10, under the same throughput, the block confirmation time of the proposed algorithm is faster than that of the DL algorithm, and the confirmation time of the proposed algorithm remains relatively stable. Here, confirmation time refers to the time interval, on average, for each block to be packaged and reach the global consensus state. To ensure a fair comparison, the same ratio of CSTs is set.

Due to the adoption of a two-phase PBFT consensus in the DL algorithm, its throughput and block confirmation latency are simultaneously affected by the number of nodes and the number of shards. PBFT has a communication complexity of $O(n^3)$, and as the number of nodes within a shard increases, the throughput decreases significantly due to the exponential increase in the communication frequency. Similarly, block confirmation latency also increases dramatically as the number of shards increases, leading to an exponential increase in the communication frequency between shards. In contrast to the DL algorithm, the proposed algorithm ensures that the confirmation latency does not increase significantly with the increase in throughput. This is achieved by using a "relevant reference" approach in the proposed algorithm, which combines the validation and consensus of the CSTs. This shortens the time required for cross-shard transaction validation and reduces the communication complexity between shards to $O(n)$. Utilizing the parallel chain DAG ledger structure, this paper concurrently processed cross-shard transactions, achieving parallelism for both intra-shard transactions and cross-shard transactions. Therefore, as the number of shards increases, the block confirmation latency in the proposed algorithm exhibits a relatively stable linear growth at a lower time level.

7   Conclusion

The paper proposes a four-layer sharding consensus algorithm, which utilizes the "relevant reference" approach based on a ledger of the DAG structure of parallel chains to verify cross-shard transactions. By unifying the validation and consensus of cross-shard transactions, the verification process for such transactions is simplified, leading to improved consensus efficiency. Additionally, a state synchronization protocol similar to the Gossip protocol is employed to ensure the consistency of the global state, allowing each shard to store only the relevant state, thereby reducing storage redundancy. A possible future improvement could involve addressing the liveness issue of cross-shard transactions and proportionally reducing the ratio of cross-shard transactions in a reasonable manner to further enhance consensus efficiency.

Acknowledgment. Grateful appreciation is extended to the mentor and the advisors for their invaluable guidance and insightful suggestions. The anonymous reviewers and experts are also acknowledged for their valuable feedback and constructive criticism, which have greatly contributed to the refinement of this paper. Finally, sincere thanks are extended to the organizations and institutions that have provided data, resources, and support for this research.

References

1. Luo, N.: Research and implementation of sharding technology of blockChain in consortium blockChain scenarios. Master's thesis, University of Electronic Science and Technology of China (2021). https://doi.org/10.27005/d.cnki.gdzku.2021.005445
2. Nakamoto, S.: Bitcoin: A peer-to-peer electronic cash system. Decentraliz. Bus. Rev. 21260 (2008). https://assets.pubpub.org/d8wct41f/31611263538139.pdf

3. Wang, Q., Li, F., Ni, X., et al.: Survey on blockchain consensus algorithms and application. J. Front. Comput. Sci. Technol. **16**(6), 1214–1242 (2022). https://doi.org/10.3778/j.issn.1673-9418.2112077

4. Lamport, L., Shostak, R., Pease, M.: The byzantine generals problem. ACM Trans. Program. Lang. Syst. **4**(3), 203–226 (1982). https://doi.org/10.1145/3335772.3335936

5. Yuan, Y., Ni, X., Zeng, S., et al.: Blockchain consensus algorithms: the state of the art and future trends. Acta Automat. Sinica **44**(11), 2011–2022 (2018). https://doi.org/10.16383/j.aas.2018.c180268

6. Huang, H., Kong, W., Peng, X., et al.: Survey of blockchain sharding techniques. J. Comput. Eng. **48**(6), 1–10 (2022). https://doi.org/10.19678/j.issn.1000-3428.0063887

7. Danezis, G., Meiklejohn, S.: Centrally banked cryptocurrencies. arXiv preprint arXiv:1505.06895 (2015)

8. Luu, L., Narayanan, V., Zheng, C., et al.: A secure sharding protocol for open blockchains. In: Proceedings of the 2016 ACM SIGSAC Conference on Computer and Communications Security, pp. 17–30. ACM, New York (2016). https://doi.org/10.1145/2976749.2978389

9. Amiri, M.J., Agrawal, D., ElAbbadi, A.: Sharper: sharding permissioned blockchains over network clusters. In: Proceedings of the 2021 International Conference on Management of Data, pp. 76–88. ACM, New York (2021). https://doi.org/10.1145/3448016.3452807

10. Dang, H., Dinh, T.T.A., Loghin, D., et al. Towards scaling blockchain systems via sharding. In: Proceedings of the 2019 International Conference on Management of Data, pp. 123–140. ACM, New York (2019). https://doi.org/10.1145/3299869.3319889

11. Amiri, M.J., Agrawal, D., ElAbbadi, A.: On sharding permissioned blockchains. In: 2019 IEEE International Conference on Blockchain (Blockchain), pp. 282–285. IEEE, Washington (2019). https://doi.org/10.1109/Blockchain.2019.00044

12. KokorisKogias, E., Jovanovic, P., Gasser, L., et al.: Omniledger: a secure, scale-out, decentralized ledger via sharding. In: 2018 IEEE Symposium on Security and Privacy (SP), pp. 583–598. IEEE, Washington (2018). https://doi.org/10.1109/SP.2018.000-5

13. AlBassam, M., Sonnino, A., Bano, S., et al.: Chainspace: a sharded smart contracts platform. arXiv preprint arXiv:1708.03778 (2017)

14. Zamani, M., Movahedi, M., Raykova, M.: Rapidchain: scaling blockchain via full sharding. In: Proceedings of the 2018 ACM SIGSAC Conference on Computer and Communications Security, pp. 931–948. ACM, New York (2018). https://doi.org/10.1145/3243734.3243853

15. Sel, D., Zhang, K., Jacobsen, H.A.: Towards solving the data availability problem for sharded ethereum. In: Proceedings of the 2nd Workshop on Scalable and Resilient Infrastructures for Distributed Ledgers, pp. 25–30. ACM, New York (2018). https://doi.org/10.1145/3284764.3284769

16. Androulaki, E., Cachin, C., DeCaro, A., et al.: Channels: horizontal scaling and confidentiality on permissioned blockchains. In: 23rd European Symposium on Research in Computer Security, pp. 111–131. Springer, Cham (2018). https://doi.org/10.1007/978-3-319-99073-6_6

17. Wang, J., Wang, H.: Monoxide: scale out blockchains with asynchronous consensus zones. In: 16th USENIX Symposium on Networked Systems Design and Implementation, pp. 95–112. NSDI, Boston (2019). https://www.usenix.org/system/files/nsdi19-wang-jiaping.pdf

18. The ZILLIQA Technical Whitepaper. https://docs.zilliqa.com/whitepaper.pdf. Accessed 28 Mar 2023
19. Castro, M., Liskov, B.: Practical byzantine fault tolerance. In: Proceedings of the Third Symposium on Operating Systems Design and Implementation, pp. 173–186. USENIX, New Orleans (1999). https://dl.acm.org/doi/10.5555/296806.296824
20. Yang, C., et al.: A novel two-layer DAG-based reactive protocol for IoT data reliability in metaverse. arXiv preprint arXiv:2304.05094 (2023)
21. Zhang, X., Li, R., Zhao, H.: A parallel consensus mechanism using PBFT based on DAG-lattice structure in the internet of vehicles. IEEE Internet Things J. **10**(6), 5418–5433 (2022). https://doi.org/10.1109/JIOT.2022.3222217
22. Song, A., et al.: Extend PBFT protocol with L-DAG. In: 2021 IEEE International Conference on Parallel and Distributed Processing with Applications, Big Data and Cloud Computing, Sustainable Computing and Communications, Social Computing and Networking (ISPA/BDCloud/SocialCom/SustainCom), pp. 963–970. IEEE, New York (2021). https://doi.org/10.1109/ISPA-BDCloud-SocialCom-SustainCom52081.2021.00135
23. Wang, Z., Tian, Y., Li, Q., et al.: Proof of work algorithm based on credit model. J. Commun. **39**(8), 185–198 (2018). https://doi.org/10.11959/j.issn.1000-436x.2018138
24. Sun, Y., et al.: A reputation based hybrid consensus for e-commerce blockchain. In: Web Services-ICWS 2020: 27th International Conference, pp. 1–16. Springer, Honolulu (2020). https://doi.org/10.1007/978-3-030-59618-7_1
25. Micali, S., Rabin, M., Vadhan, S.: Verifiable random functions. In: 40th Annual Symposium on Foundations of Computer Science, pp. 120–130. IEEE, Washington (1999). https://doi.org/10.1109/SFFCS.1999.814584
26. Gilad, Y., Hemo, R., Micali, S., et al.: Algorand: scaling byzantine agreements for cryptocurrencies. In: Proceedings of the 26th Symposium on Operating Systems Principles, pp. 51–68. ACM, New York (2017). https://doi.org/10.1145/3132747.3132757
27. Demers, A., Greene, D., Hauser, C., et al.: Epidemic algorithms for replicated database maintenance. In: Proceedings of the Sixth Annual ACM Symposium on Principles of Distributed Computing, pp. 1–12. ACM, New York (1987). https://doi.org/10.1145/43921.43922
28. Baird L, Luykx A.: The hashgraph protocol: efficient asynchronous BFT for high-throughput distributed ledgers. In: 2020 International Conference on Omni-Layer Intelligent Systems (COINS), pp. 1–7. IEEE, Barcelona (2020). https://doi.org/10.1109/COINS49042.2020.9191430

Blockchain Data Access

Online/Offline and Fine-Grained Controllable Editing with Accountability and Revocability in Blockchains

Lifeng Guo[1], Xueke Ma[1], and Wei-Chuen Yau[2]($\boxtimes$) (iD)

[1] School of Computer and Information Technology, Shanxi University, Taiyuan, China

[2] School of Computing and Data Science, Xiamen University Malaysia, 43900 Sepang, Selangor Darul Ehsan, Malaysia
wcyau@xmu.edu.my

Abstract. Editable or rewritable blockchains offer a vital solution where flexibility and adaptability are paramount. They cater to scenarios where errors, regulatory compliance, privacy concerns, governance, and developmental stages demand a certain level of malleability in recorded data. One of the techniques for achieving editable blockchains is the use of policy-based chameleon hash functions (PCH). This enables the rewriting operations to be controlled and ensures that only specific entities with attributes that meet the predefined policies can edit the contents on the blockchains. However, PCH-based editable blockchains do not prevent malicious entities to leak their rewriting trapdoors to other unauthorized parties. Therefore, tracking of malicious key abusers is desirable in such solution. Tian et al. at ACSAC 2020 proposed a blockchain that is editable and incorporates black-box accountability, allowing for the identification of individuals who maliciously modify content. However, the key delegation of their scheme has problems with the calculation $sk_{0,1} = h^{b_1 \cdot (r_1 + z_1)}$ and $sk_{0,2} = h^{b_2 \cdot (r_2 + z_2)}$. In addition, the current approaches cannot meet the efficient fine-grained accountable and revocable editing. Motivated by the research of Tian et. al, a fine-grained controllable and editable blockchain based on online/offline policy-based chameleon hash with accountability and revocability (OPCHAR) is proposed. It achieves the black-box accountability mechanism with a correct key delegation algorithm and realizes that the authorized organization can identify malicious modifiers and append them to the revocation list. Furthermore, unlike the traditional revocable attribute encryption, to prevent accused users from leaking the previously obtained chameleon hash ephemeral trapdoor, the authorized organization can generate a new ephemeral trapdoor to re-adapt transactions modified by malicious users to achieve revocability, rather than by invoking a centralized semi-trusted third party (e.g., cloud). Additionally, we use online/offline techniques to perform hash and adaption algorithms. Finally, the implementation demonstrates that our scheme has a superior performance. In particular, the hash algorithm consistently maintains a running time of 0.02 s.

J. Zhu et al. (Eds.): CBCS 2023, CCIS 2098, pp. 125–153, 2024.
https://doi.org/10.1007/978-981-97-3203-6_7

Keywords: Editable blockchain · Chameleon hash · Online/Offline · Accountability · Revocability

1   Introduction

Blockchain has been extensively used in finance, trade, sharing economy, supply chain, Internet-of-Things (IoT), and many other fields since its inception. A recent study [28] predicts that global spending on blockchain in 2024 will increase by $12.4 billion compared to spending on blockchain in 2021. The initial version of the blockchain, blockchain 1.0, is strongly associated with cryptocurrencies, the most familiar of which is Bitcoin [23]. Blockchain provides convenient technical support for finance such as virtual currency transactions and cross-border payments by building a decentralized transaction system, and the immutability of blockchain coincides with the currency system. Later, smart contracts can be stored on blockchain 2.0 which makes this technology more widely adopted. Blockchain 3.0 is to connect all people and machines to a new worldwide network.

The blockchain, which is stored by decentralized nodes within the peer-to-peer (P2P) network, can be considered as a distributed transaction ledger that does not need any trusted central authority for its maintenance. The blockchain structure is comprised of a hash chain by linking the hash of each block to its preceding block and the transactions within a block are computed using a hash algorithm to generate the Merkle tree [21] root. Both block-to-block hash links and Merkle tree hash links between transactions within a block significantly contribute to the overall immutability of the blockchain system. These cryptographic links serve as essential mechanisms that make both block-level and transaction-level modifications challenging.

With increasingly widespread applications, the contents stored on the blockchain are more diverse. Since the miners on the blockchain can only check the format of the transaction and do not audit the content, there is a lot of illegal information [22,27] that is disseminated through blockchains. If these contents need to be modified, the blockchain needs to meet controllable editability under strict constraints. Also, recent years have brought new challenges to the immutability of blockchains as a result of an increase in awareness about data protection. Both the General Data Protection Regulation (GDPR) [16] and the Personal Information Protection Law (PIPL) [11] have implemented provisions concerning the safeguarding of personal data, affirming the data owner's entitlement to request the deletion of their data. Therefore, it is urgent to come up with a controllable way to break the immutability of the blockchain and allow contents stored on the blockchain to be rewritten or edited.

At present, some studies have implemented editable blockchains using techniques of chameleon hash (CH), consensus-based mechanism, meta-transaction, and pruning [3,26,31,32]. Ateniese et al. [4] pioneered controllable editing on the coarse-grained block level using CH [19]. Later, a rewritable blockchain at the fine-grained transaction level was proposed by Derler et al. to address the limitations of Ateniese et al.'s approach, in which policy-based chameleon hash

(PCH) is their core technique. Since PCH was proposed, many schemes have realized fine-grained editable blockchains. As the policy in PCH usually uses attribute-based encryption (ABE) to achieve fine-grained modification, these schemes possess the benefits of fine-grained modify control, but also suffer from the associated drawbacks. For example, the process of generating keys is solely based on a group of users' attributes, which can be shared by multiple users simultaneously. As such, no one can distinguish the owner of the key in the ABE system. If a malicious modifier actively leaks or sells his/her key for personal interest, or multiple malicious users encode their keys in a black-box decryption device, it will cause the blockchain to suffer uncontrollable malicious modification. Thus it is necessary to implement accountability and revocability for malicious modifiers to achieve secure and controllable editing in blockchains.

1.1 Related Work

The CH-based editable blockchain was first proposed by Ateniese et al. [4]. Their scheme only implemented the all-or-nothing coarse-grained block-level modification. All modifiable transactions are hashed using the same chameleon hash public key as well as the same trapdoor owned by all modifiers, so it is difficult to trace malicious modifiers. Later Derler et al. [13] revisited their idea and introduced a transaction-level fine-grained editable blockchain based on PCH. The policy in PCH refers to the ciphertext-policy ABE (CP-ABE), so the transaction owner can formulate a modification policy to achieve fine-grained modification. This enables the completion of blockchain edits exclusively by modifiers whose attribute set complies with the modification policy. The original hash function has been substituted with an enhanced collision-resistant chameleon hash. Only modifiers that have the ephemeral trapdoor (ETD) of chameleon hash with ephemeral trapdoor (CHET) can easily find the hash collision to edit the blockchain while finding the hash collision remains difficult if the modifier does not have the ETD. The above two schemes achieve the rewritability of the permissoned blockchain, wherein nodes join the blockchain with the permission of the authority. Then, Deuber et al. [14] achieved rewritability of the permissoned blockchain using consensus-based voting. But none of the above schemes have accountability.

Huang et al.'s scheme [18] combined accountable-and-sanitizable chameleon signature with threshold CH to implement an editable consortium blockchain. Their scheme prevents abuse of editorial privileges and enables accountability. However, their scheme is applied to IoT, and hash collisions are computed cooperatively by sensors, which results in inefficient collision computation. Xu et al. proposed a revocable PCH [33] to achieve user revocation using the tree-based revocation list [24]. The drawback of their scheme is that it is inflexible concerning the joining and leaving of nodes due to the creation of a user binary tree in the initialization phase. Xu et al. [32] proposed redactable blockchains that punish malicious behavior with a monetary penalty by the central authority (CA). In each time epoch, modifiers must make a deposit stored in the CA. The random number of the signature will be shown when the number of changes to a modifier is greater than k-time. After that, the key to the modifier can be obtained by the CA and the deposit of the modifier will be confiscated as a penalty. However, the security of their scheme is overly dependent on the trusted CA. Panwar et al. [26] used dynamic group signature schemes combined with revocable FAME [1] to implement a traceable and revocable editable blockchain, but their scheme is small-universe construction, which means that user attributes are bounded in a limited system attribute space. Recently, Xu et al. [31] introduced a novel PCH, which is based on FAME using fingerprinting code and identity-based signature to achieve black-box accountability. Duan et al. [15] also used fingerprinting code to construct PCH with traceability, and their scheme differs from Xu et al.'s in that it uses a robust fingerprinting code.

Tian et al. [29] combined CHET, CP-ABE with black-box traceability (ABET), hierarchical identity-based encryption (HIBE) [6] and digital signature (DS) to realize an editable blockchain with black-box accountability. The black-box accountability of their scheme allows any public user can access the black-box to identify the modifier, while only the attribute authority has the capability to connect the modified transaction with its modifier. However, their key delegation has problems with the calculation $sk_{0,1} = h^{b_1 \cdot (r_1 + z_1)}$, $sk_{0,2} = h^{b_2 \cdot (r_2 + z_2)}$. The modifier does not know the parameters h^{b_1}, h^{b_2}, and b_1, b_2 also cannot be calculated due to the discrete logarithm problem. Hence, even if the modifier satisfies the modification policy and the identity level of the modifier is smaller than that of the transaction owner, the modifier cannot find a hash collision to edit the transaction due to the unsuccessful key delegation.

For malicious modifiers who sell modification keys for personal gain or generate black-box decryption devices, a scheme with timely accountability and revocation is needed to ensure that editable blockchains are protected from malicious modifications. However, none of the above schemes achieve black-box accountability and revocability at the same time, and even, for some schemes with revocability, the revocability is implemented based on the revocable CP-ABE without adaptive changes based on editable blockchain property of chameleon hash.

A comparison of the features between our scheme and existing editable blockchains is presented in Table 1. and it is shown that our work achieves all features and hence is functionally superior.

1.2 Contribution

We reference the idea of [29] regarding the utilization of HIBE and DS to implement black-box accountability. In addition, the authorized organization (AO) re-adapts the transactions modified by accused modifiers to realize revocation. The main contributions of our online/offline policy-based chameleon hash with accountability and revocability (OPCHAR) are listed as follows:

(1) Revocability is achieved by AO adding malicious users to the revocation list stored on the blockchain. To save blockchain resources, the revocation list

Table 1. Comparison of Existing Editable Blockchains

Scheme	Type	Granularity Level	Core Technique	Fine-Grained Control	Black-Box Accountability	Revocability
[4]	P	Block	CH	✗	✗	✗
[13]	P	Transaction	CHET	✓	✗	✗
[14]	PL	Block	Consensus Voting	✗	✗	✗
[29]	P	Transaction	CHET	✓	✓	✗
[26]	P	Transaction	CHET	✓	✗	✓
[32]	P	Transaction	CH	✓	✗	✓
[33]	P	Transaction	CHET	✓	✗	✓
[31]	P	Transaction	CHET	✓	✓	✗
Ours	P	Transaction	CHET	✓	✓	✓

[1] "Type" - P: Permissioned blockchain; PL: Permissionless blockchain.
[2] "Granularity level" - Block: The ability to modify is restricted to a whole block (all-or-nothing coarse-grained modification); Transaction: The right to modify is a particular transaction in a block.
[3] "Fine-grained control" - The modification rights have fine-grained control based on modifier attributes.
[4] "Black-box Accountability" - The identity of malicious users can be identified and traced by interacting with an access device/blackbox.
[5] "Revocability" - Revocation of modification rights for malicious modifiers.

can be updated by *Adapt* of chameleon hash instead of creating a new transaction. Then AO finds a collision with a new ETD and re-adapts transaction components to prevent the leak of ETD by malicious modifiers.

(2) The hash algorithm is separated into two phases: online and offline. The majority of calculations are performed in the offline phase. The online/offline technique improves the performance of both *Hash* and *Adapt* algorithms due to the re-encryption of ETD in the *Adapt* algorithm.

(3) Transparency is the ability to tell whether a transaction has been edited or not. Our system ensures transparency by allowing any public user to associate a transaction with its re-edited version. After obtaining malicious users, only AO can judge whether a transaction in the blockchain is modified by these malicious users.

(4) We point out the problems of the key delegation in [29]. Our scheme realizes that a transaction modifier that satisfies the modification policy and has a smaller identity hierarchy than the transaction owner can successfully edit the blockchain with correct key delegation.

2   Preliminaries

This section provides the mathematical symbols, as well as the mathematical foundation and the definitions of cryptographic components upon which our scheme is founded. The notations are defined and summarized in Table 2.

Table 2. Mathematical Notations

Notation	Description
k	Security parameter
n	The maximum depth of identity hierarchy in HIBE
(sk_{CHET}, pk_{CHET})	The public and secret key of $CHET$
(msk_{ABET}, mpk_{ABET})	The master public and secret key of $ABET$
(msk_{DS}, mpk_{DS})	The master public and secret key of DS
$\mathcal{R}$	The revocation list
$ID = (I_1, \cdots, I_j) \in (\mathbb{Z}_p)^j$	A user identity of depth j
SC	A secret credential
ID_{TO}	Identity vectors of a transaction owner (TO)
ID_{TM}	Identity vectors of a transaction modifier (TM)
sk_{TM}	The secret key of TM
$\mathbb{A} = (M_{\ell \times t}, \rho)$	An access control (A modification) policy
r_{CHET}	The random value of $CHET$
etd	The ephemeral trapdoor of $CHET$
$\mathbb{Z}_p$	The set $\{0, \ldots, p-1\}$ where computations are done modulo p
$\mathbb{Z}_p^*$	The set $\{1, \ldots, p-1\}$

2.1   Bilinear Pairings

Definition 1. *A group generator $\mathcal{G}$ with security parameter k as input, which outputs the associated parameter $(p, \mathbb{G}, \mathbb{G}_T, e, g)$ about the group. In these parameters, $\mathbb{G}$ and $\mathbb{G}_T$ are two (multiplicative) cyclic group of prime order p, and g is a generator of $\mathbb{G}$. The following three properties are satisfied by a bilinear map $e : \mathbb{G} \times \mathbb{G} \to \mathbb{G}_T$ [30].*

- *Bilinearity: $\forall g, h \in \mathbb{G}$, and $\forall a, b \in \mathbb{Z}_p$, $e\left(g^a, h^b\right) = e(g, h)^{ab}$ holds.*
- *Non-degeneracy: $\exists g \in \mathbb{G}$, such that $e(g, g)$ does not equal the identity element of $\mathbb{G}_T$.*
- *Computability: $\forall g, h \in \mathbb{G}$, the computation of the value of $e(g, h)$ is performed in an efficient manner.*

2.2   Access Structures

Definition 2. *Let attribute universe be* $\mathcal{P} = \{P_1, P_2, \ldots, P_t\}$. *If* $\forall B, C : B \in \mathbb{A}$ *and* $B \subseteq C$ *then* $C \in \mathbb{A}$, *a collection* $\mathbb{A} \subseteq 2^{\mathcal{P}}$ *is considered monotone. A monotone access structure is a collection* $\mathbb{A} \subseteq 2^{\mathcal{P}} \backslash \{\emptyset\}$. *If a set is contained in* $\mathbb{A}$, *we refer to it as the authorization set, otherwise, it is denoted as the unauthorized set [5].*

2.3   Linear Secret-Sharing Schemes

Definition 3. *A secret-sharing scheme (SSS)* Π *over an access structure* $\mathbb{A}$ *is referred to as a linear SSS (LSSS) [5] when the following condition is met:*

1. *The allocation of shares for each party can be represented as a vector* $v \in \mathbb{Z}_p^t$.
2. *A matrix denoted as* $M_{\ell \times t}$, *comprising* ℓ *rows and* t *columns, is referred to as the share-generating matrix for* Π. *A function* $\rho(i)$, *known as a monjection, is utilized to map* M_i *to the respective participant. When* $v = (s, r_2, \ldots, r_t)^T$ *is taken into account, where* $s \in \mathbb{Z}_p$ *represents the secret to be distributed, and* $r_2, \ldots, r_t \in \mathbb{Z}_p$ *are randomly selected, the resulting vector* Mv *represents* ℓ *shares of* s. *The secret share* $\lambda_i = (Mv)_i$ *is associated with party* $\rho(i)$.

LSSS exhibits the characteristic of linear reconstruction: Set $S \in \mathbb{A}$ refers to any authorized set, and $I = \{i : \rho(i) \in S\} \subset \{1, 2, \ldots, \ell\}$ is defined. Then, it is possible to determine constants $\{\omega_i \in \mathbb{Z}_p\}_{i \in I}$ such that $\sum_{i \in I} \omega_i M_i = (1, 0, \cdots, 0)$. If $\{\lambda_i\}$ represent legitimate shares of s as determined by Π, then $\sum_{i \in I} \omega_i \lambda_i = s$.

2.4   Chameleon Hash with Ephemeral Trapdoor

CHET [8] serves as the fundamental cryptographic primitive for the construction of PCH [13], which is an extension of CH. A collision can only be successfully found if users hold both of long-term and ephemeral trapdoors.

Definition 4. *The general algorithm definition of CHET in the plaintext space* $\mathcal{M}$ *comprises the following four parts:*

- *CHET.KeyGen* $(1^k) \rightarrow (sk_{CHET}, pk_{CHET})$: *It accepts a security parameter* k *and produces a long-term trapdoor* sk_{CHET} *and a public key* pk_{CHET}.
- *CHET.Hash* $(pk_{CHET}, m) \rightarrow (h_{CHET}, r_{CHET}, etd_{CHET})$: *Given a public key* pk_{CHET} *and a message* $m \in \mathcal{M}$ *as input, this algorithm produces a hash value* h_{CHET}, *a randomness* r_{CHET}, *and an ephemeral trapdoor* etd_{CHET} *as its output of this algorithm.*
- *CHET.Verify* $(pk_{CHET}, m, h_{CHET}, r_{CHET}) \rightarrow \{0, 1\}$: *Given the public key* pk_{CHET}, *a message* m, *the hash* h_{CHET}, *and randomness* r_{CHET} *as input, this algorithm generates a bit verification result* b *as its output.*
- *CHET.Adapt* $(sk_{CHET}, etd_{CHET}, m, m', h_{CHET}, r_{CHET}) \rightarrow r'_{CHET}$: *When provided with the secret key* sk_{CHET}, *the ephemeral trapdoor* etd_{CHET}, *a message* $m \in \mathcal{M}$, *a new message* $m' \in \mathcal{M}$, *the hash value* h_{CHET}, *the randomness* r_{CHET}, *this algorithm produces a new randomness denoted as* r'_{CHET} *as its output.*

2.5   Attribute-Based Encryption with Black-Box Traceability

In general, the ABET [20] primitive refers to attribute-based encryption with malicious user tracking, and is comprised of five parts. Our algorithm applies the online/offline technique, thereby dividing the encryption algorithm Enc into two components: $Enc_{Offline}$ and Enc_{Online}.

Definition 5. *The subsequent statement provides a general description of the cryptographic primitive ABET:*

- *$ABET.Setup(1^k) \rightarrow (msk_{ABET}, mpk_{ABET})$: Given the security parameter k as input to Setup of ABET cipher primitive, it outputs the master secret key msk_{ABET} and public key mpk_{ABET}.*
- *$ABET.Enc_{Offline}(mpk_{ABET}) \rightarrow IT$: This offline hash algorithm inputs mpk_{ABET}, and produces an intermediate ciphertext IT during the offline phase.*
- *$ABET.Enc_{Online}(mpk_{ABET}, IT, m, \mathbb{A}) \rightarrow CT$: This online hash algorithm takes mpk_{ABET}, an intermediate ciphertext IT which is derived from the online hash algorithm, the plaintext m and an access structure $\mathbb{A}$, and generates a ciphertext CT.*
- *$ABET.KeyGen(msk_{ABET}, S, ID) \rightarrow ssk_{ID}$: This algorithm takes msk_{ABET}, a set of attributes S and an identity vector ID as input, and outputs a private key ssk_{ID}.*
- *$ABET.Dec(mpk_{ABET}, CT, ssk_{ID}) \rightarrow m$: This algorithm for decryption requires mpk_{ABET}, a ciphertext CT, and a private key ssk_{ID} as its input. If the user meets the access policy specified in the ciphertext and the key delegation of HIBE, the algorithm will produce a decrypted message m.*
- *$ABET.Trace(mpk_{ABET}, \mathcal{D}, \tau) \rightarrow K_T$: Upon receiving mpk_{ABET}, a keylike decryption device $\mathcal{D}$, and a parameter τ which is polynomially related to k and $\tau > 0$, this algorithm outputs the set K_T of the accused users.*

2.6   Digital Signature

DS consists of $(Setup, Keygen, Sign, Verify)$, and satisfies the homomorphic properties regarding keys and signatures, which can be used to find the connection between a transaction and accused modifiers. Please consult [29] for the detailed definition.

Definition 6. *The properties of DS are as follows:*

- *Simple Key Generation. The process involves executing $DS.Setup(1^k) \rightarrow pp$ to produce the public parameter, followed by $DS.KeyGen(pp_{DS}) \rightarrow (sk_{DS}, vk_{DS})$, where $vk_{DS} \leftarrow DS.Keygen'(pp, sk_{DS})$.*
- *The linearity of keys is demonstrated by the equation $DS.Keygen'(pp, sk_{DS} + \Delta(sk_{DS})) = M_{vk}(pp, vk_{DS}, \Delta(sk_{DS}))$. Here, Δ represents the difference in keys.*

- *Linearity of Signatures.* $\{\sigma' \leftarrow Sign\,(pp, sk_{DS} + \Delta\,(sk)\,, m)\}$ and $\{\sigma' \leftarrow M_{DS}\,(pp, vk_{DS}, m, \sigma, \Delta\,(sk_{DS}))\}$ have the same distribution, where $\sigma \leftarrow Sign\,(pp, sk_{DS}, m)$ and M_{DS} are a deterministic algorithm.
- *Linearity of Verifications.* It satisfies $Verify\,(pp, M_{vk}$ $(pp, vk_{DS}, \Delta\,(sk_{DS}))\,, m, M_{DS}\,(pp, vk_{DS}, m, \sigma, \Delta\,(sk_{DS}))) = 1$ and $Verify$ $(pp, vk_{DS}, m, \sigma) = 1$.

2.7   Complexity Assumption

Our construction relies on the Decisional Bilinear Diffie-Hellman (DBDH) assumption on a prime order bilinear group. This assumption is established through a game involving an attacker $\mathcal{A}$ and a challenger $\mathcal{C}$:

The challenger initiates the game by invoking the group generation algorithm $\mathcal{G}\,(1^k) \rightarrow (p, \mathbb{G}, \mathbb{G}_T, e)$ and selects random values $a, b, s, z \in \mathbb{Z}_p^*$. Subsequently, the challenger transmits $(p, \mathbb{G}, \mathbb{G}_T, e)$ and (g, g^a, g^b, g^s) to the attacker.

In the challenge phase, the challenger flips a random coin $b \leftarrow \{0, 1\}$. If $b = 1$, $\mathcal{C}$ hands the term $e(g, g)^{abs}$ to $\mathcal{A}$. Otherwise, it hands $e(g, g)^z$. $\mathcal{A}$ then returns $b' \in \{0, 1\}$ as the guess value.

Definition 7. *The DBDH assumption is considered to hold if no polynomial-time (PPT) attacker achieves a non-negligible advantage $Adv = \Pr\,[b' = b] - 1/2$ in the security game described above.*

3   The Proposed OPCHAR System

3.1   System Architecture

Online/offline policy-based chameleon hash with accountability and revocability (OPCHAR) implements fine-grained modification control and transaction-level editable blockchain, and accountability and revocability for malicious modifiers. The system architecture, illustrated in Fig. 1, comprises four main entities: permissioned blockchain, authorized organization (AO), transaction owner (TO), and transaction modifier (TM). We illustrate the editable blockchain with three non-editable transactions and one editable transaction. However, in reality, a block can contain a large number of transactions. The following describes the specific functions of the four entities in the system:

Permissioned Blockchain: Blockchain can be classified into *permissioned* and *permissionless* blockchain based on the requirement of permission for user participation in the blockchain network. *Permissionless* blockchains are completely decentralized [7] that anyone can join or leave the network flexibly without any central authorization. On the other hand, *permissioned* blockchains follow a different approach. In a permissioned blockchain, users can only join the network after obtaining approval, which means that the network operates under the control and governance of a specific group or organization. The type of our editable

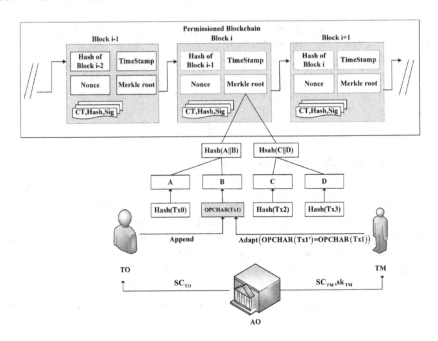

Fig. 1. Architecture of OPCHAR System

blockchain is permissioned blockchain. As shown in Fig. 1, each block consists of a block header and a block body, with the block body containing the relevant information of transactions.

Authorized Organization (AO): AO is mainly responsible for initializing the system parameters, sending secret credentials (SC) for TO and TM, and generating the decryption keys for TM based on their attributes and identity in the hierarchy via a secure channel. For the transactions modified by accused modifiers, AO finds collisions and re-updates them with a new ETD.

Transaction Owner (TO): TO appends an editable transaction as $Tx1$ marked in blue in the Fig. 1 to the blockchain, and the hash value of this transaction is computed by our OPCHAR scheme which is different from the traditional collision-resistant hash. Other transaction information consisting of the ciphertext component CT, the hash component $Hash$, and the signature component Sig is stored in the block body.

Transaction Modifier (TM): TM is a user who modify the editable transaction without changing the structure of the blockchain. Only if his decryption key satisfies the transaction modification policy in the ciphertext can he edit the transaction successfully. As shown in the Fig. 1, the editable transaction $Tx1$ is edited as $Tx1'$ by the TM, and the hash value calculated with our OPCHAR is unchanged.

3.2 The Generic Definition

The OPCHAR scheme is based on PCH, HIBE and DS to achieve an online/offline fine-grained controllable and editable blockchain with accountability. The key delegation of our scheme for accountability is inspired by [29]. OPCHAR is defined formally as follows:

- $Setup(1^k) \rightarrow (mpk, msk, \mathcal{R})$: AO accepts k as input, and produces the system public key $mpk \leftarrow (pk_{CHET}, mpk_{ABET}, mpk_{DS})$ and the system master secret key $msk \leftarrow (sk_{CHET}, msk_{ABET}, msk_{DS})$, where $(sk_{CHET}, pk_{CHET}) \leftarrow CHET.KeyGen(1^k)$, $(msk_{ABET}, mpk_{ABET}) \leftarrow ABET.Setup(1^k)$, and $(msk_{DS}, mpk_{DS}) \leftarrow DS.Setup(1^k)$. Create an empty revocation list denoted as $\mathcal{R}$.

- $KeyGen_{SC}(msk, ID) \rightarrow SC$: AO calls this algorithm which takes msk and a user identity ID as input to generate the identity secret credential SC.

- $KeyGen_{TM}(msk, S, ID_{TM}) \rightarrow sk_{TM}$: This algorithm is run by AO, and it takes as input msk, the attribute set S, the identity ID_{TM} of TM, and outputs the decryption key sk_{TM}.

- $Hash_{Offline}(mpk) \rightarrow IT$: TO calls this algorithm to calculate an intermediate ciphertext $IT \leftarrow ABET.Enc_{Offline}(mpk_{ABET})$ in the offline phase.

- $Hash_{Online}(mpk, IT, m, \mathbb{A}, ID_{TO}, SC_{TO}) \rightarrow (Hash, CT, Sig)$: In the online hash phase, this algorithm takes mpk, the intermediate ciphertext IT, a transaction m, an access policy $\mathbb{A}$, TO's identity ID_{TO}, and the secret credential SC_{TO} as input. TO produces a hash-ciphertext-signature component group $(Hash, CT, Sig)$.

- $Verify(mpk, CT, Sig, Hash) \rightarrow \{0,1\}$: The validity of a transaction can be verified by running this algorithm by any public user. It returns 1 if $1 \leftarrow DS.Verify$ and $1 \leftarrow CHET.Verify$. Otherwise, it returns 0.

- $Adapt(mpk, sk_{TM}, ID_{TM}, SC_{TM}, m', Hash, CT, Sig) \rightarrow (Hash', CT', Sig')$: It takes as input mpk, the TM's decryption key sk_{TM}, the identity ID_{TM} of TM, the secret credential SC_{TM}, a new transaction m', and a hash-ciphertext-signature component group $(Hash, CT, Sig)$ that TM wants to edit. It returns a new hash-ciphertext-signature component group $(Hash', CT', Sig')$.

- $Judge(mpk, \mathcal{T}) \rightarrow \{(T, T')\}$: By utilizing the input of mpk and a transaction set $\mathcal{T}$, any public user can establish a link between a transaction and its altered version.

- $Adapt_{AO}(mpk, msk, \mathcal{O}, Hash', CT', Sig', \mathcal{R}) \rightarrow (Hash'', CT'', Sig'', \mathcal{R}')$: AO calls this algorithm which takes mpk, msk, the black-box $\mathcal{O}$, a hash-ciphertext-signature component group $(Hash', CT', Sig')$ modified by the accused TM as input, and adapts $(Hash', CT', Sig')$ to $(Hash'', CT'', Sig'')$, and updates the revocation list $\mathcal{R}$ to $\mathcal{R}'$.

Correctness. For all k, for all $S \in \mathcal{P}$, for all $(mpk, mpsk) \leftarrow Setup(1^k)$, for all $SC \leftarrow KeyGen_{SC}(msk, ID)$, for all $sk_{TM} \leftarrow KeyGen_{TM}(msk, S, ID_{TM})$, for all $IT \leftarrow Hash_{Offline}(mpk)$, for all $m \in \mathcal{M}$, for all $(Hash, CT, Sig) \leftarrow Hash_{Online}(mpk, IT, m, \mathbb{A}, ID_{TO}, SC_{TO})$, for all $m' \in \mathcal{M}$, for all $S \in \mathbb{A}$, for all $ID_{TM} \leqslant ID_{TO}$, for all $(Hash', CT', Sig') \leftarrow Adapt(mpk, sk_{TM}, ID_{TM}, SC_{TM}, m', Hash, CT, Sig)$, for all $(Hash'', CT'', Sig'', \mathcal{R}') \leftarrow Adapt_{AO}(mpk, msk, \mathcal{O}, Hash', CT', Sig', \mathcal{R})$, we have $1 = Verify(mpk, CT, Sig, Hash) = Verify(mpk, CT', Sig', Hash') = Verify(mpk, CT'', Sig'', Hash'')$.

3.3 Security Model

In our *permissioned* blockchain, TO and AO are trusted entities, while TM is not trusted. In the best interests of TO, the transaction will be honestly and correctly appended to the blockchain. It is necessary for the ABET used in OPCHAR to satisfy IND-CCA2 security, only in this way can this scheme meet the collision-resistance. It is worth noting that ABET in our scheme does not achieve IND-CCA2, but provides selective IND-CPA, which is to avoid significant differences due to the use of IND-CPA variants during the experiment evaluations. Nevertheless, it is well-known that a CPA scheme can be readily transformed into a scheme that meets the CCA2 security requirement using the approach outlined by Canetti et al. [10]. Hence, we will analyze the following four security guarantees, including chosen plaintext security, indistinguishability, collision-resistance, and accountability. These assurances aim to make it challenging for an attacker to retrieve the trapdoor key and carry out a double-spend attack or tampering attack.

Chosen Plaintext Security. Develop a scenario in which an attacker, denoted as $\mathcal{A}$, engages in a game with a challenger, denoted as $\mathcal{C}$, in order to demonstrate the security of chosen plaintext. $\mathcal{A}$ is permitted to make inquiries about keys for attribute sets that do not meet the specified access policy $\mathbb{A}^*$. The game proceeds as outlined below:

- **Init** : $\mathcal{A}$ sends $\mathbb{A}^* = (M^*_{\ell^* \times t^*}, \rho^*)$ to $\mathcal{C}$. $\mathbb{A}^*$ is the access policy that $\mathcal{A}$ will try to attack.
- **Setup** : Here $\mathcal{C}$ calls $Setup(1^k) \rightarrow (mpk, msk)$, and sends mpk to $\mathcal{A}$. It retains msk for itself.
- **Phase1** : During this stage, $\mathcal{A}$ has the capability to dynamically request confidential keys associated with the attribute sets and identities $(ID_{TM_1}, S_1), (ID_{TM_2}, S_2), \cdots, (ID_{TM_{Q_1}}, S_{Q_1})$. The absence of any queried sets that fulfill the challenge access structure $\mathbb{A}^*$ is constrained. For each S_i and ID_{TM_i}, $\mathcal{C}$ calls $KeyGen_{TM}(msk, S_i, ID_{TM_i})$ to generate sk and transmits it back to $\mathcal{A}$.
- **Challenge** : The entity $\mathcal{A}$ asserts two messages of the same length, denoted as m_0 and m_1, and a target identity ID^*_{TO} that has not been queried before. Subsequently, $\mathcal{C}$ randomly selects a coin flip outcome $b \in \{0, 1\}$ and calls $Hash_{Offline}(mpk) \rightarrow IT$ and

$Hash_{Online} (mpk, IT, m_b, \mathbb{A}^*, ID^*_{TO}, SC^*_{TO}) \rightarrow (CT, Sig, Hash)$. The resulting tuple $(CT, Sig, Hash)$ is then transmitted to the adversary $\mathcal{A}$.

- **Phase2** : Repeat *Phase*1. The attacker requests for the secret key of $(ID_{TM_{Q_1+1}}, S_{Q_1+1}), (ID_{TM_{Q_1+2}}, S_{Q_1+2}), \cdots, (ID_{TM_{Q_1+Q_2}}, S_{Q_1+Q_2})$. The restriction is $\mathcal{A}$ can not query for the target identity ID^*_{TO} and none of the queried attribute set satisfies the challenge access structure $\mathbb{A}^*$.

- **Guess** : The attacker $\mathcal{A}$ outputs the guess $b' \in \{0,1\}$ for b. If $b' = b$, $\mathcal{A}$ wins the game. Otherwise, $\mathcal{C}$ wins the game.

Definition 8. *The superiority of $\mathcal{A}$ in the aforementioned game is denoted as $Adv^{CPA}_{\mathcal{A}}(k) = |\Pr[b' = b] - 1/2|$. The CPA security property is claimed for the OPCHAR scheme when the advantages gained by all polynomial-time attackers are deemed insignificant.*

Indistinguishability. The attacker cannot tell whether the randomness of a chameleon hash stored in the blockchain is generated by the transaction owner with $Hash_{Online}$, or by the transaction modifier with *Adapt*. The subsequent interactions represent the security game between a attacker $\mathcal{A}$ and challenger $\mathcal{C}$:

- **Setup** : $\mathcal{C}$ executes the algorithm Setup$(1^k) \rightarrow (mpk, msk)$ to produce mpk and msk. Subsequently, $\mathcal{C}$ transmits mpk to $\mathcal{A}$.
- **Challenge** : $\mathcal{A}$ specifies two transaction messages m_0 and m_1, an access policy $\mathbb{A}$, identities ID_{TO} and ID'_{TO}, and sends these parameters to $\mathcal{C}$. $\mathcal{C}$ firstly calls $Hash_{Offline}(mpk)$ to generate an intermediate ciphertext. Next, run $Hash_{Online}(mpk, IT, m_0, \mathbb{A}, ID_{TO}, SC_{TO})$ to get $(Hash_0, CT_0, Sig_0)$, and $Hash_{Online}(mpk, IT, m_1, \mathbb{A}, ID'_{TO}, SC'_{TO})$ to generate $(Hash_1, CT_1, Sig_1)$. Then, $\mathcal{C}$ calls $KeyGen_{TM}(msk, S, ID_{TO})$ to get the secret key sk_{TO}, and $Adapt(mpk, sk_{TO}, ID_{TO}, SC_{TO}, m_1, Hash_0, CT_0, Sig_0)$ to find a collision $(Hash'_0, CT'_0, Sig'_0)$, in which the transaction m_0 is adapted to m_1 by its owner ID_{TO} instead of other transaction modifiers. Finally, $\mathcal{C}$ selects a random coin b from the set $\{0,1\}$ and provides $(Hash_b, CT_b, Sig_b)$ to $\mathcal{A}$.
- **Guess** : $\mathcal{A}$ produces a prediction $b' \in \{0,1\}$ for the value of b and achieves success if $b' = b$. If $b' \neq b$, then $\mathcal{C}$ is deemed the winner of the game.

Definition 9. *The advantage of $\mathcal{A}$ is expressed as $Adv^{IND}_{\mathcal{A}}(k) = |\Pr[\mathcal{A} \rightarrow 1] - 1/2|$, where $\Pr[\mathcal{A} \rightarrow 1]$ represents the probability that $\mathcal{A}$ wins. OPCHAR is considered indistinguishable if it cannot be broken by a polynomial-time attacker $\mathcal{A}$ with a significant advantage, or $Adv^{IND}_{\mathcal{A}}(k)$ is a negligible function.*

Collision-Resistance. Any attacker cannot is unable to discover a collision for a chameleon hash that has not been computed by *Adapt* oracle even if he can access the *Adapt*.

- **Setup** : $\mathcal{C}$ initializes a message space $\mathcal{M}$, two lists $\mathcal{L}_1, \mathcal{L}_2 \rightarrow \varnothing$ and $i = 0$, and generates mpk, msk. $\mathcal{C}$ then provides mpk to $\mathcal{A}$.

- **Query** : Key queries, hash queries, and collision queries are performed by $\mathcal{A}$.
  - **Key query.** Upon receiving a specific query involving the parameters (ID_{TM}, S), where ID_{TM} is an identity and S denotes a attributes set, $\mathcal{C}$ runs $KeyGen_{TM}(msk, S, ID_{TM})$ to generate sk_{TM} and sends sk_{TM} to $\mathcal{A}$. Then set $\mathcal{L}_1 \leftarrow \mathcal{L}_1 \cup \{S\}$.
  - **Hash query.** $\mathcal{A}$ submits the transaction m, access policy $\mathbb{A}$, and the TO's identity ID_{TO}. First, AO performs $KeyGen_{SC}(msk, ID_{TO})$ to generate SC_{TO}, and then AO runs $Hash_{Offline}(mpk) \rightarrow IT$ in the offline phase and then calls $Hash_{Online}(mpk, IT, m, \mathbb{A}, ID_{TO}, SC_{TO}) \rightarrow (Hash, CT, Sig)$. $\mathcal{C}$ outputs the $(Hash, CT, Sig)$ to $\mathcal{A}$ and sets $\mathcal{L}_2 \leftarrow \mathcal{L}_2 \cup \{(m, h_{CHET}, \mathbb{A})\}$, where h_{CHET} is contained in $Hash$.
  - **Adapt Query.** $\mathcal{A}$ send m', $(Hash, CT, Sig)$, and sk_{TM} that has been queried before to $\mathcal{C}$. Then $\mathcal{C}$ finds the collision $(Hash', CT', Sig') \leftarrow Adapt(sk_{TM}, ID_{TM}, m', Hash, CT, Sig)$. If $(m, h_{CHET}) \in L_2$, then set $\mathcal{L}_2 \leftarrow \mathcal{L}_2 \cup \{(m', h_{CHET}, \mathbb{A})\}$.
- **Forgery** : If the input $(m^*, m^{*'}, h^*_{CHET}, \mathbb{A})$ from $\mathcal{A}$ satisfied $m^* \neq m^{*'} \wedge \mathbb{A} \cap \mathcal{L}_1 = \emptyset \wedge (m^*, h_{CHET}, \cdot) \notin \mathcal{L}_2$, $\mathcal{C}$ calculates $Verify(mpk, m^*, h^*_{CHET}, r^*, \sigma^*) \wedge Verify(mpk, m^{*'}, h^*_{CHET} r^{*'}, \sigma^*) \wedge (\cdot, h^*_{CHET}, \mathbb{A}) \in \mathcal{L}_2$, where $r^* \neq r^{*'}$. If the result is 1, then $\mathcal{A}$ wins. Otherwise, $\mathcal{C}$ wins.

Definition 10. *The advantage of $\mathcal{A}$ in the aforementioned game is denoted as $Adv_{\mathcal{A}}^{CR}(k) = |\Pr[\mathcal{A} \rightarrow 1]|$. OPCHAR is collision-resistance if it holds that $Adv_{\mathcal{A}}^{CR}(k)$ is negligible in k for every polynomial-time attacker $\mathcal{A}$.*

Accountability. If the accused identity never creates a message-signature pair, then $\mathcal{A}$ is unable to generate a bogus message-signature for the chameleon hash connected to the accused identity.

- **Setup** : $\mathcal{C}$ runs Setup$(1^k) \rightarrow (mpk, msk)$ and provides mpk to $\mathcal{A}$. $\mathcal{C}$ initializes a list $\mathcal{L} \rightarrow \emptyset$.
- **Query** : $\mathcal{A}$ sends the transaction $T = (h_{CHET}, m, r_{CHET}, \sigma)$, the attributes set S, the queried message m', and the identity ID' to $\mathcal{C}$. Then, $\mathcal{C}$ calls $KeyGen_{TM}(msk, S, ID')$ to generate the secret key sk_{TM}, and $Adapt(sk_{TM}, ID', SC_{TM}, m', T)$ to generate $T' = (h_{CHET}, m', r_{CHET}', \sigma')$. Then set $\mathcal{L} \leftarrow \mathcal{L} \cup \{(T, T')\}$, and output the connection pair (T', ID') to $\mathcal{A}$.
- **Challenge** : If $\mathcal{A}$ transmits (T^*, ID^*) to $\mathcal{C}$, $\mathcal{A}$ is the winner. Otherwise, the winner is $\mathcal{C}$. The restriction is $T^* \notin \mathcal{L}$.

Definition 11. *The benefit of an attacker $\mathcal{A}$ in the aforementioned game is characterized as $Adv_{\mathcal{A}}^{AC} = |\Pr[Exp_{\mathcal{A}, OPCHAR}(k) \rightarrow 1]|$. OPCHAR is accountable if for every polynomial-time attacker $\mathcal{A}$, it holds that $Adv_{\mathcal{A}}^{AC}(k)$ is negligible in k.*

4   Construction of OPCHAR Scheme

The highest level of the identity hierarchy in HIBE is denoted as n. For a user with depth j, his identity vector is $ID = (I_1, \cdots I_j) \in (\mathbb{Z}_p)^j$. AO is the root of the hierarchy, so we treat AO as the user at depth 0. We assume that the depths of TO and TM in the hierarchy are a and b, so the identity vector of the former is $ID_{TO} = (I_1, \cdots I_a) \in (\mathbb{Z}_p)^a$ and the latter is $ID_{TM} = (I_1, \cdots I_b) \in (\mathbb{Z}_p)^b$. The depth of TM is closer to the root than the depth of TO, or the depth of TM is equal to the depth of TO, that is $b \leqslant a$. $\mathcal{R}$ is the revocation list that stored in blockchain.

4.1   Concrete Construction

$Setup(1^k) \to (mpk, msk, \mathcal{R})$: This algorithm performs the following steps to get mpk, msk and $\mathcal{R}$.

1) It calls the group generation algorithm $\mathcal{G}$ and randomly chooses $g, h, u, v, w \in \mathbb{G}$, $\alpha, \beta, \delta, x \in \mathbb{Z}_p^*$, and $\{z_1, \cdots, z_n\} \in \mathbb{Z}_p$.
2) It calculates the CHET key pair $(sk_{CHET}, pk_{CHET}) = (x, g^x)$.
3) Then it sets ABET's master public key $mpk_{ABET} = \big(g, h, u, v, w, e(g, g)^\alpha,$ $e(g, h)^\delta, \{h_i^\alpha\}_{i \in [1,n]}, \quad \{g_i = g^{z_i}\}_{i \in [1,n]}, h^\alpha, h^\beta, H_1, H_2\big)$, and $msk_{ABET} = (\alpha, \beta, \delta, \{z_1, \cdots, z_n\})$, where $\{h_i = h^{z_i}\}_{i \in [1,n]}$, and $H_1 : \{0,1\}^* \to \mathbb{Z}_p$ is a hash function, and $H_2 : \mathbb{G}_T \to \{0,1\}^*$ is a pseudo-random generator.
4) An empty revocation list $\mathcal{R}$ is initialized, which is also appended to the blockchain using OPCHAR in order to enable the updating of $\mathcal{R}$.

Output $mpk = (pk_{CHET}, mpk_{ABET})$ and $msk = (sk_{CHET}, msk_{ABET})$.

$KeyGen_{SC}(msk, ID) \to SC$: It generates identity secret credentials $SC = \left(g \cdot \prod_{i=1}^{j} g_i^{I_i}\right)^\alpha$ for each user $ID = (I_1, \cdots, I_j) \in (\mathbb{Z}_p)^j$ in the blockchain.

$KeyGen_{TM}(msk, S, ID_{TM}) \to sk_{TM}$: It takes as input msk, TM's attributes set $S = \{A_1, A_2, \cdots, A_u\} \in \mathbb{Z}_p$, and the identity $ID_{TM} = (I_1, \cdots, I_b) \in (\mathbb{Z}_p)^b$. The algorithm selects $r, r_1, r_2, \cdots, r_u, R \in \mathbb{Z}_p$. It then computes $sk_0 = g^\alpha w^r$, $sk_1 = g^r$, $sk_2 = \{g^{r_i}\}_{i \in [1,u]}$, $sk_3 = \big\{(u^{A_i} h)^{r_i} v^{-r}\big\}_{i \in [1,u]}$, $sk_4 = g^R$, $sk_5 = h^\delta \left(h \cdot \prod_{i=1}^{b} h_i^{I_i}\right)^{\alpha r} \cdot h^{\beta R}$, $sk_6 = \{h_i^{\alpha r}\}_{i \in [b+1, n]}$, $sk_7 = h^r$. The AO outputs the private key $sk_{TM} = (S, sk_0, sk_1, sk_2, sk_3, sk_4, sk_5, sk_6, sk_7)$, where $\left(h \cdot \prod_{i=1}^{b} h_i^{I_i}\right)^\alpha$ can be pre-calculated in advance.

$Hash_{Offline}(mpk) \to IT$: In the offline hash phase, the algorithm generates the intermediate ciphertext IT. The TO independently calculates arbitrary number N_{IT} ($N_{IT} > \ell$) of attribute modules. For the ith attribute, choose random values $\lambda_i', x_i, t_i \in \mathbb{Z}_p$, and then compute $C_{i,1} = w^{\lambda_i'} v^{t_i}$, $C_{i,2} = (u^{x_i} h)^{-t_i}$, $C_{i,3} = g^{t_i}$. The attribute module for the ith attribute is $IT_i = \{C_{i,1}, C_{i,2}, C_{i,2}\}$.

Then, TO outputs the attribute module pool $IT = \{IT_i\}_{i \in [1,N_{IT}]}$, which was proposed in [17].

$Hash_{Online}(mpk, IT, m, \mathbb{A}, ID_{TO}, SC_{TO}) \rightarrow (Hash, CT, Sig)$: The online hash algorithm takes mpk, IT generated in the offline hash phase, a transaction m, an access structure $\mathbb{A} = (\mathrm{M}, \rho)$ and an identity $ID_{TO} = (I_1, \cdots, I_a) \in (\mathbb{Z}_p)^a$ as input.

1) Calculate the chameleon hash. TO selects $r_{CHET} \in \mathbb{Z}_p^*$, and calculates $y = pk_{CHET}^{r_{CHET}} = (g^x)^{r_{CHET}}$. Then TO randomly generates a short bit-string ephemeral trapdoor etd and calculates $h' = g^{H_1(etd)}$, $h_{CHET} = y \cdot h'^m$. Let the hash component $\text{Hash} = ((m, y, h'), h_{CHET})$.

2) Generate a signing/verification key pair. Choose $s \in \mathbb{Z}_p^*$ as the signing key sk_{DS}. The verification key $vk_{DS} = SC_{TO}^s$, where $SC_{TO} = \left(g \cdot \prod_{i=1}^{a} g_i^{I_i} \right)^\alpha$ is the secret credential of TO generated by AO.

3) Compute the ciphertext component CT by encrypting (r_{CHET}, etd) using $\mathbb{A} = (M_{\ell \times t}, \rho)$, the temporary ciphertext IT, and the identity ID_{TO}. TO randomly picks $y_2, \cdots, y_t \in \mathbb{Z}_p$, and sets a vector $\vec{v} = (s, y_2, \cdots, y_t)^T$. Then the shared vector $M\vec{v} = (\lambda_1, \cdots, \lambda_\ell)^T$ is computes by TO. For $j \in [1, \ell]$, TO calculates $C_{j,4} = \lambda_j - \lambda_j'$, $C_{j,5} = -t_j \cdot (\rho(j) - x_j)$. Later, TO computes $C = g^s$, $ct = (h^\beta)^s$, $ct_0 = r_{CHET} \oplus H_2(e(g,g)^{\alpha s})$, $ct_1 = (etd \| 0^{l-|etd|}) \oplus H_2\left(e(g,h)^{\delta s}\right)$, $ct_2 = vk_{DS}$, $ct_3 = \left(g \cdot \prod_{i=1}^{a} g_i^{I_i} \right)^s$, $ct_4 = ct_2^s$. Let the ciphertext component $CT = \left(C, C', \{C_{j,1}, C_{j,2}, C_{j,3}, C_{j,4}, C_{j,5}\}_{j \in [1,\ell]}, ct, ct_0, ct_1, ct_2, ct_3, ct_4, \mathbb{A} \right)$.

4) Generate an ephemeral key pair as (esk, epk). TO selects a random ephemeral secret key $esk \in \mathbb{Z}_p^*$ and calculates the ephemeral public key $epk = h^{esk}$. Then TO computes $\sigma = esk + s \cdot H_1(epk \| c)$, where $c = g^{s + H_1(etd \| 0^{l-|etd|})}$. Set the signature component is $Sig = (epk, c, \sigma)$.

Finally, TO outputs the hash-ciphertext-signature component group $(Hash, CT, Sig)$. Note that h_{CHET} in Hash is a leaf node of the Merkle tree.

$Verify(mpk, Hash, CT, Sig) \rightarrow \{0, 1\}$: Any public user can perform this algorithm to verify whether a transaction is valid. It outputs 1 if $h_{CHET} = y \cdot h'^m$ and $e(h^\alpha, ct_3)^\sigma = e(epk, ct_2) \cdot e(h, ct_4)^{H_1(epk \| c)}$, where these parameters are included in the hash-ciphertext-signature component group.

$Adapt(mpk, sk_{TM}, ID_{TM}, SC_{TM}, m', Hash, CT, Sig) \rightarrow (Hash', CT', Sig')$: It takes sk_{TM}, the identity $ID_{TM} = (I_1, \cdots, I_b) \in (\mathbb{Z}_q)^b$, the secret credential of TM, a new transaction m' and the hash-ciphertext-signature component group $(CT, Sig, Hash)$ as input. Then it performs the following steps:

1) Verify $Verify(Hash, CT, Sig) = 1 \wedge S \vDash \mathbb{A} \wedge ID_{TM} \notin R$. If the output is true, continue with the following algorithms; Otherwise, output $\perp$.

2) Execute the subsequent procedures to obtain etd. If the depth of TM is closer to the root than the depth of TO, that is $a > b$. TO first delegates the

secret key. Randomly pick $z \in \mathbb{Z}_p^*$, and calculate the delegation secret key: $sk_0' = sk_0 \cdot w^z = g^\alpha w^{r+z}$, $sk_1' = sk_1 \cdot g^z = g^{r+z}$, and for $i \in [1, u]$, $sk_{i,2}' = sk_{i,2} \cdot g^z = g^{r_i+z}$, $sk_{i,3}' = sk_{i,3} \cdot (u^{A_i} h)^z \cdot v^{-z}$, then $sk_4' = sk_4 = g^R$, $sk_5' = sk_5 \cdot$

$$(sk_{6,1})^{I_{b+1}} \cdot \left((h_1^\alpha)^{I_1} \cdots (h_{b+1}^\alpha)^{I_{b+1}} \cdot h^\alpha \right)^z = h^\delta \cdot \left(h_1^{I_1} \cdots h_{b+1}^{I_{b+1}} \cdot h \right)^{\alpha(r+z)} \cdot h^{\beta R},$$

$sk_6' = \{sk_{6,i} \cdot h_i^{\alpha z}\}_{i \in [b+2, n]}$, $sk_7' = sk_7 \cdot h^z = h^{r+z}$.

Then, check $\left(etd \parallel 0^{l-|etd|} \right) \overset{?}{=} ct_1 \oplus H_2\left(\dfrac{e(C, sk_5')}{e(sk_7', ct_2) e(sk_4', ct)} \right)$. The delegation procedure terminates if etd is retrieved with certainty $1 - 2^{l-|etd|}$ [9], and the delegated decryption key is denoted as sk_{TM}'.

3) Since TM's attribute set S satisfies the access structure $\mathbb{A} = (M_{\ell \times t}, \rho)$, a subset of $I = \{i : \rho(i) \in S\}$ and corresponding coefficients $w_i \in \mathbb{Z}_p$ such that $\sum_{i \in I} w_i \cdot M_i = (1, 0, \cdots, 0)$ can be calculated. Then, TM calculates $\varphi = e(C, sk_0')$, $\gamma = e\left(sk_1', w^{\sum_{i \in I} C_{i,4} w_i}\right)$, $\tau = \prod_{i \in I} \left(e(sk_1', C_{i,1}) \cdot e(sk_{2,j}', C_{i,2} \cdot u^{C_{i,5}}) \cdot \cdot e(C_{i,3}, sk_{3,j}') \right)^{w_i}$ and $r_{CHET} = ct_0 \oplus H_2\left(\dfrac{\varphi}{\gamma \cdot \tau} \right)$.

4) Derive an adaptive $r_{CHET}' = r_{CHET} + (m - m') \cdot \dfrac{H_1(etd)}{sk_{CHET}}$ with etd and r_{CHET} decrypted by the above algorithms, and compute $y' = pk_{CHET}^{r_{CHET}'} = (g^x)^{r_{CHET}'}$. Then perform the following like the algorithm $Hash$. First of all, pick $s' \in \mathbb{Z}_p^*$ and generate a signing/verification key pair $(sk_{DS}, vk_{DS}) = \left(s', SC_{TM}^{s'} \right)$. In addition, based on the access control structure $\mathbb{A}$, use the randomness s' to encrypt r_{CHET}' and etd to generate the ciphertext component CT'. Finally, generate a new signature component $Sig' = (epk', c', \sigma')$, where $epk' = h^{esk'}$, $c' = g^{s' + H_1(etd \parallel 0^{l-|etd|})}$, $\sigma' = esk' + s' \cdot H_1(epk' \parallel c')$.

TM changes the hash-ciphertext-signature component group from $(Hash, CT, Sig)$ to $(Hash', CT', Sig')$. For $Hash' = ((m', y', h'), h_{CHET})$, h_{CHET} is the hash value in the Merkle tree and has not changed. $h' = g^{H_1(etd)}$ has not been changed due to the same etd.

$Judge(mpk, \mathcal{T}) \rightarrow \{(T, T')\}$: Any individual can publicly confirm the association between a transaction and its altered version. For example, there are two hash-ciphertext-signature component groups $(Hash, CT, Sig)$ and $(Hash', CT', Sig')$ in the set $\mathcal{T}$ of transactions. A public user performs the following steps:

1) Verify whether the chameleon hash h_{CHET} of these two components are equal.
2) Verify $1 \overset{?}{=} Verify(Hash, CT, Sig)$ and $1 \overset{?}{=} Verify(Hash', CT', Sig')$.
3) Compute $\Delta(sk) = c'/c = g^{s'-s}$ (the meaning of $\Delta(sk)$ is referred to definition 6), and then verify $C' \overset{?}{=} C \cdot \Delta(sk)$.

If all three of the above verifications are passed, it proves that transaction $T' = (Hash', CT', Sig')$ is a modified version of transaction $T = (Hash, CT, Sig)$.

$Adapt_{AO}(mpk, msk, \mathcal{O}, Hash', CT', Sig', \mathcal{R}) \rightarrow (Hash'', CT'', Sig'', \mathcal{R}')$: In the event of the transaction being approved by *judge*, AO has the ability to acquire a collection of accused TMs by engaging with an access blackbox denoted as $\mathcal{O}$. If $\mathcal{O}$ is generated by the TM's delegated secret keys, it becomes challenging for the public user to accurately identify the accused TM due to the potential for shared identities among the delegated keys. Consequently, the utilization of the TM's delegated secret keys in the generation of $\mathcal{O}$ is prohibited. For a accused TM with $ID_{TM} = (I_1, \cdots, I_b) \in (\mathbb{Z}_p)^b$ and a transaction hash-ciphertext-signature component group $(Hash', CT', Sig')$, if

$$e(ct_2^{1/\alpha}, h) = e\left(\left(g \cdot \prod_{i=1}^{b} g_i^{I_i}\right)^s, h\right) = e\left(C, h \cdot \prod_{i=1}^{b} h_i^{I_i}\right), \text{ AO confirms that this}$$

transaction is modified by this TM. Then, AO add this accused modifier ID_{TM} to the revocation list $\mathcal{R}$. Note that the revocation list $\mathcal{R}$ can be encrypted with our proposed OPCHAR to realize rewriting.

Then, AO derives an adaptive r'_{CHET} with a new generated etd' in order to prevent malicious users from leaking etd obtained by previous decryption. AO decrypts $e(g,g)^{\alpha s} = \frac{\varphi}{\gamma \cdot \tau}$ using msk and as a user with all attributes, and $r_{CHET} = ct_0 \oplus H_2(e(g,g)^{\alpha s})$. Second, AO is regarded as a user of depth 0, so $e(g,h)^{\delta s} = \frac{e(C, sk_5')}{e(sk_7', ct_2)e(sk_4', ct)}$ can be computed using the delegated secret key. Then, generate a new short bit-string etd' and derive an adaptive $r'_{CHET} = r_{CHET} + (H_1(etd) - H_1(etd')) \cdot \frac{m}{sk_{CHET}}$, so update $h'' = g^{H_1(etd')}$, $y' = pk_{CHET}^{r'_{CHET}} = (g^x)^{r'_{CHET}}$. Furthermore, AO picks $s'' \in \mathbb{Z}_p^*$, and updates $C' = (C)^{s''} = g^{s \cdot s''}$, $ct' = ct^{s''} = (h^\beta)^{ss''}$, $cto' = r'_{CHET} \oplus H_2\left((e(g,g)^{\alpha s})^{s''}\right)$, $ct_1' = \left(etd' \| 0^{l-|etd'|}\right) \oplus H_2\left((e(g,h)^{\delta s})^{s''}\right)$, $ct_2' = ct_2^{s''} = vk_{DS}^{s''}$, $ct_3' = ct_3^{s''} = \left(g \cdot \prod_{i=1}^{a} g_i^{I_i}\right)^{ss''}$, $ct_4' = ct_4^{s''} = ct_2^{ss''}$. Lastly, AO generates a new hash-ciphertext-signature component group $(Hash'', CT'', Sig'')$.

4.2 Security Analysis

Theorem 1. *The security of the ABET used in OPCHAR is guaranteed against selectively chosen plaintext attack CPA, provided that the DBDH assumption holds in the oracle model.*

Theorem 2. *The OPCHAR scheme has indistinguishability if the CHET in our scheme holds the indistinguishability.*

Theorem 3. *The proposed OPCHAR achieves collision-resistance if the CHET and ABET on which our scheme depends is collision-resistant and IND-CCA2 secure. Note that OPCHAR with CPA security can be easily converted into a scheme that satisfies IND-CCA2 by the method proposed by Canetti et al. [10].*

Theorem 4. *The OPCHAR scheme achieves accountability if DS is existential unforgeability under chosen message attack EUF − CMA secure.*

The details of the proof of the above theorems are given in the Appendix.

5   Implementation and Evaluation

We compare our scheme with PCHBA [29] and ReTRACe [26] and implement them in python 3.9.0 using Charm framework [2]. The experimental PC configuration is Intel(R) Core(TM) i7-7700 CPU (@3.60GHz) and 16.00GB RAM, and we use the virtual 64bit ubuntu environment built in VirtualBox [25] to conduct experiments. We use the SS512 elliptic curve for bilinear pairing. The SS512 curve is a supersingular curve with a group order of 512 bits, which provides a security level of 80 bits [12]. To implement our scheme, we utilize the interfaces offered by the Charm framework to instantiate the pseudo-random number generator. Each experimental iteration is conducted 100 times, with the resulting average time being used as the outcome.

First, since there are problems in the key delegation of *Adapt* algorithm of PCHBA, that $h^{b_1 \cdot (r_1 + z_1)}$ and $h^{b_2 \cdot (r_2 + z_2)}$ cannot be calculated with the known parameters, we set the hierarchies of TO and TM are the same as 2, so there is no need for the key delegation. The maximum identity hierarchy of the system is 10. The user attribute set length or policy length is determined within the range of 2 to 20. The performance comparison results of *Setup, Keygen, Hash, Adapt* are shown in Fig. 2, 3. In Fig. 2(a), the computational time of ReTRACe exhibits a linear relationship with the expansion of the attribute set size, whereas the running time of OPCHAR and PCHBA remains unaffected by variations in the attribute set size, and our OPCHAR has a shorter running time than the others. In Fig. 2(b) and Fig. 3(b), the duration of execution for OPCHAR is marginally greater than that of ReTRACe, yet significantly shorter than that of PCHBA. Compared with PCHBA, the running time of OPCHAR and ReTRACe

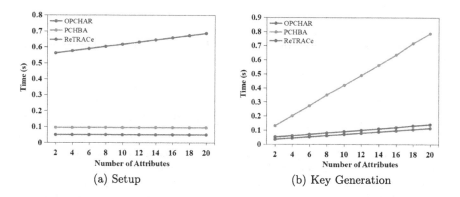

(a) Setup   (b) Key Generation

Fig. 2. Performances of *Setup* (Left) and *Keygen* (Right) Algorithms.

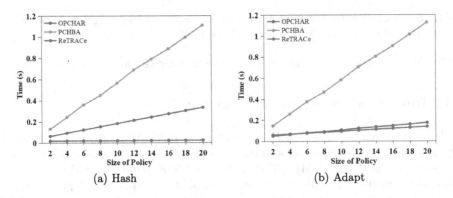

Fig. 3. Performances of *Hash* (Left) and *Adapt* (Right) Algorithms.

increases more slowly with the number of attributes. In the hash phase as shown in Fig. 3(a), our OPCHAR is the most efficient. The running time of OPCHAR barely changes with the increasing of the access policy size, and it is stable at about 0.02 s since we take the online/offline technique. Please be aware that the computational time of *Hash* in our OPCHAR is the time of $Hash_{Online}$.

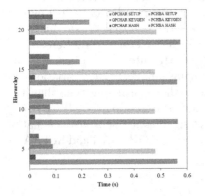

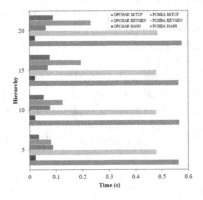

Fig. 4. Timings for OPCHAR vs. PCHBA

Fig. 5. Timing for Adapt of OPCHAR

Then, since the algorithm complexity of OPCHAR and PCHBA is related to the identity hierarchy, the comparison results of keeping the number of attributes unchanged at 10 and making the identity hierarchy incremental are shown in Fig. 4 and Fig. 5. The complexity of *Setup* is related to the maximum identity hierarchy depth. and *Keygen* is related to the identity hierarchy of TM, and *Hash* is related to the identity hierarchy of TO. Since the key delegation algorithm in *adapt* of PCHBA cannot be executed, the key delegation efficiency of our algorithm is shown separately in Fig. 5. As depicted in Fig. 4, it is evident that our OPCHAR algorithm demonstrates greater efficiency as the size of the identity hierarchy increases. In Fig. 5, we fix the identity hierarchy of TO to be 20, and the x-axis represents the identity hierarchy of TM. As the identity hierarchy of TM is closer to that of TO, the key delegation efficiency of our OPCHAR is faster.

6 Conclusion

We revisited the problems that exist in the editable blockchain of [29] and proposed an online/offline policy-based chameleon hash with accountability and revocability (OPCHAR). Any member of the public can associate a transaction with its altered versions, and the authorized organization can accuse and revoke a malicious modifier by black-box mechanism and revocation list. Moreover, the experiment demonstrates that OPCHAR exhibits greater efficiency with the online/offline hash calculation. At last, we also verfied the security of our scheme. In the coming work, we will explore how to implement computational outsourcing without breaking the decentralization of the blockchain.

Acknowledgments. The work of Lifeng Guo was supported by the National Science Foundation of Shanxi Province (202203021221012). The work of Wei-Chuen Yau was supported by the Xiamen University Malaysia Research Fund under Grant XMUMRF/2019-C4/IECE/0011.

Disclosure of Interests. The authors have no competing interests to declare that are relevant to the content of this article.

A Correctness

$$
e\left(epk, ct_2\right) \cdot e(h, ct_4)^{H_1(epk\|c)}
$$

$$
= e\left(h^{esk}, \left(g \cdot \prod_{i=1}^{a} g_i^{I_i}\right)^{\alpha s}\right) \cdot e\left(h, \left(g \cdot \prod_{i=1}^{a} g_i^{I_i}\right)^{\alpha s^2}\right)^{H_1(epk\|c)}
$$

$$
= e\left(h^{\alpha}, \left(g \cdot \prod_{i=1}^{a} g_i^{I_i}\right)^{s}\right)^{esk+s \cdot H_1(epk\|c)}
$$

$$
= e(h^{\alpha}, ct_3)^{\sigma}
$$

(1)

$$\zeta = \frac{e\left(C, sk_5'\right)}{e\left(sk_7', ct_2\right) e\left(sk_4', ct\right)}$$

$$= \frac{e\left(g^s, h^\delta \cdot \left(h_1^{I_1} \cdots h_a^{I_a} \cdot h\right)^{\alpha(r+z)} \cdot h^{\beta R}\right)}{e\left(h^{r+z}, \left(g \cdot \prod_{i=1}^{a} g_i^{I_i}\right)^{\alpha s}\right) \cdot e\left(g^R, h^{\beta s}\right)}$$

$$= \frac{e\left(h \cdot \prod_{i=1}^{a} h_i^{I_i}, g\right)^{(r+z)\alpha s} \cdot e(g, h)^{\beta R s} \cdot e(g, h)^{\delta s}}{e\left(h^{r+z}, \left(g \cdot \prod_{i=1}^{a} g_i^{I_i}\right)^{\alpha s}\right) \cdot e\left(g^R, h^{\beta s}\right)} \tag{2}$$

$$= \frac{e\left(h \cdot \prod_{i=1}^{a} h^{z_i I_i}, g\right)^{(r+z)\alpha s} \cdot e(g, h)^{\delta s}}{e\left(h, g \cdot \prod_{i=1}^{a} g^{z_i I_i}\right)^{(r+z)\alpha s}}$$

$$= e(g, h)^{\delta s}$$

$$ct_1 \oplus H_2\left(\zeta\right) = \left(etd \parallel 0^{l-|etd|}\right) \oplus H_2\left(e(g,h)^{\delta s}\right) \oplus H_2\left(\zeta\right) = etd \parallel 0^{l-|etd|} \tag{3}$$

$$\tau = \prod_{i \in I}\left(e\left(sk_1', C_{i,1}\right) \cdot e\left(sk_{2,j}', C_{i,2} \cdot u^{C_{i,5}}\right) \cdot e\left(C_{i,3}, sk_{3,j}'\right)\right)^{w_i}$$

$$= \prod_{i \in I}\left(e\left(g^{r+z}, w^{\lambda_i'} v^{t_i}\right) \cdot e\left(g^{r_i+z}, (u^{x_i}h)^{-t_i} \cdot u^{-t_i \cdot (\rho(i)-x_i)}\right) \cdot \right.$$
$$\left. e\left(g^{t_i}, \left(u^{A_i}h\right)^{r_i} v^{-r} \cdot \left(u^{A_i}h\right)^z \cdot v^{-z}\right)\right)^{w_i}$$

$$= \prod_{i \in I}\left(e\left(g^{r+z}, w^{\lambda'_i}\right) \cdot e(g^{r+z}, v^{t_i}) \cdot e\left(g^{r_i+z}, \left(u^{\rho(i)}h\right)^{-t_i}\right) \cdot \right.$$
$$\left. e\left(g^{t_i}, \left(u^{A_i}h\right)^{(r_i+z)} v^{-(r+z)}\right)\right)^{w_i} \tag{4}$$

$$= \prod_{i \in I}\left(e\left(g^{r+z}, w^{\lambda'_i}\right) \cdot e(g^{r+z}, v^{t_i}) \cdot e\left(g^{r_i+z}, \left(u^{\rho(i)}h\right)^{-t_i}\right) \cdot \right.$$
$$\left. e\left(g^{t_i}, \left(u^{A_i}h\right)^{(r_i+z)}\right) \cdot e\left(g^{t_i}, v^{-(r+z)}\right)\right)^{w_i}$$

$$= \prod_{i \in I}\left(e\left(g^{r+z}, w^{\lambda'_i}\right)\right)^{w_i}$$

$$\varphi = e\left(C, sk_0'\right) = e\left(g^s, g^\alpha w^{r+z}\right) \tag{5}$$

$$\gamma = e\left(sk_1{}', w^{\sum_{i\in I} C_{i,4}w_i}\right)$$

$$= e\left(g^{r+z}, w^{\sum_{i\in I} (\lambda_i - \lambda_i')w_i}\right) \tag{6}$$

$$= e(g,w)^{s(r+z)} \cdot e(g,w)^{-(r+z)\sum_{i\in I}\lambda_i' w_i}$$

$$\frac{\varphi}{\gamma \cdot \tau} = \frac{e\left(g^s, g^\alpha w^{r+z}\right)}{e(g,w)^{s(r+z)} \cdot e(g,w)^{-(r+z)\sum_{i\in I}\lambda_i' w_i} \cdot \prod_{i\in I}\left(e\left(g^{r+z}, w^{\lambda'_i}\right)\right)^{w_i}}$$

$$= \frac{e\left(g^s, g^\alpha\right) \cdot e\left(g^s, w^{r+z}\right)}{e(g,w)^{s(r+z)} \cdot e(g,w)^{-(r+z)\sum_{i\in I}\lambda_i' w_i} \cdot e(g,w)^{(r+z)\sum_{i\in I}\lambda_i' w_i}} \tag{7}$$

$$= e(g,g)^{\alpha s}$$

B Security Analysis

B.1 Security Proof of Theorem 1

Proof. To prove Theorem 1, we assume that there exists a polynomial time attacker $\mathcal{A}$ with a non-negligible advantage to attack the chosen plaintext security of OPCHAR. In this scenario, there exists a challenger $\mathcal{C}$ who takes advantage of $\mathcal{A}$ with a substantial advantage to attack the DBDH problem. Here is the game played between $\mathcal{A}$ and $\mathcal{C}$:

Init : $\mathcal{A}$ sends the challenge access policy $\mathbb{A}^* = \left(M^*_{\ell^* \times t^*}, \rho^*\right)$ to $\mathcal{C}$.

Setup : The simulator $\mathcal{S}$ chooses random values $a, b, s, z \in \mathbb{Z}_p^*$, $g \in \mathbb{G}$, and computes terms $g^a, g^b, g^s, e(g,g)^{abs}, e(g,g)^z$ of the assumption. Then $\mathcal{S}$ sends $g^a, g^b, g^s, e(g,g)^{abs}, e(g,g)^z$ to the challenger $\mathcal{C}$. $\mathcal{C}$ randomly picks $x', q_1, q_2, \delta, \{z_1, z_2, \cdots, z_k\} \in \mathbb{Z}_p^*$, then calculates $g = g$, $u = g^b$, $h = g^a$, $w = g^{s/q_2}$, $v = g^{s/q_1}$, and $e(g,g)^\alpha = e(g,g)^{ab}e(g,g)^{x'}$, which implies $\alpha = ab + x'$. $\mathcal{C}$ sends $mpk_{CHET} = \left\{g, u, h, w, v, e(g,g)^\alpha, e(g,h)^\delta, \{h_i^\alpha = h^{z_i\alpha}\}_{i=1}^k \{g_i = g^{z_i}\}_{i=1}^k, h^\alpha, h^\beta, H_1, H_2\right\}$ to $\mathcal{A}$.

Phase1 : $\mathcal{A}$ asks $\mathcal{C}$ for the secret key of the attribute set and the identity (ID_{TM}, S), where $S = \{A_1, A_2, \cdots, A_u\}$ and $ID_{TM} = (I_1, \cdots, I_b)$. When S satisfies the challenge access policy $\mathbb{A}^*$, $\mathcal{C}$ responds with $\bot$. Otherwise, $\mathcal{C}$ randomly chooses $r, r_1, r_2, \cdots, r_m, R \in \mathbb{Z}_p$, and calculates $sk_0 = g^\alpha w^r$, $sk_1 = g^r$, $sk_4 = g^R$, $sk_5 = h^\delta \cdot \left(h \cdot \sum_{i=1,}^b h_i^{I_i}\right)^{\alpha r} \cdot h^{\beta R}$, $sk_6 = \{h_i^{\alpha r}\}_{i\in[b+1,n]}$, $sk_7 = h^r$. For $i \in I = \{i|i\in[l^*] \wedge \rho^*(i)\in S\}$, $\mathcal{C}$ computes $\left\{sk_{2,i} = \prod_{j\in[1,t^*]} g^{r_i M^*_{i,j}}, sk_{3,i} = \prod_{j\in[1,t^*]}\left(u^{A_i}h\right)^{r_i M^*_{i,j}}v^{-r}\right\}_{i\in[1,u]\wedge\rho^*(i)\in S}$, otherwise, $\mathcal{C}$ computes $\left\{sk_{2,i} = g^{r_i}, sk_{3,i} = \left(u^{A_i}h\right)^{r_i}v^{-r}\right\}_{i\in[1,u]\wedge\rho^*(i)\notin S}$. $\mathcal{C}$ sends the secret key $sk_{(S,ID)} = \left\{sk_0, sk_1, \{sk_{2,i}, \ sk_{3,i}\}_{i\in u}, sk_4, sk_5, sk_6, sk_7\right\}$.

Challenge : $\mathcal{A}$ declares two messages m_0, m_1 with the same length and a target identity ID_{TO}^* that have not been queried before, and submits them to $\mathcal{C}$. For the access matrix $M_{l^* \times t^*}^*$, $\mathcal{C}$ randomly picks $v_2, v_3, \ldots, v_{t^*} \in \mathbb{Z}_p$, then $\overrightarrow{y} = (s, y_2, \cdots, y_{t^*})^T$. $\mathcal{C}$ calculates the shared vector $(\lambda_1, \cdots, \lambda_{\ell^*})^T = M^* \overrightarrow{y}$ and selects at least l^* attribute modules $IT_i = \{C_{i,1}, C_{i,2}, C_{i,2}\}$ from the intermedia ciphertext pool IT which is generated in $Hash_{Offline}$, where $C_{i,1} = w^{\lambda'_i} v^{t_i}$, $C_{i,2} = (u^{x_i} h)^{-t_i}$, $C_{i,3} = g^{t_i}$. Then for $j \in [1, l^*]$, calculate $C_{j,4} = \lambda_j - \lambda'_j$,

$$C_{j,5} = -t_j \cdot (\rho^*(j) - x_j), \text{ and } C = g^s, \ ct = (h^\beta)^s, \ ct_2 = \left(g \cdot \sum_{i=1,}^{a} g_i^{I_i}\right)^{as},$$

$$ct_3 = \left(g \cdot \sum_{i=1,}^{a} g_i^{I_i}\right)^s, \ ct_4 = \left(g \cdot \sum_{i=1,}^{a} g_i^{I_i}\right)^{as^2}. \text{ To perform the operation, a ran-}$$

dom number r is chosen and a coin is flipped to obtain a random bit $b \in 0, 1$. Following that, the value of $ct1, ct0$ is computed as $ct_1 = r \oplus H_2\left(e(g, h)^{\delta s}\right)$, $ct_0 = m_b \oplus H_2\left(e(g, g)^{abs} \cdot e(g, g)^{x's}\right) = m_b \oplus H_2\left(T \cdot e(g, g)^{x's}\right)$. $\mathcal{C}$ returns $CT = \left(C, \{C_{j,1}, C_{j,2}, C_{j,3}, C_{j,4}, C_{j,5}\}_{j \in [1, \ell]}, ct, ct_0, ct_1, ct_2, ct_3, ct_4\right)$ to the attacker $\mathcal{A}$.

Phase2 : It is identical with *Phase*1. The restriction is $\mathcal{A}$ cannot query for the target identity ID_{TO}^* and none of the queried set S meet the requirements of the specified challenge access structure $\mathbb{A}^*$.

Guess : After receiving the guess b' from $\mathcal{A}$, which belongs to the set $\{0, 1\}$, $\mathcal{C}$ proceeds as follows: If $b' = b$, $\mathcal{C}$ makes a guess that $T = e(g, g)^{abs}$, indicating that $\left(g, g^a, g^b, g^s, e(g, g)^{abs}\right)$ forms a valid DBDH tuple. Otherwise, if $b' \neq b$, $\mathcal{C}$ makes a guess that $T = e(g, g)^z$, implying that $\left(g, g^a, g^b, g^s, e(g, g)^z\right)$ represents a random tuple.

If $\mathcal{A}$ can attack the CPA security of our OPCHAR scheme with a non-negligible advantage, then there is a polynomial time $\mathcal{C}$ who can break DBDH with the same advantage. However, it is known that DBDH problem is computationally difficult to break. Hence, we can conclude that OPCHAR provides selective CPA security.

B.2   Security Proof of Theorem 2

Proof. If there exists a polynomial-time attacker $\mathcal{A}$ who can break the indistinguishability security of OPCHAR with a non-negligible advantage, then it is feasible to construct a polynomial-time challenger $\mathcal{C}$ to compromise the indistinguishability of CHET that our scheme based with the same probability. The game between $\mathcal{A}$ and $\mathcal{C}$ is as follows:

Setup : $\mathcal{C}$ runs Setup(1^k) $\rightarrow$ (mpk, msk) and sends mpk to the attacker $\mathcal{A}$, where $mpk \leftarrow (mpk_{ABET}, mpk_{CHET})$, $msk \leftarrow (msk_{ABET}, msk_{CHET})$.

Challenge : $\mathcal{A}$ specifies two transaction m_0 and m_1, an access policy $\mathbb{A}^* = \left(M_{\ell^* \times t^*}^*, \rho^*\right)$, identities ID_{TO} and ID_{TO}', and sends these parameters to $\mathcal{C}$. $\mathcal{C}$ firstly calls $Hash_{Offline}(mpk)$ to generate an intermediate ciphertext pool IT and selects ℓ^* attribute modules IT_{attr}. Then run $Hash_{Online}(mpk, IT, m_0, \mathbb{A}, ID_{TO}, SC_{TO})$ to get the (h_0, r_0) contained in $(Hash_0, CT_0, Sig_0)$, and run $Hash_{Online}(mpk, IT, m_1, \mathbb{A}, ID'_{TO}, SC'_{TO})$ to generate (h_1, r_1) contained in $(Hash_1, CT_1, Sig_1)$. Futhermore, $\mathcal{C}$ generates the secret key sk_{TO} from running $KeyGen_{TM}(msk, S, ID_{TO})$, where S satisfied the access policy. $\mathcal{C}$ inputs sk_{TO} to $Adapt(mpk, sk_{TO}, ID_{TO}, SC_{TO}, m_1, CT_0, Sig_0, Hash_0)$ for the collision finding and generates (h'_0, r'_0), and note that the transaction m_0 is adapted to m_1 by its owner ID_{TO} instead of other transaction modifiers. Finally, $\mathcal{C}$ randomly selects a coin b from the set $\{0, 1\}$ and provides (h_b, r_b) to $\mathcal{A}$.

Guess :$\mathcal{A}$ returns a guess b'. $\mathcal{A}$ is the winner if $b' = b$.

If the CHET holds the indistinguishability, then our OPCHAR scheme also holds this security.

B.3   Security Proof of Theorem 3

Proof. To demonstrate the security of collision resistance, we employ a series of games. For $i \in [0, 3]$, $Pr[S_i]$ is defined as the success probability of the attacker $\mathcal{A}$ in the Game i. Furthermore, the number of queries of $\mathcal{A}$ to the hash oracle is denoted by q.

The specific process of the games goes as follows.

Game 0: This refers to the initial collision-resistance security game as outlined in Sect. 3.3, in which an adversary denoted as $\mathcal{A}$ engages in a simulation with a challenger denoted as $\mathcal{C}$ within the context of OPCHAR. So, we can get that

$$\text{Adv}_{OPCHAR,\mathcal{A}}^{CR}(k) = \Pr[S_0] \tag{8}$$

Game 1: Game 1 is similar to Game 0, except that challenger $\mathcal{C}$'s task is to predict the index $i^* \in [1, q]$ that corresponds to the hash query in the **Query**. $\mathcal{A}$ attack the hash output $(Hash^*, CT^*, Sig^*)$ by $\mathcal{C}$ by $\mathcal{C}$. Then, $\mathcal{C}$ stores $(Hash^*, CT^*, Sig^*)$ and the ephemeral trapdoor etd^*. If $\mathcal{C}$ guesses wrong during the simulation, the game aborts. If $\mathcal{C}$ guesses correctly, then $\mathcal{A}$ wins the Game 1. Therefore, we can get that

$$\Pr[S_0] = q \cdot \Pr[S_1] \tag{9}$$

Game 2: In this game, when $\mathcal{C}$ recieves an adapt query for $(Hash, CT^*, Sig)$ from $\mathcal{A}$, $\mathcal{C}$ directly adapt using etd^* instead of decrypting the component C to get the ephemeral trapdoor. Others are like Game 1. If the ABET scheme is perfectly correct, then the winning probability for $\mathcal{A}$ in this game is equivalent to that in Game 1. So

$$\Pr[S_1] = \Pr[S_2] \tag{10}$$

Game 3: As Game 2 except the simulation of the hash queries. In the i^*-th $Hash$ query, the challenger $\mathcal{C}$ encrypts $0^{|etd^*|}$ by the ABET instead of the ephemeral trapdoor etd^* to get C^* and sends C^* to the attacker $\mathcal{A}$.

Claim 1. *If ABET scheme composing OPCHAR is IND-CCA2 secure, Game 2 and Game 3 are indistinguishable and*

$$|\Pr[S_3] - \Pr[S_2]| \leqslant Adv_{ABET,\mathcal{C}}^{IND-CCA2}(k). \tag{11}$$

Proof. To proof claim 1, we construct an IND-CCA2 challenger $\mathcal{C}_1$ to perform interpolation between Game 2 and Game 3 effectively and set $\mathcal{C}$ as an attacker against ABET. The following proof is consistent with the Game 2 and Game 3, where etd^* is encrypted in Game 2 and $0^{|etd^*|}$ is encrypted in Game 3, and $\mathcal{C}$ can not tell them.

- $\mathcal{C}_1$ runs *ABET.Setup* and send mpk_{ABET} to $\mathcal{C}$. Then $\mathcal{C}$ completes the remainder of *Setup* and sends public parameter $mpk = (pk_{CHET}, mpk_{ABET}, mpk_{DS})$ to $\mathcal{A}$.
- For key generation queries from $\mathcal{A}$, $\mathcal{C}$ sends them to $\mathcal{C}_1$. Then $\mathcal{C}_1$ runs *ABET.Keygen* to generate the attributes decryption key ssk and sends ssk to $\mathcal{C}$. Then $\mathcal{C}$ sends (ssk, sk_{CHET}) to $\mathcal{A}$.
- When $\mathcal{A}$ issues adapt queries $(Hash, CT, Sig)$ to $\mathcal{C}$, $\mathcal{C}$ sends CT to $\mathcal{C}_1$. Then $\mathcal{C}_1$ decrypt the ciphertext to get etd and returns etd to $\mathcal{C}$. $\mathcal{C}$ then runs *CHET.adapt* to find collision $(Hash', CT', Sig')$ and outputs collision to $\mathcal{A}$.
- Upon input a hash query of $(m, \mathbb{A})$ from $\mathcal{A}$, where none of the decryption keys in key generation query satisfy the policy $\mathbb{A}$. $\mathcal{C}$ runs *CHET.Hash* to generate $(h_{CHET}, r_{CHET}, etd)$ and then sends etd and $\mathbb{A}$ to $\mathcal{C}_1$. $\mathcal{C}_1$ encrypts etd to get the ciphertext component CT and returns CT to $\mathcal{C}$. $\mathcal{C}$ guesses the index i^* of hash query that will be attack by $\mathcal{A}$. In the i^*-th hash query, $\mathcal{C}$ runs *CHET.hash* to generate $(h_{CHET}^*, r_{CHET}^*, etd^*)$ and saves etd^*. Then $\mathcal{C}$ sends $(m_0, m_1) = (etd^*, 0^{|etd^*|})$ and the access policy $\mathbb{A}$ to $\mathcal{C}_1$. Then $\mathcal{C}_1$ flips a random coin $b \in \{0,1\}$, and runs $ABET.Enc_{offline}(mpk_{ABET}) \to IT^*$ and $ABET.Enc_{Online}(mpk_{ABET}, IT^*, m_b, \mathbb{A}) \to CT^*$ to encrypt m_b and returns CT^* to $\mathcal{C}$. $\mathcal{C}$ stores and outputs $(Hash^*, CT^*, Sig^*)$ to $\mathcal{A}$. If $\mathcal{C}$ guesses wrong, the game aborts. Note that $\mathcal{C}$ can generate the signature component Sig honestly.
- Then $\mathcal{A}$ queries the collision again. If $\mathcal{C}$ recieves an adapt query $(m', Hash, CT^*, Sig)$, $\mathcal{C}$ first verifies whether *verify* $(mpk, Hash^*, CT^*, Sig^*)$ outputs 1. If the result is equal to 1, $\mathcal{C}$ directly runs *CHET.Adapt* with etd^* instead of decrypting the ciphertext CT.

If $\mathcal{C}_1$ encrypts $m_0 = etd^*$, then the game is consistent with Game 2; Otherwise, $\mathcal{C}_1$ encrypts $m_1 = 0^{|etd^*|}$, and we simulate Game 3. At last, we complete the proof of Claim 1.

Claim 2. *In Game 3, for all PPT attackers $\mathcal{A}$, if CHET is collision-resistance, then*

$$|\Pr[S_3]| \leqslant Adv_{CHET,\mathcal{C}}^{CR}(k) \tag{12}$$

Proof. To proof Claim 2, let $\mathcal{C}$ as a PPT attacker who can break the collision-resistance of CHET, and we construct a collision resistance challenger $\mathcal{C}_2$.

- C_2 runs $CHET.Setup\left(1^k\right)$ to get sk_{CHET} and pk_{CHET} of CHET, and sends PK_{CHET} and SK_{CHET} to C. Then, C runs $ABET.setup\left(1^k\right)$ and $DS.setup\left(1^k\right)$ to complete the remaining steps of $Setup$, and sends the system public key $mpk = (pk_{CHET}, mpk_{ABET}, mpk_{DS})$ to A.
- When A query a key generation to C, C can honestly generate a decryption key sk with self-generated msk_{ABET} and sk_{CHET} sent by C_2.
- If A issues an adapt query of $(m', Hash, CT, Sig)$, C firstly verify whether the output of $Verify\,(mpk, Hash, CT, Sig)$ is equal to 1. If it passes the verification, C performs the decryption algorithm $ABET.Dec$ to get etd, then C performs the adapt query to C_2 for (h, r, m, m', etd), where (h, r, m) are contained in $Hash$ component. C_2 runs $CHET.Adapt$ to get the collision r' and returns r' to C. Finally, C sends $(Hash', CT', Sig')$ to A. Note that the hash value in $Hash$ has not been changed.
- For a hash query $(m, \mathbb{A})$ from A, C performs a hash query of m to C_2. C_2 outputs the hash result (h, r, etd) to C. Then C runs $ABET.Enc_{Offline}$ and $ABET.Enc_{Online}$ to encrypt etd and completes the remainder of $Hash$, then C sends $(Hash, CT, Sig)$ to A. In the i^*-th hash query, after obtaining (h^*, r^*, etd^*) from C_2, C saves etd^* and encrypts $0^{|etd^*|}$ to get the ciphertext CT^*. At last, C returns $(Hash^*, CT^*, Sig^*)$ to A.
- A does the adapt query again. For the received $(m', Hash, CT^*, Sig)$, C directly performs the adapt query in form of (m, m', h, r, etd^*) to C_2 without the decryption of CT^*, C finds the collision r' and sends r' to C. In the end, C returns $(Hash^*, CT^*, Sig^*)$ to A.

If A can output a collision $\left(Hash^*, CT^*, Sig^*, Hash^{*\prime}, CT^{*\prime}, Sig^{*\prime}\right)$ for the attacked i^*-th query, where the hash value h_{CHET} in $Hash^*$ and $Hash^{*\prime}$ are the same. Then C can output a collision $\left(h^*, m^*, r^*, m^{*\prime}, r^{*\prime}\right)$ to C_2. Eventually, we proof the Claim 2.

We can compute the following with Eqs.(8)–(12):

$$
\begin{aligned}
Adv^{CR}_{OPCHAR,A} &= \Pr\left[S_0\right] = q \cdot \Pr\left[S_1\right] = q \cdot \Pr\left[S_2\right] \\
&\leqslant Adv^{IND-CCA2}_{ABET,C}(k) + \Pr\left[S_3\right] \\
&\leqslant dv^{IND-CCA2}_{ABET,C}(k) + Adv^{CR}_{CHET,C}(k)
\end{aligned}
\tag{13}
$$

B.4   Security Proof of Theorem 4

The concrete proof is similar to the proof of theorem $B.3$ of [29].

References

1. Agrawal, S., Chase, M.: FAME: fast attribute-based message encryption. In: Proceedings of the 2017 ACM SIGSAC Conference on Computer and Communications Security, pp. 665–682 (2017)
2. Akinyele, J.A., et al.: Charm: a framework for rapidly prototyping cryptosystems. J. Cryptogr. Eng. **3**, 111–128 (2013)

3. Ashritha, K., Sindhu, M., Lakshmy, K.: Redactable blockchain using enhanced chameleon hash function. In: 2019 5th International Conference on Advanced Computing & Communication Systems (ICACCS), pp. 323–328. IEEE (2019)
4. Ateniese, G., Magri, B., Venturi, D., Andrade, E.: Redactable blockchain–or–rewriting history in bitcoin and friends. In: 2017 IEEE European Symposium on Security and Privacy (EuroS&P), pp. 111–126. IEEE (2017)
5. Beimel, A.: Secure schemes for secret sharing and key distribution (1996)
6. Boneh, D., Boyen, X., Goh, E.-J.: Hierarchical identity based encryption with constant size ciphertext. In: Cramer, R. (ed.) EUROCRYPT 2005. LNCS, vol. 3494, pp. 440–456. Springer, Heidelberg (2005). https://doi.org/10.1007/11426639_26
7. Cai, W., Wang, Z., Ernst, J.B., Hong, Z., Feng, C., Leung, V.C.: Decentralized applications: the blockchain-empowered software system. IEEE Access 6, 53019–53033 (2018)
8. Camenisch, J., Derler, D., Krenn, S., Pöhls, H.C., Samelin, K., Slamanig, D.: Chameleon-hashes with ephemeral trapdoors. In: Fehr, S. (ed.) PKC 2017. LNCS, vol. 10175, pp. 152–182. Springer, Heidelberg (2017). https://doi.org/10.1007/978-3-662-54388-7_6
9. Canetti, R., Fuller, B., Paneth, O., Reyzin, L., Smith, A.: Reusable fuzzy extractors for low-entropy distributions. J. Cryptol. 34, 1–33 (2021)
10. Canetti, R., Halevi, S., Katz, J.: Chosen-Ciphertext Security from Identity-Based Encryption. In: Cachin, C., Camenisch, J.L. (eds.) EUROCRYPT 2004. LNCS, vol. 3027, pp. 207–222. Springer, Heidelberg (2004). https://doi.org/10.1007/978-3-540-24676-3_13
11. People's Republic of China, N.P.C.: "Personal information protection law, Aug 20 (2021). http://www.npc.gov.cn/npc/c30834/202108/a8c4e3672c74491a80b53a172bb753fe.shtml
12. Cui, H., Wan, Z., Deng, R.H., Wang, G., Li, Y.: Efficient and expressive keyword search over encrypted data in cloud. IEEE Trans. Dependable Secure Comput. 15(3), 409–422 (2016)
13. Derler, D., Samelin, K., Slamanig, D., Striecks, C.: Fine-grained and controlled rewriting in blockchains: Chameleon-hashing gone attribute-based. Cryptology ePrint Archive (2019)
14. Deuber, D., Magri, B., Thyagarajan, S.A.K.: Redactable blockchain in the permissionless setting. In: 2019 IEEE Symposium on Security and Privacy (SP), pp. 124–138. IEEE (2019)
15. Duan, P., Wang, J., Zhang, Y., Ma, Z., Luo, S.: Policy-based chameleon hash with black-box traceability for redactable blockchain in iot. Electronics 12(7), 1646 (2023)
16. European Union, R.: General Data Protection Regulation, Jul 13. (2016), https://gdpr-info.eu/
17. Hohenberger, S., Waters, B.: Online/offline attribute-based encryption. In: Krawczyk, H. (ed.) PKC 2014. LNCS, vol. 8383, pp. 293–310. Springer, Heidelberg (2014). https://doi.org/10.1007/978-3-642-54631-0_17
18. Huang, K., et al.: Building redactable consortium blockchain for industrial internet-of-things. IEEE Trans. Industr. Inf. 15(6), 3670–3679 (2019)
19. Krawczyk, H., Rabin, T.: Chameleon hashing and signatures. Cryptology ePrint Archive (1998)
20. Liu, Z., Cao, Z., Wong, D.S.: Blackbox traceable cp-abe: how to catch people leaking their keys by selling decryption devices on ebay. In: Proceedings of the 2013 ACM SIGSAC Conference on Computer & Communications Security, pp. 475–486 (2013)

21. Merkle, R.C.: A certified digital signature. In: Brassard, G. (ed.) CRYPTO 1989. LNCS, vol. 435, pp. 218–238. Springer, New York (1990). https://doi.org/10.1007/0-387-34805-0_21

22. Middleton, C.: Bitcoin blockchain contains porn, say researchers. Not news, say coders, Mar 21 (2018). https://internetofbusiness.com/bitcoin-blockchain-contains-illegal-porn-say-researchers/

23. Nakamoto, S.: Bitcoin: A peer-to-peer electronic cash system. Decentralized Bus. Rev. 21260 (2008)

24. Naor, D., Naor, M., Lotspiech, J.: Revocation and tracing schemes for stateless receivers. In: Kilian, J. (ed.) CRYPTO 2001. LNCS, vol. 2139, pp. 41–62. Springer, Heidelberg (2001). https://doi.org/10.1007/3-540-44647-8_3

25. Oracle: VirtualBox. https://www.virtualbox.org/

26. Panwar, G., Vishwanathan, R., Misra, S.: Retrace: revocable and traceable blockchain rewrites using attribute-based cryptosystems. In: Proceedings of the 26th ACM Symposium on Access Control Models and Technologies, pp. 103–114 (2021)

27. Schellekens, M.: Does regulation of illegal content need reconsideration in light of blockchains? Inter. J. Law Inform. Technol. 27(3), 292–305 (2019)

28. Taylor, P.: Global blockchain solutions spending 2017-2024, May 23 (2022).https://www.statista.com/statistics/800426/worldwide-blockchain-solutions-spending/,

29. Tian, Y., Li, N., Li, Y., Szalachowski, P., Zhou, J.: Policy-based chameleon hash for blockchain rewriting with black-box accountability. In: Annual Computer Security Applications Conference, pp. 813–828 (2020)

30. Boneh, D., Boyen, X.: Efficient selective-ID secure identity-based encryption without random oracles. In: Cachin, C., Camenisch, J.L. (eds.) EUROCRYPT 2004. LNCS, vol. 3027, pp. 223–238. Springer, Heidelberg (2004). https://doi.org/10.1007/978-3-540-24676-3_14

31. Xu, S., Huang, X., Yuan, J., Li, Y., Deng, R.H.: Accountable and fine-grained controllable rewriting in blockchains. IEEE Trans. Inf. Forensics Secur. 18, 101–116 (2022)

32. Xu, S., Ning, J., Ma, J., Huang, X., Deng, R.H.: K-time modifiable and epoch-based redactable blockchain. IEEE Trans. Inf. Forensics Secur. 16, 4507–4520 (2021)

33. Xu, S., Ning, J., Ma, J., Xu, G., Yuan, J., Deng, R.H.: Revocable policy-based chameleon hash. In: Bertino, E., Shulman, H., Waidner, M. (eds.) ESORICS 2021. LNCS, vol. 12972, pp. 327–347. Springer, Cham (2021). https://doi.org/10.1007/978-3-030-88418-5_16

Cross Chain and Interoperability
of Blockchain

Optimized Cross-Chain Mechanisms for Secure and Reliable Domain Information Synchronization in Blockchain-Driven Networks

Linkai Zhu[1], Xiaolian Zhu[1], Lihui Sun[1], Shanwen Hu[2(✉)], Siyu Chen[1], and Xiaomin Guo[1]

[1] School of Information Technology, Hebei University of Economics and Business, Shijiazhuang 050061, China
{linkai,xiaolianzhu,sunlihui}@hueb.edu.cn
[2] Faculty of Data Science, City University of Macau, Macau 999078, China
D23092100358@cityu.mo

Abstract. This research introduces an innovative consortium blockchain system designed to enhance the scalability and reliability of DNS resolution on a global scale. At its core, the system utilizes a mainchain for essential communication, supported by various sidechains that synchronize domain information. Initially relying on atomic swaps for transaction security, the system has undergone significant advancements to improve cross-chain interactions. Key enhancements include a dualphase voting and verification process for improved transaction validation, a reputation-based committee election system to prevent malicious activities, and an enhanced sidechain protocol with advanced hashing and a Random Beacon for quicker consensus building. These developments target the security challenges in cross-chain data exchanges, thereby bolstering the transaction mechanism's resilience and efficiency. The result is a more secure, efficient, and adaptable cross-chain framework, optimally designed to meet the evolving requirements of domain resolution in today's rapidly changing digital landscape.

Keywords: Blockchain · Synchronization · Domain Name System (DNS)

1 Introduction

The Domain Name System (DNS), a pivotal element of the Internet's architecture, plays a crucial role in translating human-readable domain names into machine-readable IP addresses. This process is essential for ensuring the seamless functioning and accessibility of the Internet. With the exponential growth of the Internet, the DNS faces increasing demands. These demands encompass not only the sheer volume of domain name queries but also evolving challenges in the realms of security, privacy, and operational efficiency.

J. Zhu et al. (Eds.): CBCS 2023, CCIS 2098, pp. 157–166, 2024.
https://doi.org/10.1007/978-981-97-3203-6_8

Addressing the aforementioned DNS challenges necessitates a paradigm shift, and herein lies the potential of blockchain technology. Blockchain's core characteristics-decentralization, immutability, and transparency-make it a formidable candidate for redefining DNS infrastructure. A blockchain-based DNS system promises enhanced security and resilience, reducing vulnerabilities to cyber-attacks and ensuring a more trustworthy domain name resolution process, particularly vital in an era of escalating cybersecurity threats.

The current landscape of domain synchronization is dominated by centralized or semi-centralized models, which inherently suffer from several drawbacks. These include susceptibility to single points of failure, potential data inconsistencies, and heightened risk of targeted cyber-attacks. Furthermore, the integration of blockchain technology in domain synchronization is still in its nascent stages, with existing solutions struggling with issues of scalability, cross-chain interoperability, and efficient handling of sensitive data across diverse blockchain platforms.

To address these issues, this paper introduces a novel cross-chain solution, underpinned by a consortium blockchain framework. This framework is designed to leverage the strengths of blockchain while mitigating its limitations, particularly in the context of DNS. The proposed model features a mainchain responsible for orchestrating cross-chain interactions and multiple sidechains dedicated to specific domain synchronization tasks. Key innovations of this model include an advanced two-stage voting and verification protocol for enhanced security, a reputation-based committee election system for decentralized governance, and state-of-the-art encryption techniques for heightened data privacy. This approach aims to revolutionize domain synchronization, offering a scalable, secure, and efficient mechanism for managing DNS queries in a blockchain environment.

In this research, we present the following key contributions:

1. We introduce an innovative cross-chain architecture based on blockchain technology, specifically designed to enhance domain information synchronization within a domain synchronization network powered by blockchain.
2. We develop a unique two-phase voting and verification procedure to improve the accuracy and dependability of cross-chain transaction validation, offering a more stringent and trustworthy verification framework.
3. We establish a novel committee election system, rooted in reputation metrics, on the primary blockchain. This system aims to mitigate the negative influence of untrustworthy participants in the validation process, thus ensuring more secure and dependable cross-chain interactions.

The primary objective of this study is to present and elaborate on the newly proposed cross-chain architecture, highlighting its advantages in creating a more secure, reliable, and efficient domain synchronization network. Furthermore, we aim to conduct a comprehensive assessment of its performance relative to current methodologies. Our goal is to provide a significant advancement in the domain of DNS domain resolution, contributing to a more fortified and efficient global internet infrastructure.

2   Related Work

2.1   Cross-Chain Solutions

The Notary Mechanism. The Notary Mechanism, as elucidated in sources [1,2], serves as a cornerstone for transaction validation, ensuring their accuracy and security. However, this approach introduces a level of centralization and adds to the operational complexities, which might, in turn, impinge upon the system's overall efficiency.

Hash Time-Locked Contracts (HTLCs). A breakthrough in the form of HTLCs, detailed in [3], has paved the way for atomic swaps between blockchains without the need for intermediary notaries. This innovation significantly lowers the risks tied to notary node failures or adversarial actions, and it helps in cushioning the transactions from the impacts of market fluctuations. Importantly, HTLCs have the added advantage of reducing the transactional load, thereby streamlining the efficiency and enhancing the user interface in cross-chain transactions.

The Sidechain Mechanism. The sidechain scheme, as investigated in references [4–6], represents a strategic method to facilitate cross-chain transactions. It effectively links a main blockchain with auxiliary chains, maintaining the main chain's operational integrity while offering enhanced scalability and fault tolerance. A caveat, however, is the potential decline in system efficiency due to the resource allocation from the main chain.

The Relay Chain Mechanism. Advancing beyond the sidechain concept, the Relay Chain mechanism, which involves using an external public blockchain, orchestrates transactions across diverse blockchain systems. While it brings benefits in terms of scalability and fault tolerance, it also encounters challenges related to centralization and the intricacies of transaction processing.

These mechanisms, each with its unique attributes and applications, collectively enrich the blockchain field, striking a balance between ensuring secure, authentic transactions and achieving seamless cross-chain interoperability.

2.2   Domain Information Synchronization Techniques

Blockchain-Enhanced DNS Models. In the dynamic field of Domain Name System (DNS) development, the intersection between traditional domain name services and blockchain's advanced framework is increasingly prominent. This convergence has given rise to blockchain-based DNS systems, which markedly differ from the conventional centralized DNS models. These new systems offer a decentralized approach, significantly enhancing resilience and security [7,8]. Insights into the advantages and challenges of this integration are discussed in a ScienceDirect article, focusing on the decentralization aspect of blockchain within DNS and the obstacles to its broader adoption [9,10].

Architectural Designs in Blockchain DNS. Further, a comprehensive analysis on ResearchGate delves into the specific architectural designs of blockchain-powered DNS. This study highlights the ability of blockchain to reliably manage databases in decentralized environments, where traditional trust mechanisms are absent [11,12]. Moreover, there is a growing discourse around blockchain's potential role in the evolution of domain names. This conversation centers on how blockchain technology can significantly enhance the security and transparency of the DNS, which are vital for the uninterrupted operation of the internet [13]. Current research and development efforts are focused on addressing the limitations of traditional DNS frameworks, employing the robust capabilities of blockchain to forge a more secure and reliable internet infrastructure.

2.3 Sidechain

Sidechains, integral to blockchain innovation, function as independent protocols linked to a main blockchain. They enhance the main blockchain's scalability and interoperability while operating autonomously. Pegged sidechains, introduced by Back et al. (2014), enable asset transfer across multiple blockchains, addressing scalability challenges [14]. Building on this, Johnny et al. (2016) introduced "Strong Federations," reducing centralized third-party reliance and enhancing blockchain interoperability [15]. Lerner (2015) developed Rootstock (RSK), a smart contract platform aligned with Bitcoin, focusing on scalability and speed [16]. In 2016, ConsenSys developed BTC Relay, a bridge between Bitcoin and Ethereum, facilitating secure transaction verification and enhancing network communication [17]. Lastly, Kiayias and Zindros (2019) introduced a Proof-of-Work Sidechain mechanism at the International Conference on Financial Cryptography and Data Security, furthering blockchain network interoperability [18].

3   System Architecture

3.1   The Domain Information Synchronization Cross-Chain Framework

The framework presented here introduces a cross-chain architecture that utilizes a consortium blockchain, designed to achieve efficient and secure domain information synchronization within a blockchain-based domain synchronization network, as illustrated in Fig. 1. Central to this architecture is the concept of a mainchain, serving as a relay platform, with various sidechains connected to it for enabling cross-chain interactions. This consortium blockchain is characterized by its permissioned nature, allowing only verified entities to participate, a key aspect in protecting the sensitive data involved in DNS resolution. The aim of this framework is to meet the growing demands of global DNS resolution, fostering a distributed but cohesive method for managing domain information securely and dependably.

To meet the expanding global demands of DNS domain resolution, the framework proposed in this article adopts a cross-chain model aimed at enhancing

Mainchain

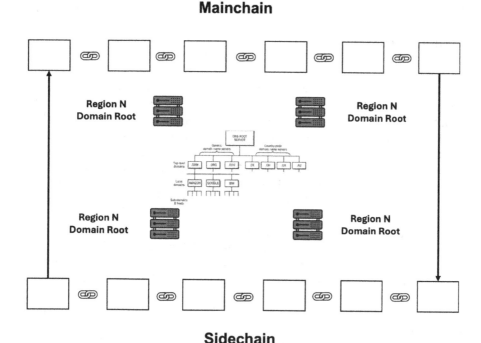

Fig. 1. The Domain Information Synchronization Cross-Chain Framework

the synchronization efficiency of domain information across different regional domain roots. This model is based on a consortium blockchain and utilizes a Proof-of-Stake (PoS) consensus protocol to manage transactions both within and across the chains. Under the guidance of this model, the framework provides a structured mechanism for synchronizing domain information between various regional roots. The adoption of the PoS consensus protocol ensures the security and efficiency of the transaction verification process, thereby supporting a reliable domain information sharing environment within the global digital ecosystem.

Specifically, this cross-chain model, through the features of the consortium blockchain, allows participants to interact in a controlled environment, which is crucial for maintaining the security of sensitive data involved in DNS resolution. Moreover, the PoS consensus protocol ensures that the contributions of network participants are aligned with their stakes, thereby enhancing the security and stability of the network. This mechanism not only reduces the energy consumption in the transaction verification process but also increases the speed and efficiency of transaction processing.

The framework also takes into account the heterogeneity and dynamism of different regional networks, adapting to a variety of network environments through cross-chain technology. This method of cross-chain communication allows for efficient and secure synchronization of information between regional domain roots, meeting the growing demands of global DNS resolution. Through this advanced cross-chain architecture, we provide a reliable and efficient solution for the global expansion of DNS domain resolution.

This research introduces an approach that incorporates blockchain technology to enhance the security and stability of domain name systems, specifically designed to meet the essential needs of key organizations and institutions. Utilizing the decentralization and immutability inherent in blockchain, this method significantly improves data integrity and system robustness in DNS operations. The implementation of distributed storage technology is central to this strategy, serving as the core of a decentralized management system for off-chain DNS domain data. This approach effectively mitigates single point of failure risks and reduces the impact of centralized control and potential cyber threats, thereby elevating the system's dependability and accessibility.

The research further introduces an innovative multi-stakeholder governance model for root zone management, which distinctly separates authorization and publication functions. Reflecting the collaborative nature of DNS, this model involves various independent entities in data handling and distribution processes. Such a framework not only enhances system robustness but also addresses the challenges of centralization, fitting well with the globally distributed governance of DNS infrastructure.

In maintaining domain name system consistency and dependability, the role of sidechain and cross-chain technologies is crucial. These technologies effectively meet key DNS needs, such as high availability, and tackle issues related to latency and throughput, vital for DNS systems to function efficiently.

By integrating blockchain and distributed storage within a multi-stakeholder governance structure, the research satisfactorily meets the requirements for a secure, scalable, and decentralized DNS system. This holistic approach presents a modern solution to traditional DNS system challenges, suitably matching the needs of the rapidly changing digital world.

3.2   Mainchain as a Relay Platform

The mainchain operates as the nexus for cross-chain interactions within the proposed framework. Initially, a simplistic atomic swap transaction was employed on the mainchain to safeguard sensitive data transactions among participants. However, to bolster the security framework and ensure rigorous validation of cross-chain transactions, a two-stage voting and verification mechanism has been proposed to replace the initial atomic swap transaction. Moreover, a reputation scoring-based committee election mechanism is introduced on the mainchain to ensure that only credible and responsible members partake in the voting and transaction validation processes. These modifications aim to mitigate the potential adverse impacts of dishonest members and foster a more secure and reliable cross-chain communication infrastructure.

3.3 Communication

In the cross-chain ecosystem, pivotal operations include transactions between the mainchain and sidechains. While each sidechain functions autonomously, they maintain connectivity with the mainchain for inter-chain communications. To streamline this process, a sophisticated sidechain protocol has been developed, focusing on accelerating the selection of voting committees and the consolidation of votes. This protocol utilizes advanced hash functions and implements a Random Beacon mechanism, ensuring rapid, secure committee elections and efficient vote aggregation within a harmonized network framework. Furthermore, to address security concerns inherent in sensitive data exchanges during cross-chain activities, the protocol integrates stringent data encryption and privacy safeguards. These enhancements are crucial in accelerating the transaction speed within the cross-chain framework, equipping it to effectively meet the demands of contemporary domain resolution systems in an increasingly digital global landscape.

3.4 Two-Stage Voting and Verification Mechanism

The Two-Stage Voting and Verification Mechanism is essential for a secure and efficient system to verify cross-chain transactions. This mechanism is designed for detailed scrutiny and confirmation of transactions, leveraging a committee's collective evaluation and supervision. It employs a dual-level assessment - an initial basic screening followed by a more thorough investigation for transactions that pass the first phase. This method not only bolsters the validation process's integrity and security but also significantly minimizes the chances of unauthorized transactions entering the system. By ensuring that only transactions undergoing this stringent two-phase verification are approved, this mechanism notably improves the security and reliability of the cross-chain context. The subsequent discussion delves into the intricacies of this mechanism, elucidating its functionality and integration within the wider cross-chain framework to fortify system safety and reliability. The features of the Two-Stage Voting and Verification Mechanism

- Role of Committee: Tasked with auditing and validating cross-chain transactions.
- Data-Driven Reputation Scoring: Calculates members' scores based on historical behavior and contributions.
- Meritocratic Election System: Establishes a merit-based system with higher scores increasing election likelihood.
- Risk Mitigation: Mitigates risks from dishonest members in voting and transaction validation.
- Enhancing Security and Stability: Critical for maintaining integrity and trustworthiness of the cross-chain framework.
- Detailed Algorithmic Workflow: In-depth explanation of the reputation score computation and its impact on elections.
- Underpinning Framework Robustness: Reputation scoring strengthens the robustness of the cross-chain framework.

3.5   Reputation Scoring-Based Committee Election

We elucidate the proposed Reputation Scoring-based Committee Election mechanism, a crucial facet of the mainchain architecture. This mechanism is pivotal for ensuring that only credible, responsible members are elected to the committee tasked with auditing and validating cross-chain transactions. By employing a data-driven approach, the mechanism computes reputation scores for each member based on their historical behavior and contributions, thereby establishing a meritocratic system for committee election. Higher reputation scores augment a member's likelihood of being elected to the committee, thus providing a systematic mitigation strategy against the potential adversarial effects of dishonest members on the voting process and cross-chain transaction validation. The meticulous design of this mechanism underpins the integrity and trustworthiness of the cross-chain framework, thereby significantly enhancing the security and stability of cross-chain interactions facilitated through the mainchain. Through a detailed exposition of the algorithmic workflow and the underlying rationale, this section presents a comprehensive understanding of how reputation scoring undergirds the robustness of the proposed cross-chain framework.

4   Performance Evaluation

4.1   Experimental Setup

To assess the effectiveness and dependability of the proposed cross-chain transfer protocol, a detailed experimental framework was established. This segment outlines the specifics of the hardware and software setups, the configuration of the network, and the variables adjusted during the testing phase.

The tests were carried out using a server cluster, with each server powered by an Intel Xeon E5-2620 v4 CPU. This processor, operating at 2.1 GHz and featuring 8 cores, provided ample computational capacity to replicate the functioning of numerous blockchain nodes. These servers were also equipped with 32 GB of DDR4 RAM and a 1 TB solid-state drive, ensuring efficient data processing and storage capabilities.

4.2   Evaluation of Cross-Chain Evidence

The Fig. 2. shows the relationship between the size of the cross-chain evidence and the proportion of honest nodes in the network. As expected, the evidence size increases with the proportion of honest nodes because a higher proportion requires more signatures to be collected, thereby increasing the total size of the cross-chain evidence. As the network grows and the number of honest nodes increases, the evidence size will continue to grow. This could have scalability implications for the blockchain, particularly for large networks. Efficient encoding and compression techniques might be necessary to manage this growth. This demonstrates how the protocol's communication and storage overheads can scale with the trustworthiness of the network participants in a PoS sidechain protocol.

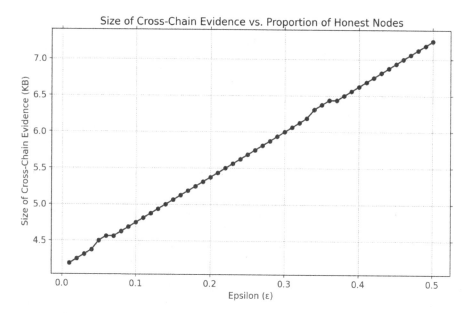

Fig. 2. The relationship between the size of the cross-chain evidence and the proportion of honest nodes in the network.

5   Conclusion

This paper introduces a blockchain-based cross-chain framework to advance global DNS resolution. Key enhancements include a two-phase voting and verification process, a reputation-based committee election mechanism, and an advanced sidechain protocol with refined hash functions and a Random Beacon mechanism. These developments collectively enhance the security, reliability, and efficiency of cross-chain transactions, addressing the challenges of sensitive data exchange. This innovative approach marks a significant advancement in domain resolution infrastructure, showcasing the transformative potential of blockchain technology in modern digital ecosystems.

Acknowledgment. This research is supported by Science Research Project of Hebei Education Department: (BJK2024111).

References

1. Buterin, V.: R3 Report - chain interoperability. Technical Report, R3 Corda (2016)
2. Adams, H., Zinsmeister, N., Robinson, D.: Uniswap v2 Core. Technical Report (2020)
3. WEF: Bridging the governance gap: interoperability for blockchain and legacy systems. Technical Report (2020)
4. Lerner, S.: RSK whitepaper. Technical Report, RSK (2015)

5. Poon, J., Buterin, V.: Plasma: scalable autonomous smart contracts. Technical Report, Plasma (2017). https://plasma.io/
6. Singh, A., Click, K., Parizi, R.M., Zhang, Q., Dehghantanha, A., Choo, K.K.R.: Sidechain technologies in blockchain networks: an examination and state-of-the-art review. J. Netw. Comput. Appl. **149**, 102471 (2020)
7. Al-Mashhadi, S., Manickam, S.: A brief review of blockchain-based DNS systems. Int. J. Internet Technol. Secured Trans. **10**(4), 420–432 (2020)
8. Fu, Y., Li, C., Yu, F.R., Luan, T.H., Zhao, P., Liu, S.: A survey of blockchain and intelligent networking for the metaverse. IEEE Internet Things J. **10**(4), 3587–3610 (2022)
9. Bagay, D.: Blockchain-based DNS building. Procedia Comput. Sci. **169**, 187–191 (2020)
10. Chen, W., Yang, X., Zhang, H., et al.: Big Data Architecture for Scalable and Trustful DNS based on Sharded DAG Blockchain. J. Sign. Process. Syst. **93**, 753–768 (2021). https://doi.org/10.1007/s11265-021-01645-3
11. Liu, Y., Zhang, Y., Zhu, S., Chi, C.: A comparative study of blockchain-based DNS design. In: Proceedings of the 2019 2nd International Conference on Blockchain Technology and Applications, pp. 86–92 (2019, December)
12. Nawrocki, M., Koch, M., Schmidt, T.C., Wählisch, M.: Transparent forwarders: an unnoticed component of the open DNS infrastructure. In: Proceedings of the 17th International Conference on emerging Networking EXperiments and Technologies, pp. 454–462 (2021, December)
13. Hesselman, C., et al.: The DNS in IoT: opportunities, risks, and challenges. IEEE Internet Comput. **24**(4), 23–32 (2020)
14. Back A., Corallo M., Dashjr L., et al.: Enabling blockchain innovations with pegged sidechains [EB/OL] (2014). http://diyhpl.us/~bryan/papers2/bitcoin/sidechains.pdf
15. Johnny D., Andrew P., Jonathan W., et al.: Strong federations: an interoperable blockchain solution to centralized third party risks [EB/OL] (2016). https://arxiv.org/pdf/1612.05491.pdf
16. Lerner S.D.: RSK white paper overview [EB/OL] (2015)
17. ConsenSys: BTC relays documentation [EB/OL] (2016). http://btc-relay.readthedocs.io/en/latest/
18. Kiayias, A., Zindros, D.: Proof-of-Work sidechains. In: Bracciali, A., Clark, J., Pintore, F., Rønne, P.B., Sala, M. (eds.) FC 2019. LNCS, vol. 11599, pp. 21–34. Springer, Cham (2020). https://doi.org/10.1007/978-3-030-43725-1_3

Innovation and Application
of Blockchain Technology

A Review of Goal Search Algorithms for Multi-robot Systems Based on Blockchain

Jiansheng Peng[1](✉), Fengbo Bao[2], Jingsong Guo[2], Chengjun Yang[3], Yong Xu[3], and Yong Qin[3]

[1] Guangxi University of Science and Technology, Hechi 54700, China
sheng120410@163.com
[2] Guangxi University of Science and Technology, Liuzhou 54500, China
[3] Hechi University, Hechi 54700, China
{05062,xuyong}@hcnu.edu.cn

Abstract. The main focus of this paper is to review the task allocation and goal search of multi-robot systems. This paper will sort out the development and research status of multi-robot and blockchain, first introducing the application field of multi-robot and the task allocation to be made when the multi-robot system performs tasks. Then introduce the advantages of using blockchain technology for task distribution of multi-robot systems; Then, the target to search algorithm of multi-robot system and the improvement method of the algorithm is described. Finally, the problems of tasking allocation and target to search algorithms in multi-robot systems are analyzed, and prospected.

Keyword: Blockchain · Multi-robot · Task allocation · Goal search algorithm

1 Introduction

Research on multi-robot systems began as early as the end of the last century for example: ACTRESS is an autonomous distributed robotic system containing multiple robotic elements. Each element can make independent decisions based on its surroundings and can communicate with other robots. Movement coordination between robots is achieved through communication protocols [1]. The GOFER project is to control the operation of moving multiple robots in an indoor environment, where multiple robots can move freely in an indoor environment after they have been assigned tasks [2]. The CEBOT system consists of multiple autonomous robot units with simple functions that can work together to perform tasks [3]. ALLIANCE is a fully distributed behavior-based architecture focused on solving fault-tolerant collaboration problems in small teams of heterogeneous mobile robots [4]. M+ decentralised multi-robot system protocol that serves to rationally assign tasks to each robot when multiple robots are required to perform them [5]. Murdoch's publish or subscribe system provides a solution for autonomous heterogeneous robot teams to cope with dynamic task allocation and facilitates collaborative work among multiple robots [6]. ASYMTRE describes an approach from heterogeneous multi-robot teams to find a solution to a problem by automatically synthesis tasks, with

J. Zhu et al. (Eds.): CBCS 2023, CCIS 2098, pp. 169–184, 2024.
https://doi.org/10.1007/978-981-97-3203-6_9

the advantage that heterogeneous multi-robot can synthesized new task solutions for combinations of robots from different [7]. A large number of academics papers and publications have been published by national and international researchers on multi-robot systems. Figure 1 shows the statistical results obtained by searching the subject term "Multiple robots" in Wed of Science from January 1, 2019 to May 2023.

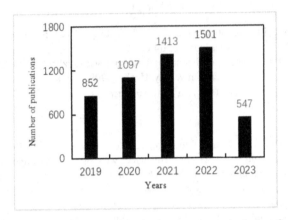

Fig. 1. Statistical articles on multi-robot system papers in the last five years.

It can be observed that publishing articles in this field is becoming more and more popular. There are no shortage of IEEE journals and top journals in the field of process control. The main research interests include areas such as automatic control systems for multiple robots, task allocation and goal search algorithms.

The concept of blockchain was first introduced to the Bitcoin white paper published by Satoshi Nakamoto in 2009 [8]. Two important indicators of blockchain technology are security and trust [9], and the services of trust and security are achieved through cryptography. The creation of peer-to-peer decentralised networks of nodes enables trust between unknown peers [10]. In blockchain technology, cryptocurrency plays a crucial role as a virtual currency that is the medium through which end-user exchanges is achieved [11]. Data is encrypted and decrypted by using a public key, which is a public key that all nodes have for other nodes in the decentralised network and is used to trace the source of the message, and a private key, which can only is useful for the nodes themselves, to encrypt the message. Literature [12] explains blockchain technology, describes its architecture, and compares some typical consensus mechanisms in blockchain.

Researchers combine blockchain technology with multi-robot systems and use the properties of blockchain to solve problems such as distrust, transaction data tampering and information sharing in multi-robot systems. For example, blockchain technology is used in the literature [13] to optimize the heterogeneous multi-robot computing resources and the different sensing capabilities they have, and the data sampled by the heterogeneous multi-robot is verified through blockchain technology and packaged into a chain for other robots to the literature [14] use blockchain technology to achieve decentralized control of spherical amphibious multi-robots and establishes a peer-to-peer communication network. The experiment proves the feasibility of blockchain technology in realizing decentralized control in multi-robot systems. The literature [15] illustrates that blockchain technology can provide innovative solutions to problems arising from multi-robot systems, making them safer, more autonomous and more flexible. Literature [16] introduces a distributed control system based on blockchain, deploys a multi-robot goal search application, and experimental results show that multi-robots can quickly complete goal search under the control of blockchain technology. Literature [17] uses blockchain technology to realize information interaction in order to decentralize control of a decentralized multi-robot system.

2 The Role of Blockchain Technology in Multi-robot Systems

In this section, the basic principles of multi-robot technology are briefly described. Multi-robot systems are currently used in many fields, for example: exploration [18], surveillance [19], search [20], rescue [21] and other areas. Multi-robot systems consist of two or more independent robots that work together to perform tasks in the same workspace. Multi-robot systems are classified based on the characteristics of individual robots. Multi-robot systems can be divided into homogeneous multi-robot systems and heterogeneous multi-robot systems. A single robot with the same function is called a homogeneous multi-robot system, and vice versa, it is called a heterogeneous multi-robot system.

Multi-robot systems can be divided into two types if classified according to control architecture [22]. One is a centralized architecture in which only one central node is responsible for collecting messages from the entire multi-robot system and formulating a set of actions and decisions to be executed based on these messages. The characteristic is that by controlling a single node, a global view of the entire system can be taken and tasks can be assigned. The speed of task execution depends only on how quickly individual nodes can build decisions. Disadvantages Communication bandwidth limits the distance from centralised decision making, making multi-robot systems limited in their scopes of work. And the excessive computational load placed on a single node makes it more prone to failure, and when the master node is hacked, the entire system will stop working or crash. Decentralised architectures unlike centralised architectures where all control and decision making is concentrated in one node, instead some or all nodes work together to decide on collective actions and decisions and can be divided into hierarchical and distributed architectures [23]. Advantages because it is relatively decentralised in terms of control, multi-robot systems do not stop working properly when individual nodes fail and are attacked, and show good robustness in terms of operational autonomy. Disadvantages. It has a very complex architecture, so it can be slow in distributing tasks compared to centralised control.

In a multi-robot system, there is not only a safe working platform, but also how to reasonably allocate tasks to individual robots is also a challenge. Involving how to effectively and reasonably allocate tasks to different robots in order to achieve optimal overall system performance or specific optimization goals. The literature [24] proposes a self-organizing approach that allows a group of robots to assign themselves to sequentially interdependent tasks, and to improve robot efficiency by switching between subgroups of robots if the sub-task robots do not perform the group's tasks well, without relying on global knowledge or centralized components and without the need for inter-robot communication. The approach is adaptive and allows for the reallocation of robots when the environment changes. The literature [25] details a framework that focuses on heterogeneous collections of multiple robot variants operating in complex and dynamic environments, where a new robot can arrive at a given location when one robot fails. Use the role played by the robot to allocate tasks, and the tasks can be reasonably transferred to other robots. Literature [26] describes that to improve task efficiency in a multi-robot system, reasonable task allocation is required, especially when the same task is completed by different robots, task conflicts must be reasonably resolved. This research adopts the task decomposition method to decompose the original task into subtasks and coordinate their operation tasks by assigning these subtasks to individual robots. It is easy to see from reading the literature that multi-robot systems first decompose tasks when they are assigned. Task decomposition is a part of task allocation. It mainly divides the task into multiple subtasks that can be completed independently by a single robot based on the characteristics and requirements of the task.

After decomposition through tasks, how to reasonably assign subtasks to single robots is a key step for multi-robot systems to complete their work efficiently. There are currently two main forms used for task allocation, one is a market-based task allocation method, where the literature [27] proposes a single robot to obtain and complete subtasks through bidding and negotiation between them, with the advantage of maximising task revenue while minimising task cost, and this method has been applied in real-life scenarios; where the literature [28] proposed an auction based task allocation method, described the specific process of the auction in detail, and tested it in two different fields. The advantages and disadvantages of these two task allocation methods are summarized in Table 1.

Table 1. The multi-robot system adopts a comparison of the advantages and disadvantages of the two task allocation algorithms.

Task allocation methods	References	Advantages
Based on a market approach	[27]	Maximising task benefits while minimising task costs
Based on the auction method	[28]	Consider only the robot's own needs for the task

To sum up, the task allocation of most multi-robot systems is to split the task into multiple subtasks, and finally assign the subtasks in order or out of order, which requires optimal task allocation based on the function and cost of the robot. A common problem with market and auction-based task allocation is that it does not protect against malicious attacks on task allocation by malicious nodes. Considering the environment in which multi-robot systems are becoming more and more popular, future control methods for multi-robot systems are expected to develop toward distributed architectures that can provide excellent robustness when multi-robot systems perform goal searches. Reasonable task allocation is crucial before multi-robot systems perform goal search. If there are malicious nodes participating in task allocation, the task may not be completed. Therefore, some scholars have proposed using blockchain technology to restrict malicious nodes in multi-robot systems.

Blockchain is composed of blocks arranged in a specific order, and each block contains a certain amount of transaction information. In a blockchain, participating nodes are responsible for recording and packaging transactions into a block. When all participating nodes pass the verification block and finally reach a consensus, the block will be broadcast to all participating nodes. In order to ensure the security and integrity of transactions, all blockchain nodes will hold a copy of the ledger and maintain it. This nature of the blockchain not only eliminates the risk of single node failure, but also ensures the openness and traceability of transactions. Because blockchain can provide a secure platform of trust entities, it has multiple applications in many technologies.

In a multi-robot system, task distribution may be attacked by malicious nodes. Some people have proposed a solution that uses blockchain technology to combine with the multi-robot system. This method significantly reduces the attacks of malicious nodes on the multi-robot system, and effectively improves the trust between system nodes and the security of transactions through the decentralization, transparency and non-tampering characteristics of the blockchain. In the literature [29], tasks are allocated to heterogeneous multi-robot systems through blockchain technology, and individual robots are given tasks based on bids to the tasks, and since individual robots are verified in the blockchain system, the individual The risk of a robot being compromised is greatly reduced because the individual robots are verified in the blockchain system. Experimental results show that the task allocation scheme that introduces blockchain in a multi-robot system has higher security and response speed. Literature [30] applies blockchain technology to market-based methods of tasking allocation, solving the problem of malicious attacks of market-based methods of multi-robot systems due to the presence of malicious nodes, making task allocation fail. In task allocation systems based on market and auction algorithms, task allocation failures may occur due to the emergence of malicious nodes. According to the nature of the blockchain, existing malicious nodes can be identified between nodes, and then the multi-robot system can complete reasonable task distribution.

Tasks that blockchain can take on in multi-robot systems. In industrial multi-robot systems, the literature [31] proposed a platform called RobotChain, which combines blockchain technology with industrial robots to make the event logs generated by the robots during their work immutable and difficult to be tampered with by malicious nodes. To achieve anomaly detection, the operating principle of this method is that the robot registers its identity in the blockchain. The robot that registers its identity uploads its own data information to the blockchain through smart contracts for abnormality detection by the system. Although literature [32] proposed a blockchain-based swarm robot framework, the proposed technology may become unstable when Byzantine robots are introduced into the group. Literature [33] proposed a new architecture that can still reach consensus among robots in the presence of Byzantine robots. Experimental results show that Byzantine robots will not have much impact on multi-robot systems. In order to solve the safety problem of underwater multi-robot systems, literature [17] proposed a solution based on the blockchain framework. Experiments show that a single robot can securely transmit and obtain information data through the blockchain. This method realizes the collaborative work of multi-robot systems in complex environments. Literature [29] adopts a multi-robot architecture based on blockchain, and enables information sharing between individual robots through reasonable architecture design. Each robot bids for decomposed tasks based on its own functions and computing capabilities, and uses blockchain technology to share bidding information. Experimental test results show that the designed architecture realizes blockchain-based data sharing in a multi-robot system and can add new robots to the multi-robot system. In response to epidemics in remote areas (such as the recent COVID-19), literature [34] proposed a conceptual framework for applying blockchain in multi-robot systems and summarized the challenges and opportunities involved in this field. The study categorizes tasks ranging from outbreaks to robots taking action.

In summary, the blockchain-based multi-robot architecture can ensure a secure source of reliable data and solve the adverse impact of malicious nodes on task distribution in a multi-robot system. However, judging from the shortcomings of the blockchain itself, long-term maintenance of block transactions of all network nodes will put great pressure on the storage space of a single robot, and may cause a single robot to not process data in a timely manner, causing the impact of the blockchain. Overall system throughput. Therefore, it is necessary to address these deployment challenges to fully realize the potential of blockchain applications in multi-robot systems.

3   Goal Search Algorithms for Multiple Robots

When the multi-robot system performs target search, first, multi-target tasks are assigned to the multi-robot system in a blockchain-based environment. Secondly, a single robot obtains task allocation information through the blockchain, and then conducts a reasonable target search based on the specific task information. A single robot uploads target search information to the blockchain to provide reference information for other robots. Since target search is a key step for multi-robots to complete tasks, Sect. 3 focuses on the target search algorithm of multi-robot systems. In view of the characteristics of multi-robot system target search, three types of target search algorithms including grid algorithm, sampling algorithm and bionic algorithm are described and summarized. In addition, the researchers also made improvements to address their respective shortcomings and analyzed and summarized the advantages of the improvements.

3.1   Grid Based Goal Search

The main method of grid-based goal search is to grid the environment where multiple robots are located. Obstacles are represented by black grids, movable spaces are represented by white grids, and specific grids mark the starting point and start point of the robot's movement. The robot scans the environment grid and calculates the path to the best solution based on its own algorithm.

Dijkstra's algorithm solves the shortest path problem between two points [35]. This algorithm gradually expands the weight of the shortest path by continuously selecting the vertex closest to the starting point until it covers the end position in the graph. In order to calculate the shortest path between starting points, the algorithm continuously traverses the network map. Therefore, it is not difficult to see from its calculation characteristics that the algorithm requires a large amount of calculation and takes a long time to calculate.

Literature [36] proposed the A* complete planning algorithm to achieve target shrinkage of multi-robot systems in static environments; the literature [37] completed a multi-robot goal search in a dynamic environment by using Dijkstra's goal search algorithm, i.e. the goal search is performed for robots that have already completed their task allocation, and the algorithm checks the multi-robot paths of a time window, allowing for re-routing when overlapping paths of multiple robots occur.

The A* algorithm uses a heuristic function, that is, certain evaluation indicators to guide the operation of the algorithm, so that the goal search traverses toward the end point [38]. The presence of the evaluation index function causes the A* algorithm to not traverse all grids of the map like the Dijkstra algorithm, thus saving goal search time and reducing the computational effort for multiple robots.

In order to enable multi-robot systems to perform target search in complex environments, literature [39] improved the dynamic cost function of the A* algorithm so that the algorithm can perform path planning in unknown environments. In order to solve the problem of increasing the calculation amount of the A* algorithm due to the excessive size of the grid map, the literature [40] adopts the combination of the A* algorithm and other algorithms. First, the target search of multiple robots is divided into several areas, then plan the end point that a single robot wants to reach, and finally use the fused A* algorithm to plan the shortest distance for a single robot to reach the end point. Experimental results show that although the fused A* algorithm shortens the path planning distance, the calculation efficiency is reduced, and there are many polylines in the planned path. In order to solve the problem that the path curvature is too large, causing the robot's turning action to be too high, the literature [41] improved the heuristic function based on the traditional A* algorithm. Experimental results show that the path becomes smoother after the algorithm is improved.

The D* algorithm is developed on the basis of the A* algorithm and is more suitable for complex working environments [42]. It also belongs to the heuristic algorithm, but compared to some other heuristics, the D* algorithm is less computational and simpler to implement. The $f(n)$ estimation function is used in the D* algorithm, that is, $f(n) = g(n) + h(n)$. $h(n)$ uses the Euclidean distance as the heuristic function, which is two-dimensional or three-dimensional. The true distance of the point. The selection of the valuation function can be based on the actual choice of different valuation functions. Unlike the A* algorithm it can be used to detect dynamic obstacles and create temporary paths near dynamic obstacles, the paths will change as the dynamic obstacles change.

The D* algorithm searches for paths faster and with shorter paths than the A* algorithm, but the D* algorithm does not improve on the disadvantages of having many path folds and planning routes close to the edges of obstacles. Its improvement is mainly reflected in two aspects: improving path smoothness and improving algorithm calculation speed. By optimizing the node selection method, the D* algorithm is optimized in a single pass to improve the algorithm search speed. The introduction of the concept of secondary nodes in literature [43] removes the expansion of useless nodes and improves the problem of many path folds. After path generation, the path is smoothed on the basis of this path. The literature [44] smoothed the generated path by introducing three times B splines.

In the grid-based goal search algorithm, there are three different traditional algorithms. As shown in Table 2, some scholars have proposed corresponding improvement measures to address their shortcomings.

Table 2. Effects of improvement based on grid path algorithm

Name of algorithm	Limitations	Reference	Advantages
Dijkstra [35]	Large computational effort for undirected search, small search area	[36]	Enables heterogeneous multiple robots for goal search
		[37]	Paths can be plotted through moving obstacles
A* Algorithms [38]	Computationally intensive and unsmooth planning paths	[39]	Possibility to plan paths in unknown environments
		[40]	Multiple robots can search for targets over a wide geographical area
		[41]	Improved smoothness of the path
D* Algorithms [42]	Planned paths with many twists and turns and close to obstacles	[43]	Improving algorithmic search efficiency
		[44]	Smooths out the path

3.2 Sampling-Based Goal Search Algorithm

The Probabilistic Road Map algorithm (PRM) generates random nodes in the graph, and by connecting nodes that do not overlap with obstacles, many kinds of paths are formed [45]. The key to this algorithm is finding the right number of randomly generated sampling nodes; too many will result in increased computational cost, too few will result in planning paths that do not pass through narrow passages.

To address the problems arising from the original algorithm, literature [46] the author proposed a probabilistic roadmap algorithm based on hybrid potential. Experiments have shown that by utilizing hybrid potential and map segmentation, the improved algorithm significantly improves the success rate of planning. Literature [47] increased the narrow channel by identifying narrow channels and increasing the mid-way density, the efficiency of goal search as well as the success rate was improved. In some applications, the computational effort to obtain a priori wayfinding may be too large causing goal search failure, limiting the online planning capability of the algorithm.

The Rapid Exploration Random Tree (RRT) method is to grow branches of equal length like a tree in a space. When a branch overlaps an obstacle, the branch will automatically disappear. If there is no contact with the obstacle, branches will grow around it. This branch branches out of other branches, and so on until the end is reached [48].

In the literature [49] the RRT* algorithm with an opportunity constraint formulation was proposed to solve the goal search problem of swarms of UAVs in cities, capable of establishing safe trajectories in a future space shared by traditional commercial aviation and UAVs. This algorithm is simple, has strong environmental adaptability, and can be used for real-time online goal search. However, the RRT* algorithm explores the space in a completely random direction, and the search efficiency is low. The RRT algorithm lacks optimisation algorithm capability for paths. In response to the limitations of the RRT algorithm, the literature [50] proposed the Bi-RRT algorithm to improve the path exploration rate by extending the random number at the same time by having the root node at the start and target points respectively.

The artificial potential field algorithm (APF) [51] is based on the interaction force phenomenon of the magnetic force field, allowing a mutually repelling force between the moving robot and obstacles. It is mainly used in local target search of robots to prevent them from colliding with stationary or moving obstacles. The biggest disadvantage of the artificial potential field algorithm is that it is easy to fall into the local optimal solution problem. The researchers have carried out a number of optimization measures. The literature [52] the oscillation effect on the artificial potential field is overcome by set up a virtual local target. Literature [53] proposed the introduction of gain limitations in the repulsive force field based on the artificial potential field (APF) algorithm. Experimental results show that this method enables the robot to reach the target smoothly when encountering obstacles in a narrow strip, effectively avoiding collisions and falling into local minima. Artificial potential field algorithms are often used in local algorithms in the multi-robot field to prevent collisions in multi-robot systems by utilizing the repulsive forces between robots and obstacles or other robots. Although the artificial potential field algorithm can effectively prevent collisions, it requires creating simulation fields of gravity and repulsion for obstacles and robots in the environment, which results in are a large amounts of calculations.

The improvement measures for the target algorithm based on traditional sampling are mainly to make the sampling space of the algorithm as small as possible, so as to reduce the calculation amount of the algorithm. Table 3 summarizes the improvement measures and effects of the sampling algorithm.

Table 3. Measures and effects of improvement based on sampling algorithm

Name of algorithm	Limitations	Reference	Advantages
PRM [45]	It is difficult to choose the number of sampling nodes, which determines the computational cost	[46]	Success rate of the algorithm is above 95% for both local and global planning
		[47]	Improved efficiency and success rate of route plan

(continued)

Table 3. (*continued*)

Name of algorithm	Limitations	Reference	Advantages
RRT [48]	High randomness of search and lack of ability to optimisation algorithm	[49]	Capable of being used in multi-drone applications, making goal search more efficient
		[50]	Improve path exploration rates
APF [51]	When the mobile robot is in the vicinity of an obstacle, the planned path oscillates and is prone to local minima	[52]	Overcoming oscillatory effects in artificial potential fields
		[53]	Solving local minima of optimal paths and smoothing paths
PRM [45]	It is difficult to choose the number of sampling nodes, which determines the computational cost	[46]	Success rate of the algorithm is above 95% for both local and global planning

3.3 Biomimetic-Based Goal Search Algorithm

The Ant Colony Algorithm (ACO) was discovered based on observing the foraging habits of ants. When foraging, ants tend to choose paths with high pheromone concentrations. According to the characteristics of the ant colony algorithm, it is not difficult to find that it has a certain fault tolerance, but the algorithm will also have local optimal solution problems. Literature [55] proposed an intelligent gain based on the ant colony algorithm, and the improved algorithm solved the problem of falling into a local optimal solution. Experiments show that the improved algorithm has a certain improvement in path speed, but the path optimization effect is not obvious.

Genetic algorithm (GA) is a global optimization algorithm inspired by the genetic mechanism of organisms in the natural reproduction and evolution process [56]. Mainly including the processes of path cod and constructing fitness functions. The genetic algorithm has a low calculation rate and consumes a lot of computing resources. In order to solve the limitations of traditional genetic algorithms, literature [57] proposed an improved adaptive genetic algorithm. Compared with the traditional genetic algorithm, not only the amount of calculation is reduced, but also the planned path is shortened. Literature [58] introduces a co-evolution improvement mechanism, which improves the calculation speed of the algorithm by reasonably adjusting the operator and fitness function, avoids robot collisions, and makes the algorithm more suitable for multi-robot target search.

The particle swarm algorithm (PSO) is inspired by the behavior of birds looking for food, by simulating the process of a group of birds sharing current location information with each other when looking for food [59]. However, the path planned by the particle swarm algorithm will have unnecessary curves. Literature [60] proposed the use of high-order Bezier curves to reduce the number of path bends. Experiments show that the new strategy has good effects in smoothing paths, and multiple comprehensive simulation experiments on mobile robot smooth target search also confirm the excellent performance of the new strategy. Literature [61] proposed an improved method for the goal search problem of multiple mobile robots in a dynamic dual warehouse. This method transforms the robot's shortest path problem under dual warehouses into a time-varying nonlinear programming problem to reduce the difficulty. This improved method effectively reduces the complexity of the problem and provides a successful solution for multi-robot system goal search in a dual warehouse environment.

The neural network algorithm proposed based on the study of the working mechanism of the human brain shows excellent learning and fault tolerance capabilities [62]. In order to describe the movement path of the robot, the neural network algorithm takes the sensor information and the state of the robot's last movement as input by establishing a neural network model [62]. The neural network method gives the robot the ability to adapt to new environments, but it requires the construction of a data set training model in advance, and the training time is long. The literature [63] combined neural networks of genetic algorithms for mobile robot goal search, and experimental results demonstrated the feasibility of the method; the literature [64] fused neural networks of hybrid particle swarm algorithms to achieve mobile robot goal search.

Based on the improvement of the bionic goal search algorithm, researchers have also made a lot of improvement measures for the limitations of the algorithm itself, as shown in Table 4, a summary of the bionic path algorithm.

Table 4. Improvement measures and effects based on bionic path algorithm.

Name of algorithm	Limitations	Reference	Advantages
ACO [54]	Prone to local optimum problems	[55]	Some improvement in gaining path speed
GA [56]	Slow convergence and poor local search capability	[57]	Improved the search efficiency of the algorithm
		[58]	The improved algorithm can be applied to multirobot goal search
PSO [59]	Most of its applications are based on empirical and experimental data	[60]	Improved spatial search capability of PSO algorithm and smooth planning paths
		[61]	Solving the path planning problem for multiple mobile robots in a dynamic double decker warehouse
Neural network algorithms [62]	Requires prior construction of data set training model and longer training time	[63]	Improved planning capability of neural networks
		[64]	Improved efficiency of the algorithm
ACO [54]	Prone to local optimum problems	[55]	Some improvement in gaining path speed

Neural networks have more obvious drawbacks, but a superior network architecture often enables algorithms with strong environmental adaptability. As the application scenarios of mobile robots increase and the complexity of the working environment they face increases further, the advantages of neural networks will be further demonstrated. Therefore, the application of neural networks of mobile robots is of great importance, and future work will require a great deal of research into this application scenario.

Existing goal searches algorithms and their refinements have been applied to mobile robot goal search, but most research has used planning algorithms for individual mobile robots, with relatively few algorithms for multi-robot collaborative planning. Goal search algorithms is a key technology for mobile robots, and current goal search algorithms have limitations that still require significant work to improve the performance and applicability of the algorithms.

The first are more efficient algorithm fusion. Most of the research work on algorithms is based on improving the characteristics of the algorithm itself, and relatively little research has been done on algorithm fusion; the second is dynamic goal search with multi-sensor fusion, and existing goal search algorithms are mostly used for offline planning, i.e. assuming a constant environment The existing goal search algorithms is mostly used for offline planning, i.e. goal search assuming a constant environment. However, the actual application scenario is often dynamic, and the mobile robot needs to avoid dynamic obstacles in time; the third is goal search in complex environments, and the existing goal search algorithms often replace the initial position and target position with points in the planning process, which is a relatively simple way, and some traditional goal search algorithms are only applicable to two-dimensional environments, and most algorithms will be less efficient when the environment dimension increases and obstacles increase. As the dimensionality of the environment increases and the number of obstacles increases, the efficiency of most algorithms may decrease. By improving the performance and applicability of goal search algorithms, mobile robots can be more widely used in various fields.

4   Summary and Outlook

A multi-robot system is a system composed of multiple robots with simple or complex functions that work in coordination with each other to perform required automation tasks in many different spatial domains. Multi-robot systems are mainly used to solve complex task problems that cannot be completed by a single robot. But from a control perspective, how to safely and efficiently assign tasks to individual robots is a key issue. Therefore, multi-robot systems require a platform that enables secure communication and trusted data transmission between individual individuals. To sum up, blockchain technology can provide a safe and trustworthy information interaction platform for multi-robot systems. Therefore, integrating blockchain technology into multi-robot systems has certain development prospects.

Through blockchain technology, the task distribution and target search of multi-robot systems can be decentralized, untrusted individual nodes can be effectively managed, and the system can be prevented from being harmed by Byzantine entities. Additionally, blockchain technology can verify robot identities and establish secure communication networks between entities. However, using blockchain has certain limitations.

For example, there is the problem of the number of robots in a multi-robot system. In a multi-robot system, increasing the number of robots means that the system has stronger sensing and information sharing capabilities, and therefore a better understanding of the environment around the multi-robot system. However, for a multi-robot system using blockchain technology, consensus must be reached among multiple robots. As the number of robots increases, the consensus time may take longer. On the other hand, if the number of multi-robot systems is too small, once one of the robots is in crisis, blockchain security issues will arise. If robotic operations involve sensing, processing and storing large amounts of data, blockchain will have latency issues. Using blockchain technology, this data is stored in immutable and sequentially ordered blocks. Due to the limit on the number of blocks produced by a node, there will be some delay in the creation of new blocks. For latency-sensitive, mission-critical robots, delays in communication, processing, and consensus can be the biggest hurdles.

As blockchain technology matures, corresponding problems will also be solved. For example, if there is a delay in uploading information to the chain, important information can be uploaded to the chain in advance through smart contracts to avoid information delays caused by the consensus mechanism. In general, applying blockchain to multi-robot systems is a new research direction, which can well solve the trust problem between individual robots in multi-robot systems. Blockchain can also be used as a tool for multi-robot systems. The memory is used to store important transaction information.

Acknowledgments. The authors are highly thankful to the National Natural Science Foundation of China, to the Innovation Fund of Chinese Universities Industry-University-Research, to the Research Project for Young and Middle-aged Teachers in Guangxi Universities, and to the Special research project of Hechi University. This research was financially supported by the project of outstanding thousand young teachers' training in higher education institutions of Guangxi, Guangxi Colleges and Universities Key Laboratory of AI and Information Processing (Hechi University), Education Department of Guangxi Zhuang Autonomous Region.

Disclosure of Interests. The author has no competing interests related to the content of this article.

References

1. Asama, H., Matsumoto, A., Ishida, Y.: Design of an autonomous and distributed robot system: ACTRESS. In: Proceedings of IROS 1989, Tsukuba, Japan, pp. 283–290, September 1989
2. Caloud, P., Choi, W., Latombe, J.-C., Le Pape, C., Yim, M.: Indoor automation with many mobile robots. In: Proceedings of IROS 1990, Ibaraki, Japan, pp. 67–72, July 1990
3. Fukuda, T., Ueyama, T., Kawauchi, Y., Arai, F.: Concept of cellular robotic system (CEBOT) and basic strategies for its realization. Comput. Electr. Eng. **18**(1), 11–39 (1992)
4. Parker, L.E.: ALLIANCE: an architecture for fault tolerant, cooperative control of heterogeneous mobile robots. In: Proceedings of IROS 1994, Munich, Germany, pp. 776–783, September 1994
5. Botelho, S.C., Alami, R.: M+: a scheme for multi-robot cooperation through negotiated task allocation and achievement. In: Proceedings of ICRA 1999, Detroit, MI, USA, pp. 1234–1239, May 1999

6. Gerkey, B.P., Matarić, M.J.: Murdoch: Publish/subscribe task allocation for heterogeneous agents. In: Proceedings of Agents 2000, Barcelona, Spain, pp. 203–204, June 2000
7. Tang, F., Parker, L.E.: ASyMTRe: automated synthesis of multi-robot task solutions through software reconfiguration. In: Proceedings of ICRA 2005, Barcelona, Spain, pp. 1501–1508, April 2005
8. Bitcoin, N.S.: A peer-to-peer electronic cash system (2009)
9. Curran, K., Curran, J.: Blockchain security and potential future use cases. In: Blockchain for Cybersecurity and Privacy, pp. 75–83 (2020)
10. Pal, P., Ruj, S.: BlockV: a blockchain enabled peer-peer ride sharing service. In: 2019 IEEE International Conference on Blockchain (Blockchain), pp. 463–468. IEEE (2019)
11. Rehman, M.H.U., Salah, K., Damiani, E., Svetinovic, D.: Trust in blockchain cryptocurrency ecosystem. IEEE Trans. Eng. Manag. **67**(4), 1196–1212 (2020)
12. Zheng, Z., Xie, S., Dai, H., et al.: An overview of blockchain technology: architecture, consensus, and future trends. In: 2017 IEEE International Congress on Big Data (BigData Congress), pp. 557–564. IEEE (2017)
13. Queralta, J.P., Westerlund, T.: Blockchain-powered collaboration in heterogeneous swarms of robots. arXiv preprint arXiv:1912.01711 (2019)
14. Guo, S., Cao, S., Guo, J.: Study on decentralization of spherical amphibious multi-robot control system based on smart contract and blockchain. J. Bionic Eng. **18**(6), 1317–1330 (2021)
15. Castelló Ferrer, E.: The blockchain: a new framework for robotic swarm systems. In: Arai, K., Bhatia, R., Kapoor, S. (eds.) FTC 2018. AISC, vol. 881, pp. 1037–1058. Springer, Cham (2019). https://doi.org/10.1007/978-3-030-02683-7_77
16. Mokhtar, A., Murphy, N., Bruton, J.: Blockchain-based multi-robot goal search. In: 2019 IEEE 5th World Forum on Internet of Things (WF-IoT), pp. 584–589. IEEE (2019)
17. Karthik, S., Chandhar, N.P., Akil, M., et al.: Bee-bots: a blockchain based decentralised swarm robotic system. In: 2020 6th International Conference on Control, Automation and Robotics (ICCAR), pp. 145–150. IEEE (2020)
18. Pei, Y., Mutka, M.W.: Steiner traveler: relay deployment for remote sensing in heterogeneous multi-robot exploration. In: Proceedings of ICRA 2012, Saint Paul, MN, USA, pp. 1551–1556, May 2012
19. Mendonça, R., Marques, M.M., Marques, F., et al.: A cooperative multi-robot team for the surveillance of shipwreck survivors at sea. In: OCEANS 2016 MTS/IEEE Monterey, pp. 1–6. IEEE (2016)
20. Murphy, R.R., Lisetti, C.L., Tardif, R., et al.: Emotion-based control of cooperating heterogeneous mobile robots. IEEE Trans. Robot. Autom. **18**(5), 744–757 (2002)
21. Gutiérrez, M.A., Nair, S., Banchs, R.E., et al.: Multi-robot collaborative platforms for humanitarian relief actions. In: 2015 IEEE Region 10 Humanitarian Technology Conference (R10-HTC), pp. 1–6. IEEE (2015)
22. Jose, K., Pratihar, D.K.: Task allocation and collision-free goal search of centralized multi-robots system for industrial plant inspection using heuristic methods. Robot. Auton. Syst. **80**, 34–42 (2016)
23. Amato, C., Konidaris, G., Cruz, G., et al.: Planning for decentralized control of multiple robots under uncertainty. In: 2015 IEEE International Conference on Robotics and Automation (ICRA), pp. 1241–1248. IEEE (2015)
24. Brutschy, A., Pini, G., Pinciroli, C., et al.: Self-organized task allocation to sequentially interdependent tasks in swarm robotics. Auton. Agents Multi-Agent Syst. **28**(1), 101–125 (2014)
25. Gunn, T., Anderson, J.: Effective task allocation for evolving multi-robot teams in dangerous environments. In: 2013 IEEE/WIC/ACM International Joint Conferences on Web Intelligence (WI) and Intelligent Agent Technologies (IAT), vol. 2, pp. 231–238. IEEE (2013)

26. Yan, Z., Jouandeau, N., Cherif, A.A.: A survey and analysis of multi-robot coordination. Int. J. Adv. Robot. Syst. **10**(12), 399 (2013)

27. Zlot, R., (Tony) Stentz, A., Bernardine Dias, M., Thayer, S.: Multi-robot exploration controlled by a market economy. In: Proceedings of ICRA 2002, Washington, DC, USA, pp. 3016–3023, May 2002

28. Gerkey, B.P., Matarić, M.J.: Sold! Auction methods for multirobot coordination. IEEE Trans. Robot. Autom. **18**(5), 758–768 (2002)

29. Basegio, T.L., Michelin, R.A., Zorzo, A.F., Bordini, R.H.: A decentralised approach to task allocation using blockchain. In: El Fallah-Seghrouchni, A., Ricci, A., Son, T. (eds.) EMAS 2017. LNCS, vol. 10738, pp. 75–91. Springer, Cham (2018). https://doi.org/10.1007/978-3-319-91899-0_5

30. Krämer, L., Ahlbäumer, R., Roidl, M.: Two-stage market-based task allocation for blockchain-based cyber-physical production systems. In: 2022 IEEE International Conference on Blockchain (Blockchain), pp. 282–289. IEEE (2022)

31. Lopes, V., Alexandre, L.A.: Detecting robotic anomalies using robotchain. In: 2019 IEEE International Conference on Autonomous Robot Systems and Competitions (ICARSC), pp. 1–6. IEEE (2019)

32. Melnik, E.V., Klimenko, A.B., Ivanov, D.Y.: A blockchain-based technique for making swarm robots distributed decision. In: Journal of Physics: Conference Series, vol. 1333, no. 5, p. 052013. IOP Publishing (2019)

33. Strobel, V., Castelló Ferrer, E., Dorigo, M.: Blockchain technology secures robot swarms: a comparison of consensus protocols and their resilience to byzantine robots. Front. Robot. AI **7**, 54 (2020)

34. Alsamhi, S.H., Lee, B.: Blockchain for multi-robot collaboration to combat COVID-19 and future pandemics. arXiv 2020. arXiv preprint arXiv:2010.02137

35. Thomas, H.C., Charles, E.L., Ronald, L.R., et al.: Section 24.3: Dijkstra's Algorithm. Introduction to Algorithms, pp. 595–601. MIT Press and McGraw-Hill (2001)

36. Bai, X., Yan, W., Cao, M., et al.: Distributed multi-vehicle task allocation in a time-invariant drift field with obstacles. IET Control Theory Appl. **13**(17), 2886–2893 (2019)

37. Chen, X., Zhang, X., Huang, W., et al.: Coordinated optimal goal search of multiple substation inspection robots based on conflict detection. In: 2019 Chinese Automation Congress (CAC), pp. 5069–5074. IEEE (2019)

38. LaValle, S.M.: Planning Algorithms. Cambridge University Press, Cambridge (2006)

39. Erokhin, A., Erokhin, V., Sotnikov, S., Gogolevsky, A.: Optimal multi-robot path finding algorithm based on A*. In: Silhavy, R., Silhavy, P., Prokopova, Z. (eds.) CoMeSySo 2018. AISC, vol. 860, pp. 172–182. Springer, Cham (2019). https://doi.org/10.1007/978-3-030-00184-1_16

40. Tang, Y., Zhou, R., Sun, G., et al.: A novel cooperative goal search for multirobot persistent coverage in complex environments. IEEE Sens. J. **20**(8), 4485–4495 (2020)

41. Min, H., Xiong, X., Wang, P., et al.: Autonomous driving goal search algorithm based on improved A* algorithm in unstructured environment. Proc. Inst. Mech. Eng. Part D J. Automob. Eng. **235**(2–3), 513–526 (2021)

42. Stentz, A.: Optimal and efficient path planning for partially known environments. In: Hebert, M.H., Thorpe, C., Stentz, A. (eds.) Intelligent Unmanned Ground Vehicles. SECS, vol. 388, pp. 203–220. Springer, Boston (1997). https://doi.org/10.1007/978-1-4615-6325-9_11

43. Wang, S.J., Hu, L.K., Wang, Y.F.: Goal search of indoor mobile robot based on improved D* algorithm. Comput. Eng. Des. **41**(04), 1118–1124 (2020). https://doi.org/10.16208/j.iss n1000-7024.2020.04.036

44. Zhu, X.X., Sun, B., Zhu, D.Q.: Three-dimensional dynamic goal search of AUV based on improved D* algorithm. Control Eng. China **28**(04), 736–743 (2021). https://doi.org/10.14107/j.cnki.kzgc.20190179

45. Kavraki, L.E., Kolountzakis, M.N., Latombe, J.-C.: Analysis of probabilistic roadmaps for goal search. In: Proceedings of ICRA 1996, Minneapolis, MN, USA, pp. 3020–3025, April 1996

46. Ravankar, A.A., Ravankar, A., Emaru, T., et al.: HPPRM: hybrid potential based probabilistic roadmap algorithm for improved dynamic goal search of mobile robots. IEEE Access **8**, 221743–221766 (2020)

47. Zhong, J., Su, J.: Robot goal search in narrow passages based on probabilistic roadmaps. Int. J. Robot. Autom. **28**(3) (2013)

48. LaValle, S.M.: Rapidly-exploring random trees: a new tool for goal search. Technical report TR 98-11, Iowa State University, Ames, IA, USA, October 1998

49. Berning, A.W., Girard, A., Kolmanovsky, I., et al.: Rapid uncertainty propagation and chance-constrained goal search for small unmanned aerial vehicles. Adv. Control Appl. Eng. Ind. Syst. **2**(1), e23 (2020)

50. Kuffner, J., LaValle, S.M.: RRT-Connect: an efficient approach to single-query goal search. In: IEEE International Conference on Robotics and Automation, San Francisco, pp. 473–479 (2000)

51. Tanner, H.G., Kumar, A.: Towards decentralization of multi-robot navigation functions. In: Proceedings of ICRA 2005, Barcelona, Spain, pp. 4132–4137, April 2005

52. Li, G., Yamashita, A., Asama, H., et al.: An efficient improved artificial potential field based regression search method for robot goal search. In: 2012 IEEE International Conference on Mechatronics and Automation, pp. 1227–1232. IEEE (2012)

53. Wu, Z., Su, W., Li, J.: Multi-robot goal search based on improved artificial potential field and B-spline curve optimization. In: 2019 Chinese Control Conference (CCC), pp. 4691–4696. IEEE (2019)

54. Colorni, A., Dorigo, M., Maniezzo, V.: Distributed optimization by ant colonies. In: Proceedings of the first European Conference on Artificial Life, vol. 142, pp. 134–142 (1991)

55. Sangeetha, V., Ravichandran, K.S., Shekhar, S., et al.: An intelligent gain-based ant colony optimisation method for goal search of unmanned ground vehicles. Def. Sci. J. **69**(2), 167–172 (2019)

56. Bremermann, H.J.: The evolution of intelligence: the nervous system as a model of its environment. University of Washington, Department of Mathematics (1958)

57. Wang, H., Zhao, X., Yuan, X.: Robot goal search based on improved adaptive genetic algorithm. Electron. Opt. Control. **29**(05), 72–76 (2022)

58. Qu, H., Xing, K., Alexander, T.: An improved genetic algorithm with co-evolutionary strategy for global goal search of multiple mobile robots. Neurocomputing **120**, 509–517 (2013)

59. Eberhart, R., Kennedy, J.: A new optimizer using particle swarm theory. In: MHS 1995, Proceedings of the Sixth International Symposium on Micro Machine and Human Science, pp. 39–43. IEEE (1995)

60. Song, B., Wang, Z., Zou, L.: An improved PSO algorithm for smooth goal search of mobile robots using continuous high-degree Bezier curve. Appl. Soft Comput. **100**, 106960 (2021)

61. Ma, Y., Wang, H., Xie, Y., et al.: Goal search for multiple mobile robots under double-warehouse. Inf. Sci. **278**, 357–379 (2014)

62. Wang, W., Wei, S.M., Yang, Y.F., et al.: Goal search for a mobile robot using neural networks. J. Beijing Univ. Technol. **36**(09), 1287–1291 (2010)

63. Liu, L., Wang, Y.N., Kuang, F., et al.: Goal searchof mobile robot based on neural network and genetic algorithm. Jisuanji Yingyong Yanjiu Appl. Res. Comput. **24**(2), 264–265 (2007)

64. Gong, M.M.: Research on goal search method of mobile robot based on neural network. Harbin Institute of Technology (2017)

A Blockchain-Based Distributed Anonymous Weighted Voting System

Mingyuan Chen[1,2], Bin Chen[1,2(✉)], Zejun Lin[1,2], Litao Ye[1,2], Shijie Zhang[1,2], and Shengli Zhang[1,2]

[1] School of Electronic and Information Engineering, Shenzhen University, Shenzhen 518060, Guangdong, China
bchen@szu.edu.cn
[2] Blockchain Technology Research Center, Shenzhen University, Shenzhen 518060, Guangdong, China

Abstract. Given the growing complexity of decision-making scenarios, the singular and unalterable electronic voting approach depending on centralized authorities is no longer satisfying the requirements of practicality. To address these limitations and accommodate evolving decision-making scenarios, this work proposes an anonymous weighted voting system. The proposed system employs distributed Elgamal encryption to encrypt the voting weights. This encryption method possesses a homomorphic property that allows for vote counting in a ciphertext state, thereby ensuring computational privacy. Additionally, the system utilizes blind and ring signatures to enhance the protection of voter identity, simultaneously ensuring the authenticity and legitimacy of the votes. The integration of blockchain smart contract technology automates the vote counting process and promotes transparency, eliminating the need for centralized vote counting agencies. Through analysis and experimentation, the proposed voting system is proved to be both feasible and secure.

Keywords: Blockchain · Anonymous Weighted Voting · Distributed Elgamal Encryption

1 Introduction

Traditional paper voting has become increasingly inadequate in modern society due to its inefficiency, high cost, and vulnerability to tampering [1]. As a result, electronic voting (e-voting) has gained attention as a potential alternative. However, in the internet environment, e-voting is susceptible to hacker attacks, compromising the voting process and the privacy of voters [2]. Many current e-voting solutions rely on third-party organizations to ensure security and privacy [3], but the misconduct of insiders within these organizations can undermine the credibility of the vote. Additionally, the complexity of decision-making scenarios in society requires a more adaptable voting method [4]. Weighted voting can offer greater flexibility [5].

The emergence of Bitcoin [6] has brought significant attention to blockchain technology. The characteristics of blockchain, including decentralization, data immutability,

J. Zhu et al. (Eds.): CBCS 2023, CCIS 2098, pp. 185–197, 2024.
https://doi.org/10.1007/978-981-97-3203-6_10

and traceability, have the potential to enhance the credibility of e-voting systems [7, 8]. Smart contracts automate the process, reducing the need for central control and increasing transparency. In response to the advancements in blockchain, researchers have been working towards the development of decentralized e-voting systems. Zhao [9] integrates e-voting with blockchain technology based on the bitcoin network. Lee et al. [10] propose an alternative strategy that involves a trusted third party to ensure the security of voters' ballots in blockchain e-voting. Additionally, several companies, such as Blockchain Voting Machine [11], Follow My Vote [12], and TIVI [13], have proposed voting systems that incorporate blockchain.However, all of these schemes utilize blockchain as a bulletin board for storing ballots [14]. McCorry et al. [15] designed an Ethernet-based voting scheme that utilizes smart contracts on the blockchain to automate vote counting and employs ring-signature to protect voter privacy. However, this scheme is only suitable for two-elections voting scenarios and has limited application scenarios. Zhang's study [16] utilizes Elgamal encryption to ensure secure voting in distributed systems and blockchain to eliminate the need for conventional ballot counters. However, it requires ballot decryption for counting and does not maintain voter privacy.

A voting system is proposed in this work for integrating cryptographic techniques and blockchain technology to guarantee anonymity and security. The system incorporates the Elgamal encryption algorithm [17] to encrypt the weights of the ballots, enabling vote counting on encrypted data while preserving the confidentiality of the weights. The distributed Elgamal encryption ensures that decryption of the vote result necessitates the involvement of multiple parties, preventing any individual from decrypting it independently. To verify the eligibility of each voter and prevent double voting, linkable ring signatures [18] are utilized. Blind signature [19] is employed to safeguard the privacy of the voter and ensure the authenticity of the ballot. The counting process is automated and made transparent through the utilization of smart contracts, eliminating the requirement for centralized counting agencies.

2 System Design

2.1 System Model

The specific responsibilities and functions associated with each role are illustrated in Fig. 1.

- Vote initiators: Vote initiators are responsible for establishing the voting agenda, regulations, and commencing the voting procedure. They compile and distribute a list of qualified voters. Additionally, they employ blind signatures as a means of verifying encrypted ballots.
- Proxy: To address the potential privacy problem that may occur when the voter directly interacts with the vote initiator, blind signatures are implemented in a reliable open-source proxy software to ensure the voter's anonymity. The proxy service functions as an intermediary, employing the distributed Elgamal encryption algorithm to encrypt the voter ballot. It assists the voter in blinding the encrypted ballots and unblinding the blind signatures.

- Voters: In the democratic process, individuals possess the fundamental right to exercise their voting preferences. To ensure the integrity of the voting system and protect the privacy of voters, a linkable ring signature is employed.
- Blockchain: Blockchain ensures that voting data is stored permanently and cannot be altered. Blockchain-based smart contracts automatically verify and count votes, and subsequently disclose the results once the voting period concludes.

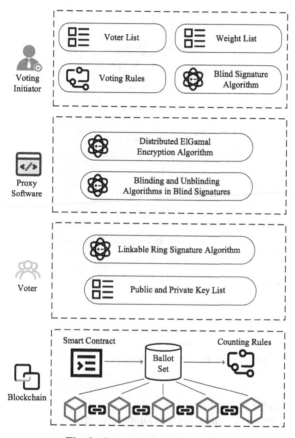

Fig. 1. Roles in the voting system

The interaction of the four roles is shown in Fig. 2. The vote initiator deploys the voting smart contract and has the authority to initiate and conclude the vote. The voter interacts with the voting initiator through the agent software and directly with the smart contract.

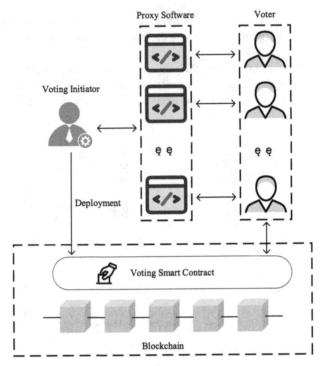

Fig. 2. The Architecture of the voting system

2.2 System Processes

Creation Phase

Vote initiators are responsible for establishing the key components of the voting process, such as the list of candidates, the list of eligible voters, the weight for each voter, and the designated start and end times for the voting period.

Initiation Phase

The Elgamal algorithm is established by selecting prime p and its generating element g. The private key for the Elgamal cryptographic algorithm is generated by the n voters involved in voting: $\{s_1, s_2, \ldots, s_n\}$. A public key is generated from a private key:

$$pk_i = g^{s_i} \bmod p \tag{1}$$

The process involves integrating several individual public keys into an aggregate public key:

$$PK = \prod_{i=1}^{n} pk_i \bmod p = \prod_{i=1}^{n} g^{s_i} \bmod p = g^{\sum_{i=1}^{n} s_i} \bmod p \tag{2}$$

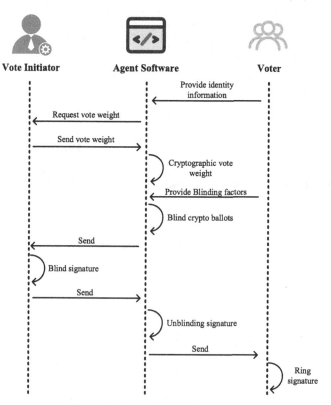

Fig. 3. The ballot generation process

Ballot Generation Phase

At this stage, the exchange of information between the initiator of the vote and the proxy software needs to include their respective signatures to ensure that the information is sent by the other party and has not been altered. The voting weight of $\{m_1, m_2, \ldots, m_n\}$ is allocated among a group of n voters. The vote weights are indexed as $\{\alpha^{m_1}, \alpha^{m_2}, \ldots, \alpha^{m_n}\}$. The ElGamal encryption method is used to generate the ciphertext (C_{i1}, C_{i2}) (Fig. 3):

$$C_{i1} = g^{r_i} \bmod p \tag{3}$$

$$C_{i2} = PK^{r_i} * \alpha^{m_i} \bmod p = g^{\sum_{j=1}^{n} s_j * r_i} * \alpha^{m_i} \bmod p \tag{4}$$

The proxy software employs a blind factor from a voter blinding the encrypted ballot and acquires the blinded message. Subsequently, the proxy software transmits the blinded message to the vote initiator. The vote initiator cannot extract the original information from the blinded message, thereby preventing the association of a specific encrypted ballot with a particular voter. Consequently, the vote initiator executes a blind signature on the blinded message. The blind signature is forwarded to the proxy software by the vote initiator, which employs the blind factor to reverse the blinding process and retrieve the signature value of S of the original message. The agent software subsequently sends S to the voter, who performs a ring signature on S to obtain the ring signature value RS. The complete ballot is (C_{i1}, C_{i2}, S, RS).

Voting and Counting Phase

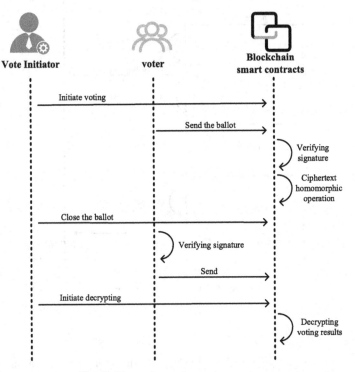

Fig. 4. The voting and counting process

Voters will call the voting function of the smart contract with the candidate they want to vote for and their ballot (C_{i1}, C_{i2}, S, RS) as input parameters. After RS and S are verified, the ballot (C_{i1}, C_{i2}, S, RS) is recorded on the chain. The ciphertext (C_1, C_2) is obtained by performing homomorphic multiplication from n voters (Fig. 4):

$$C_1 = \prod_{i=1}^{n} C_{i1} = g^{\sum_{i=1}^{n} r_i} \bmod p \tag{5}$$

$$C_2 = \prod_{i=1}^{n} C_{i2} = PK^{\sum_{i=1}^{n} r_i} * \alpha^{\sum_{i=1}^{n} m_i} \bmod p = g^{\sum_{j=1}^{n} s_j * \sum_{i=1}^{n} r_i} * \alpha^{\sum_{i=1}^{n} m_i} \bmod p \tag{6}$$

Decryption Phase

Each voter calculates the intermediate results by using the corresponding private key:

$$C_1^{-s_i} mod p = g^{-\sum_{j=1}^{n} r_j * s_i} \bmod p \tag{7}$$

The intermediate results are sent to the blockchain smart contract to achieve the final decryption result:

$$C_2 * \prod_{i=1}^{n} C_1^{-s_i} \bmod p = C_2 * g^{-\sum_{j=1}^{n} s_j * \sum_{i=1}^{n} r_i} \bmod p$$

$$= g^{\sum_{j=1}^{n} s_j * \sum_{i=1}^{n} r_i} * \alpha^{\sum_{i=1}^{n} m_i} * g^{-\sum_{j=1}^{n} s_j * \sum_{i=1}^{n} r_i} \bmod p = \alpha^{\sum_{i=1}^{n} m_i} \bmod p \tag{8}$$

The result for a particular candidate is:

$$\log_{\alpha} \alpha^{\sum_{i=1}^{n} m_i} \bmod p = \sum_{i=1}^{n} m_i \bmod p \tag{9}$$

3   Security Analysis

3.1   Correctness

By employing smart contracts to automate and ensure transparent execution, the system guarantees adherence to the prescribed rules in voting process. To validate the integrity of each ballot, it is required that the initiator of the vote provides their signature. In practice, the computational complexity of forging such a signature poses a significant challenge for potential attackers. Additionally, the verification mechanism of the ring signature ensures that only eligible voters can successfully cast their votes. Consequently, the system records legitimate ballots while rejecting any illegitimate ones.

3.2   Anonymity

By employing proxy services and blind signature, the system guarantees the preservation of voter anonymity towards the vote initiator, thereby preventing the association of a specific voter with their ballot. Furthermore, the utilization of distributed Elgamal encryption ensures that the voter's identity cannot be deduced from the ballot weights.

3.3   Fairness

The distributed Elgamal encryption algorithm guarantees that no individual entity possesses the ability to decrypt the ballot or voting results in isolation. Consequently, the precise tally of votes remains undisclosed until the voting process concludes.

3.4 Verifiability

The voting system operates on a blockchain platform, which ensures the permanent and secure recording of each ballot and voting outcome. Participants can independently verify that their vote has been accurately recorded and can also confirm the accuracy of the overall tally. This transparent and publicly verifiable process establishes a strong basis of trust in the integrity of the voting results.

3.5 Non-controversial

The ring signature verification procedure ensures that only legitimate voters are eligible to participate in the voting process. The transparent and automatic nature of the smart contract allows all participants to thoroughly examine it, ensuring a comprehensive understanding of the contract's operations and facilitating an undisputed voting process.

3.6 Non-reusability

The utilization of linkable ring signatures enables the validation of a signature's origin from a particular collective of signers. Furthermore, if a single signer generates signatures for two separate messages, the correlation between them can be detected. This effectively hinders users from submitting multiple votes and guarantees that each voter is limited to a single vote.

3.7 Receipt-Freeness

In this system, the ballots submitted by voters undergo encryption throughout phases of ballot storage and counting. The decryption process necessitates the involvement of all participants, thereby preventing voters from reconstructing their ballots or furnishing proof of their voting content to other.

4 Experiment

Table 1 presents the equipment employed in the experiment. There are two parts in this section. The first part seeks to validate the system's compliance with anticipated outcomes through an analysis of experimental findings. The second part assesses the duration of each step within the system.

4.1 Experimental Verification

Voting Schemes

Table 2 displays a voting scenario consisting of three candidates, namely Candidate A, Candidate B, and Candidate C, along with ten voters identified as Voter 1 to Voter 10. The table further presents candidates and the corresponding weights assigned by each voter.

Table 1. Equipment and Parameters

Categories	Name/Parameters
Server Operating Systems	Ubuntu Server 18.04.1 LTS 64bit
Server CPU	Intel Xeon Platinum 8269
Server RAM	4 GB
Server Hard Drive Capacity	60 GB
Blockchain	FISCO BCOS v2.9.1
Smart Contract Language	Solidity v0.6.10
Middleware	WeBASE

Table 2. A example of voting scheme

Voter	Candidate A	Candidate B	Candidate C
Voter 1	-1	0	0
Voter 2	-2	0	0
Voter 3	3	0	0
Voter 4	4	0	0
Voter 5	0	-3	0
Voter 6	0	5	0
Voter 7	0	6	0
Voter 8	0	0	1
Voter 9	0	0	2
Voter 10	0	0	3
sum	4	8	6

In Table 2, Candidate A, Candidate B and Candidate C are expected to receive 4 votes, 8 votes, and 6 votes respectively.

Voting Result

The off-chain component of the program is implemented using the C++ programming language and the Crypto++ library. The on-chain component of the smart contract is developed using Solidity. Subsequently, the voting results in Table 3 are achieved in accordance with the voting scheme in Table 2. Based on the result of the experiment, the tally of votes for each of the three candidates corresponded precisely to the anticipated number of votes.

Table 3. The voting result

Candidate	Candidate A	Candidate B	Candidate C
Number of votes	4	8	6

4.2 Performance Testing

In order to evaluate the efficiency of each stage in the voting process, a series of tests were conducted using three candidates and ten voters. The outcomes of these tests were then averaged over ten repetitions.

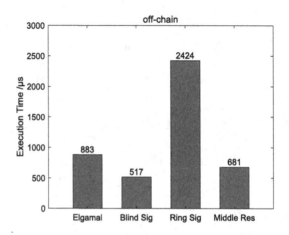

Fig. 5. Average off-chain execution time for each step

The execution time required for each step off-chain is shown in Fig. 5. The distributed Elgamal encryption exhibits an average execution time of 883 μs, while blind signatures demonstrate an average execution time of 617 μs. The computation of the intermediate result necessitates an average execution time of 681 μs. The ring signature requires an average execution time of 2424 μs. The ring signature uses the longest average time in the off-chain situation.

The average on-chain execution time required for each step is shown in Fig. 6. In the on-chain part, the homomorphic operation (HO) has an average execution time of 86.019 ms. The blind signature verification (BSV) takes an average of 66.395 ms. The ring signature verification (RSV) has an average execution time of 185.937 ms. The decrypting the result takes an average of 270.576 ms. The BSV uses the shortest average time in the on-chain situation. It is about 30 times of the longest one, ring signature, in the off-chain situation. The increased duration can be attributed to the time required for interacting with the blockchain, the consensus process, and the less efficient execution of smart contracts.

In order to optimize execution efficiency when dealing with a substantial number of participants, it is possible to employ a hybrid approach that combines both on-chain

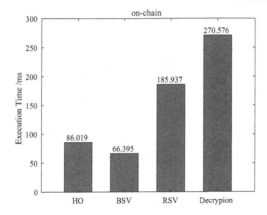

Fig. 6. Average on-chain execution time for each step

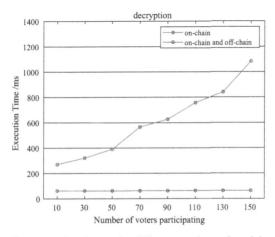

Fig. 7. Decryption time under different numbers of participants

and off-chain. The method is to put the decryption process off-chain. This process can by executed by the vote initiator. Then, the outcomes are sent to the blockchain smart contract for recording the voting results. The average duration of execution is illustrated in Fig. 7 for the combination of on-chain and off-chain methods. Under the on-chain method, the decryption results exhibit a linear relationship with the number of participants, as evidenced by the increase in average execution time. Specifically, when there are 10 participants, the average execution time is measured at 270.576 ms, whereas with 150 participants, it is approximately 1100 ms. On the other side, the average execution time of the combination method is hard to see changes comparing with that of the on-chain method. This is because the most time-consuming processes are put off-chain.

5 Conclusion

This work proposes an anonymous weighted voting system that effectively addresses the contemporary society's requirements for diversified and secure e-voting systems. This is achieved through the integration of distributed Elgamal encryption, ring signature, blind signature technology, and blockchain technology. Furthermore, the combination of on-chain and off-chain processing strategies optimizes the system's efficiency and applicability. Experimental verification has demonstrated the system's security and feasibility, offering an innovative and efficient solution for e-voting and providing valuable insights for the design and implementation of future voting systems.

Acknowledgement. China University Industry-Research-Innovation Fund [2022BL076], Shenzhen University Graduate Education Reform Research Project [SZUGS2023JG02], 2023 Shenzhen University Teaching Reform Research Project [JG2023097], Foundation of Shenzhen [20220809155455002, 20200823154213001, 20220810142731001].

References

1. Aggarwal, S., Kumar, N.: Voting system. In: Aggarwal, S., Kumar, N., Raj, P. (eds.) Advances in Computers, vol. 121, pp. 495–500. Elsevier (2021)
2. Risnanto, S., Rahim, Y.A., Mohd, O., Kusmadi, Asep Effendi, R., Perdana, R.S.: E-voting: security, threats and prevention. In: 2021 15th International Conference on Telecommunication Systems, Services, and Applications (TSSA), Bali, Indonesia, pp. 1–8 (2021)
3. Palas Nogueira, J., de Sá-Soares, F.: Trust in e-voting systems: a case study. In: Rahman, H., Mesquita, A., Ramos, I., Pernici, B. (eds.) MCIS 2012. LNBIP, vol. 129, pp. 51–66. Springer, Heidelberg (2012). https://doi.org/10.1007/978-3-642-33244-9_4
4. Casella, A.: Storable votes. Games Econ. Behav. **51**(2), 391–419 (2005)
5. Yang, Y., Zhao, Y., Zhang, Q., Ma, Y., Gao, Y.: Weighted electronic voting system with homomorphic encryption based on SEAL. Chin. J. Comput. **43**(04), 711–723 (2020)
6. Nakamoto, S.: Bitcoin: a peer-to-peer electronic cash system. Decent. Bus. Rev., 21260 (2008)
7. Pawlak, M., Poniszewska-Marańda, A.: Trends in blockchain-based electronic voting systems. Inf. Process. Manag. **58**(4), 102595 (2021)
8. Çubukçu Çerasi, C., Özsapci, B.: A blockchain based electronic voting system development (2022)
9. Zhao, Z., Chan, T.H.H.: How to vote privately using bitcoin. In: Qing, S., Okamoto, E., Kim, K., Liu, D. (eds.) ICICS 2015. LNCS, vol. 9543, pp. 82–96. Springer, Cham (2016). https://doi.org/10.1007/978-3-319-29814-6_8
10. Lee, K., James, J.I., Ejeta, T.G., et al.: Electronic voting service using block-chain. J. Digit. Forensics Secur. Law JDFSL **11**(2), 123 (2016)
11. Takabatake, Y., Kotani, D., Okabe, Y.: An anonymous distributed electronic voting system using Zerocoin. IEICE Tech. Rep. **116**(282), 127–131 (2016)
12. Yu, B., et al.: Platform-independent secure blockchain-based voting system. In: Chen, L., Manulis, M., Schneider, S. (eds.) ISC 2018. LNCS, vol. 11060, pp. 369–386. Springer, Cham (2018). https://doi.org/10.1007/978-3-319-99136-8_20
13. Zaghloul, E., Li, T., Ren, J.: D-BAME: distributed blockchain-based anonymous mobile electronic voting. IEEE Internet Things J. **8**(22), 16585–16597 (2021)
14. Yang, X., Yi, X., Nepal, S., et al.: Blockchain voting: publicly verifiable online voting protocol without trusted tallying authorities. Future Gener. Comput. Syst. **112**, 859–874 (2020)

15. McCorry, P., et al.: A smart contract for boardroom voting with maximum voter privacy. IACR Cryptology ePrint Archive (2017)
16. Zhang, B., Li, J., Hu, K., et al.: Distributed encrypted voting system based on blockchain. Comput. Sci. **49**(S02), 6 (2022). https://doi.org/10.11896/jsjkx.211000212
17. Elgamal, T.: A public key cryptosystem and a signature scheme based on discrete logarithms. IEEE Trans. Inf. Theory **31**(4), 469–472 (1985). https://doi.org/10.1109/TIT.1985.1057074
18. Liu, J.K., et al.: Linkable spontaneous anonymous group signature for ad hoc groups (extended abstract). IACR Cryptol. ePrint Arch. (2004), 27 (2004)
19. Chaum, D.: Blind Signatures for untraceable payments. In: Chaum, D., Rivest, R.L., Sherman, A.T. (eds) Advances in Cryptology, p. 199–203. Springer, Boston, MA (1983). https://doi.org/10.1007/978-1-4757-0602-4_18

A Blockchain-Based Privacy-Preserving Trust and Reputation Management for Internet of Vehicles

Hongyu Wang[1,2] , Haitao Yang[2], Wei Zhong[1], Linfang Deng[2], and Fei Tong[2,3,4(✉)]

[1] Wiscom System Co., LTD., Nanjing, China
[2] School of Cyber Science and Engineering, Southeast University, Nanjing, China
ftong@seu.edu.cn
[3] Jiangsu Province Engineering Research Center of Security for Ubiquitous Network, Nanjing, China
[4] Purple Mountain Laboratories, Nanjing, China

Abstract. Since the internet of vehicles (IoV) effectively facilitates the sharing of information between vehicles and roadside units (RSU), traffic efficiency, pedestrians and vehicle safety have been greatly improved. However, due to the openness of IoV and the high-speed mobility of vehicles, both nodes and privacy are at risk of being attacked. In this regard, we propose a privacy-preserving trust and reputation management system based on blockchain. The system uses a feedback collection model that can resist several kinds of attacks and realizes privacy protection to calculate the reputation of vehicles and RSU in IoV. The calculation process of vehicles' reputation is encapsulated in smart contract. Vehicles calculate the reputation of RSUs through collaborative filtering technique, which can ensure that the calculated reputation value is reliable. At the same time, the survival time of vehicles' reputation is introduced to prevent the occurrence of hiding attack effectively. The evaluation based on the Hyberledger Fabric platform shows that scheme can manage reputation effectively and reduce memory consumption.

Keywords: Internet of Vehicles · Privacy Preserving · Trust and Reputation Management · Blockchain · Smart Contract

1 Introduction

In recent years, the vehicular ad-hoc networks (VANETs) have undergone major changes, transforming the traditional VANETs into IoV. Both the vehicles and the roadside units (RSUs) are important components of internet of vehicles (IoV), and vehicles can communicates with RSUs through the on-board unit (OBU). So vehicles can get the latest road condition messages from the RSUs, and they can also upload road-related messages to the RSUs, thereby releasing the pressure on the road, enhancing driving safety, and achieving better service quality for intelligent transportation system. The main features of IoV include

© The Author(s), under exclusive license to Springer Nature Singapore Pte Ltd. 2024
J. Zhu et al. (Eds.): CBCS 2023, CCIS 2098, pp. 198–222, 2024.
https://doi.org/10.1007/978-981-97-3203-6_11

high confidence, controllability, manageability and operational efficiency [3,9]. However, its openness and high-speed mobility make node security and data sharing a challenge. On the one hand, the entities in IoV are all semi-trusted, and they may spread false information intentionally or unintentionally. On the other hand, the high-speed mobility makes vehicles unfamiliar with nearby entities.

The trust and reputation management system is proposed to make sure nodes take responsibility for behaviors. Reputation value is based on behavior history of node. Positive behaviors will bring the vehicle a good reputation, on the contrary, malicious behaviors will reduce the reputation of the vehicle. Trust and reputation management system thus requires behavioral analysis of nodes because of potential attacks, and employs aggregation models to ensure node trust. Li et al. [18] and Dias et al. [5] both used the vehicle's reputation value to determine whether the behavior is trustworthy or not. However, the system can hardly resist to malicious vehicles with high reputation value. In [19], the authors evaluated the trustworthiness of both vehicles and data. But he did not consider the RSUs as semi-trusted entities, and while considering malicious RSUs, collusion between malicious RSUs and malicious vehicles will also affect the evaluation of vehicles. What's more, vehicles may be reluctant to share messages to infrastructure, such as centrally managed RSUs architecture, for fear of single points of failure and manipulation of personal data. To this end, blockchain technology has been introduced to the IoV, as blockchain provides a decentralized framework that supports and ensures secure communication between nodes in intelligent transportation systems [2,10]. The vehicle's reputation value is stored on blockchain, which vehicles can access by communicating with RSU. In this way, the vehicles can have a general understanding of the unfamiliar vehicle.

In the past, the research of miners in IoV was not comprehensive enough. Yang et al. [29] proposed an evaluation scheme based on blockchain to measure message credibility, but the miners were elected from vehicles, which did not take into account the power of the vehicles. The miners in the system need to be online for long periods of time, whereas the vehicles are only online when they are in use. On this foundation, the authors in [28] made some improvements, by citing the concept of message credibility and using the Bayesian inference to generate result of the message. The system, on the other hand, cannot guarantee that the vehicle correctly assesses the message's credibility and submission grade. Similar to [28], Zhang et al. [31] formalized a reputation management scheme that employs blockchain to store reputation values, thereby minimizing the influence of malicious vehicles and malicious RSUs. One of the shortcomings of their work was that they did not consider privacy. What's more, they failed to fully evaluate semi-trusted objects in IoV, and they didn't recognize the challenges that evaluating multiple entities posed to system security. In fact, when the type of semi-trusted objects increases, the system may be subjected to more types of attacks, and it is necessary to comprehensively analyze the semi-trusted objects in the system.

Based on the shortcomings of existing work, we propose a blockchain-based privacy-preserving trust and reputation management system, called BPTRM.

It is built based on beta distribution and pseudonym technique. For message, BPTRM uses Bayesian inference to aggregate the opinions of different vehicles to verify the authenticity of the messages. For vehicles, BPTRM judges their behaviors according to the combination of their exchanged messages and reputation values, meanwhile protecting their identity privacy. The reputation value of each vehicle can be updated according to its behavior consequence. For RSUs, beta distribution is adopted to describe their reputation value distribution through collaborative filtering. What's more, BPTRM can filter redundant messages, which can reduce message processing latency and local storage overhead. Therefore, the reputation value of both vehicles and RSUs can be evaluated effectively to protect against multiple attacks by these entities.

The main contributions of this paper are as follows:

- We propose a comprehensive trust and reputation management system, not only for credibility of the messages but also for trust and reputation of the vehicles and the RSUs. The proposed algorithms are written into smart contracts to ensure the accuracy and effectiveness of vehicles' trust and reputation value. The time-to-live of vehicles' trust and reputation value is defined, which is changed according to the updated result of trust and reputation value to reduce the occurrence of harboring attacks.
- In BPTRM, vehicles employ a collaborative filtering technique to evaluate the trust and reputation values of RSUs, which not only calculates the trust and reputation value of RSUs based on their direct communication, but also takes into consideration the indirect trust and reputation factors, allowing compromised RSUs to be detected in time.
- We have implemented the proposed BPTRM based on Hyperledger Fabric v2.3 [1] and evaluated the performance of the system extensively. The results show that the authenticity of messages has been effectively improved. Malicious vehicles and compromised RSUs can be detected in time and suppressed effectively by the proposed trust and reputation management algorithms.

The rest of the paper is organized as follows. Section 2 presents the related works in the trust and reputation management system of IoV. We describe our proposed system model and BPTRM in Sects. 3 and 4, respectively. Section 5 shows the security analysis of the system, and Sect. 6 evaluates the proposed system. Finally, the paper is concluded in Sect. 7.

2   Related Work

The previous research on trust and reputation management system is briefly surveyed from two perspectives in this paper: trust and reputation system and management architecture.

2.1   Trust and Reputation System

A complete trust and reputation system consists of three parts: feedback collection, feedback aggregation (reputation calculation), and reputation dissemination. The first two are essential, and the third is based on the scenario requirement. A brief overview of feedback collection and feedback aggregation models in the IoV is provided below.

Feedback Collection: Feedback collection primarily refers to the detection and records of negative behavior, which is the foundation of reputation system. Existing feedback collection models are classified into three categories:

1. *Entity-centric:* Entity-centric feedback collection model focuses on the reliability of the vehicle itself. Li et al. [18] and Dias et al. [5] both used reputation of vehicle to determine whether the behavior is trustworthy or not. However, due to the high speed of vehicles, gathering enough messages for feedback aggregation to assess the real-time credibility of a specific vehicle is difficult. Another serious problem that has not been solved is how to identify and defend against different attacks, namely, high reputation value vehicles can also send incorrect messages due to sensor failure or controlled by attackers.
2. *Data-centric:* Data-centric feedback collection model focuses on the reliability of received data. Researchers focus on how to adopt various techniques to accurately detect vehicle misconduct and collect feedback, such as detectors [13], machine learning [8,23,30], Bayesian inference [22,28,31], etc. The disadvantages of this model are latency and data sparsity, where large amounts of message data from different vehicles may contain redundant messages, resulting in delay or overrun of critical messages.
3. *Hybrid:* The hybrid feedback collection model not only takes the trust of vehicles into consideration but also calculates the reliability of the message data [21]. Thus, this model inherits the benefits and drawbacks of the entity-centric and data-centric feedback collection models. In [19], the authors propose a trust management scheme to measure the reliability of vehicles and message. The data is perceived by various vehicles and the results are aggregated to identify the reliability of the received data. The proposed scheme does not defend against different attacks. On the whole, the hybrid model also inherits some disadvantages of both and creates new problems. First, the hybrid model means that there will be more redundant messages, and there will be higher requirements for the simplicity and efficiency of smart contracts. Secondly, multiple semi-trusted entities make the system vulnerable to more types of attacks, and the evaluation of security brings greater challenges.

Feedback Aggregation (Reputation Value Calculation): The central component of reputation systems is feedback aggregation. The following are some examples of commonly used models.

1. *Sum and Mean:* The common feedback aggregation is the mean of simple summation or the weighted summation. Dahiya et al. [4] used summation mean to filter the potential malicious feedback, thus generating dynamic reputation scores for each node. Firdaus et al. [6] took message credibility as a

weight factor and summed the mean value to generate node reputation values. The advantage of this model is that it makes full use of observations, which means it gets more messages. On the contrary, it is also a weakness, using every observation in the data set, which means it does not filter for feedback that differs greatly. In addition, the mean is sensitive to extreme values.

2. *Three-weight Subjective Logic:* Positive, negative, and uncertainties was stated in the subjective logic to denote the "opinion" of subjective belief. Three-weighted subjective logic (TWSL) model can calculate more accurate and reliable reputation value with appropriate weight. In [14,15,25], the authors all adopted TWSL to calculate reputation value. However, the existence of multiple recommendation factors makes the calculation process redundant and complex. The difficulty to confirm the factors is a common problem in trust and reputation management, but the multiple recommendation factors in the subjective logic formula make this problem more prominent.

3. *Bayesian:* In the Bayesian reputation system, the beta distribution has two free parameters (α and β) that indicate the quantity of positive and negative comments, respectively, is typically used to describe the reputation value. Due to the flexibility and simpleness of beta distribution, it can be used for simulating the reputation distribution. By updating the parameters of beta distribution through statistical data, the reputation value is calculated. Significant differences in statistical properties allow unfair ratings to be separated [26]. Gong et al. [7] adopted the reputation distribution based on beta distribution, direct and indirect reputation parameters are timely based on the results of each communication. However, due to the lack of time for distributed feedback collection, the indirect reputation may not be feasible for calculating vehicle reputation.

2.2   Management Architecture

The management architecture of the trust and reputation system is critical to the system's normal operation. We discuss below two architectures: centralized and distributed ones.

1. *Centralized Management:* Centralized management reputation systems are characterized by the existence of a credible or partially credible centralized authority. The centralized authority collects users' feedback, aggregates to compute reputation value, and stored the reputation value for access. The advantages of the centralized scheme is its ease of implementation. Furthermore, the central authority is universally trusted. In [12], the authors proposed a lightweight trust model based on five parameters in vehicle-to-vehicle and vehicle-to-infrastructure communication process to calculate the trust of nodes and data, and treated RSU as the network's trusted authority, so RSU assigned the initial trust value of vehicles and alerted the user to the presence of malicious vehicles. The RSU deployed on the side of the road may fail, then the whole reputation system is compromised. As a result, the single point of failure problem makes centralized solutions vulnerable.

2. *Decentralized Management:* In decentralized management reputation systems, the aggregation may consist of multiple nodes working together. Blockchain is a typical application, which can be well combined with the security of IoV due to its decentralized, tamper-proof, traceability, and other security attributes. Kumar et al. [17] and Hildebrand et al. [11] investigate the benefits of blockchain technology and explain how blockchain can assist IoV in providing more secure, efficient, and intelligent services. At the same time, the openness and transparency of the blockchain necessitate that the nodes' identities be concealed, i.e., that they remain anonymous. By operating anonymously in the system, no third party can track it over time. Schaub et al. [24] introduced the first blockchain-based privacy-preserving reputation system. There is no trusted third parties, trusted nodes, or subjective trust relationships to guarantee security. Liu et al. [20] exploited the identity-based group signature technique to achieve conditional privacy, calculated trust using a logistic regression-based approach, and designed a mixed consensus algorithm to reduce the cost caused by traditional blockchain. However, hiding behavior may occur because feedback is commonly stored locally and uploaded by the node that generated it.

3   System Model

In this section, we illustrate the proposed blockchain-based scenarios of IoV, and discuss the main components and threat model in detail.

3.1   Main Components

We build a network model, of which the main components are vehicles, RSUs, and the blockchain network. The overall framework is shown in Fig. 1.

1. *Vehicles:* Vehicles are the basis of IoV, and equipped with OBU. The main responsibility of OBU is communicating with RSU as well as neighboring vehicles, which are also equipped with OBU. As revealing vehicles' information publicly may cause some privacy and security issues, we use a pseudonym scheme to hide the real identities of vehicles and generate public and private key pairs by themselves. In this way, the communication messages can be protected by the pseudonym, which reduces the risk of privacy disclosure and improves system security.
2. *RSUs:* RSUs are communication-based units installed near roads, which handle requests from vehicles within radio transmission range. RSUs are licensed and directly connected to the blockchain network. They group messages by events, run smart contracts, store local ledgers and return results to vehicles when requested. An event represents a road accident that occurred somewhere at some time. The messages from the RSU is not completely reliable, and the vehicle needs to judge the quality of service (QoS) of the RSU through the trust and reputation assessment.

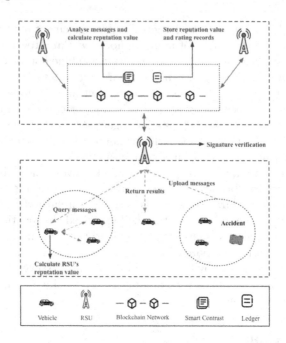

Fig. 1. Blockchain-Based Scenarios of IoV

3. *Blockchain Network:* In our proposed model, we implement a permissioned blockchain (PB), only licensed nodes can be connected to the blockchain, which provides decentralized and trusted execution of vehicles' reputation value evaluation algorithm and tamper-proof trusted data storage. PB maintains two ledgers, namely *CreditLedger* and *RecordLedger*. The former contains messages related to vehicles' reputation value and the latter keeps records of their behavior. The blockchain file system is as shown in Fig. 2. We deploy three smart contracts in PB, namely message smart contract *(MSC)*, reputation smart contract *(RSC)* and query smart contract *(QSC)*, which respectively hold the logic of messages analysis and vehicles' reputation value calculation, as well as query messages from vehicles.

3.2   Threat Model

Depending on the attack nodes, we divide the attacks into two categories: malicious vehicle attacks and compromised RSU attacks.

Malicious Vehicle Attacks: Vehicles share incorrect messages to mislead other vehicles or improve their reputation. Therefore, malicious vehicle attacks can be divided into the following four types:

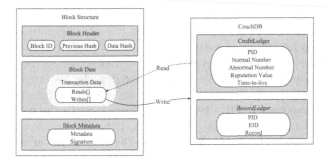

Fig. 2. Blockchain File System

1. *Messages Spoofing Attack:* Vehicles send incorrect messages, including false messages, repeated messages, and outdated messages, to improve their reputation or reduce the reputation of others, causing other nodes to misjudge.
2. *Collusion Attack:* Malicious vehicles conspire to increase their reputation value for a later-on attack, which is defined as a collusion attack.
3. *Random Rating Attack:* In this attack, the vehicle submits randomly generated feedback even though it does not know the authenticity of the message. In a system that encourages feedback submissions, this is beneficial to the vehicle.
4. *Harboring Attack:* After a vehicle is attacked, the detected relevant messages are not submitted for the purpose of protecting its reputation value and interests. It is difficult for other nodes to detect because the impact of this attack on the system takes a long time to be reflected.

Compromised RSU Attacks: RSU exposed by the roadside is vulnerable to attack and the compromised RSU attacks can be divided into the following three types:

1. *Black Hole Attack:* In this type of attack, the RSU simply discards the vehicle's request packet and does not respond, leaving the vehicle waiting for a response.
2. *Duplicate Attack:* After receiving the request, the RSU sends the information to the same vehicle repeatedly to deplete the resources of vehicle.
3. *Energy Depletion Attack:* It means that the RSU sends information to the same vehicle at high frequencies, thus depleting the resources of the target vehicle.
4. *Collusion Attack:* A malicious RSU may partner with a few malicious vehicles, and malicious vehicles give it a high recommendation reputation value, so that the RSU can launch attacks against more vehicles.

4   BPTRM

Reputation management schemes typically require vehicles to trust some entity, such as a centralized authority or other vehicles, for guarantees such as security and privacy. Trust means that the vehicle trusts the trusted entity that the vehicle will operate in a pre-agreed manner, so trust refers to the relationship between the entities, and reputation is a quantitative indicator based on this relationship, representing credibility. The trust and reputation management system evaluates the trustworthiness level by collecting and judging the historical behaviors of nodes. In order to comprehensively evaluate nodes in the blockchain-based IoV scenario, the proposed BPTRM system contains two parts: the vehicle trust and reputation management module (V-TRM) and the RSU trust and reputation management module (R-TRM). Notations in this section are given in Table 1.

Table 1. Notations

Notation	Description
c_i^j	Credibility of the message about E_j reported by V_i
R_i	Reputation value of V_i
Δd	Distance between V_i and the location of E_j
γ	Distance influencing factor
$\mathbb{C}^j$	Set of vehicles' message credibility about E_j
N	Number of elements in $\mathbb{C}^j$
$P(E_j|\mathbb{C}^j)$	Conditional probability based on $\mathbb{C}^j$
$P(E_j), P(\overline{E_j})$	Prior probabilities of E_j and $\overline{E_j}$
$P(c_i^j|E_j), P(c_i^j|\overline{E_j})$	Related and complementary to c_i^j
T, F	positive message and negative message
Thr_m	Threshold for determining whether an event is true
$record_i^j$	Rating of message which reported E_j by V_i
a_i, b_i	Total number of normal and abnormal behaviors of V_i
T_i	Time-to-live for the reputation value R_i
μ	Penalty factor
λ	Time decay factor
a_{ik}^d, b_{ik}^d	Total number of normal and abnormal behaviors of RSU_k observed by V_i
R_{ik}^d, R_{uk}^d	Direct reputation values of V_i and its neighborhood V_u to RSU_k
R_{uk}^{id}	Indirect reputation recommendation from V_u
T_{send}, T_{now}	Message sending time and current time
ω, φ	Weight coefficient of direct and indirect reputation

4.1 V-TRM

The V-TRM refers to the processes that RSU invokes smart contracts to analyze the information reported by vehicles, then calculates and updates the reputation value of vehicles in a timely manner based on past historical behavior. The main processes are illustrated in Fig. 3 and shown as follows:

Step 1: Message Uploading. When the vehicle detects the relevant road event, in order to protect data integrity, the message is signed with its pseudonym

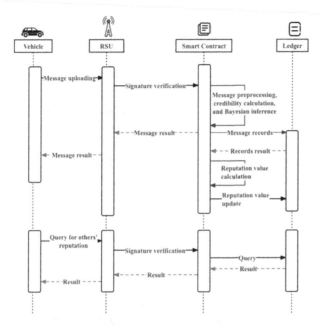

Fig. 3. The Process of V-TRM

which generated by itself. After a period of time, the vehicle can be re-registered with a new pseudonym under the reputation value. Then vehicle uploads the messages to the RSU. Timestamp labels have also been added to prevent replay attack. The data format is $(PID_i, OrgData_j, SigData_j, Timestamp)$, where PID_i is the pseudonym of the vehicle i (denoted as V_i). $OrgData_j$ is the original message data of event j (denoted as E_j) reported by V_i, $SigData_j$ is the signature of $OrgData_j$ by PID_i, and $Timestamp$ is the timestamp of $SigData_j$.

Step 2: Feedback Collection. When receiving a message, RSU needs to group the message according to the event, i.e., those messages reporting the same event are grouped together. Then MSC is called to process messages as follows to properly judge the behavior of the vehicle and get the correct feedback, which is also summarized in Algorithm 1.

1. *Signature Verification:* The following step works when the message has passed the signature verification; otherwise, the message is directly discarded.
2. *Message Preprocessing:* Firstly, the RSU checks *RecordLedger* to confirm whether V_i has reported this event before. If not reported before, the timestamp in the message is then compared with the current time to check the message's timeliness and ensure there is no concealment. If the message has been found either reported before or outdated, the behavior of sending this message is considered to be abnormal, and then MSC turns to process the next message.

3. *Message Credibility Calculation:* Since the preprocessed messages may not be exactly correct, so we design a message credibility calculation method, and take V_i's reputation value into consideration:

$$c_i^j = R_i + e^{-\gamma \cdot \Delta d}, \tag{1}$$

where c_i^j is the credibility of the message about E_j reported by V_i, R_i is the reputation value of V_i, Δd is the distance between V_i and E_j, and γ is the distance influencing factor used to control the effect of Δd on c_i^j.

4. *Bayesian Inference:* After calculating the credibility of all messages, a credibility set $\mathbb{C}^j = \left\{ c_1^j, c_2^j, ..., c_i^j \right\}$ is gained. Then RSU uses $\mathbb{C}^j$ to aggregate all messages based on Bayesian inference:

$$P(E_j|\mathbb{C}^j) = \frac{P(E_j) \cdot \prod_{i=1}^{N} P(c_i^j|E_j)}{P(E_j) \cdot \prod_{i=1}^{N} P(c_i^j|E_j) + P(\overline{E_j}) \cdot \prod_{i=1}^{N} P(c_i^j|\overline{E_j})},$$
$$P(c_i^j|E_j) = c_i^j, \tag{2}$$
$$P(c_i^j|\overline{E_j}) = 1 - c_i^j,$$

where $P(E_j)$ and $P(\overline{E_j})$ are the prior probabilities of E_j and $\overline{E_j}$, respectively, N denotes the sum of elements in $\mathbb{C}^j$, $P(c_i^j|E_j)$ and $P(c_i^j|\overline{E_j})$ are related and complementary to c_i^j, $P(E_j|\mathbb{C}^j) \in [0,1]$, and $P(E_j|\mathbb{C}^j)$ is the conditional probability based on $\mathbb{C}^j$. When $P(E_j|\mathbb{C}^j)$ exceeds the threshold Thr_m, E_j is considered to have actually occurred; otherwise, it does not occur.

In this way, RSU is able to know whether E_j is true or not, and then obtains the aggregated result and broadcasts it to all vehicles in its area. At the same time, RSU can identify whether the messages are positive or not based on the aggregated result, and distinguish whether the behavior is normal or not.

Step 3: Feedback Aggregation (Reputation Value Calculation)

1. *Ledgers Update:* Before performing feedback aggregation, we need to update the ledgers first:

$$record_i^j = \begin{cases} T, & \text{positive message} \\ F, & \text{negative message} \end{cases}, \tag{3}$$

where $record_i^j$ means the rating of message which reported E_j by V_i, and it is stored in the *RecordLedger*;

$$\begin{cases} a_i^{new} = a_i^{old} + 1, & \text{normal behavior} \\ b_i^{new} = b_i^{old} + \mu, & \text{abnormal behavior} \end{cases}, \tag{4}$$

where a_i and b_i represent the total number of normal and abnormal behaviors of V_i, respectively, and it is stored in the *CreditLedger*. In order to punish V_i which behaves abnormal, we introduce the penalty factor μ.

Algorithm 1: Feedback Collection Algorithm

Input: Messages list grouped by event ***Messages_List***, distance influencing factor γ

Output: Record messages list ***Record_List***, the true state of event E_j

1 Initialize ***Record_List*** $= \phi$;

2 Create an empty list of reported event ***verified_list*** ;

3 **for** m_i in ***Messages_List*** **do**

4   **if** m_i *passes the signature verification* **then**

5   ***verified_list*** $\leftarrow m_i$;

6 Create an empty list of negative messages record ***neRecord_list*** and a list of messages that participate in Bayesian inference ***bayesMe_list*** ;

7 **while** m_i in ***verified_list*** **do**

8   **if** m_i *is not reported before* **then**

9   **if** m_i *is not outdated* **then**

10   Calculate message credibility c_i^j according to Eq. (1) ;

11   ***bayesMe_list*** $\leftarrow m_i, c_i^j$;

12   **else**

13   ***neRecord_list*** $\leftarrow m_i$;

14   **else**

15   ***neRecord_list*** $\leftarrow m_i$;

16 Calculate probability P_j by ***bayesMe_list*** according to Eq. (2) ;

17 **if** $P_j > Thr_m$ **then**

18     $E_j = T$;

19 **else**

20     $E_j = F$;

21 **foreach** m_i in ***bayesMe_list*** **do**

22   Set $report_i$ is rating of the event in m_i ;

23   **if** $report_i == E_j$ **then**

24   ***Record_List*** $\leftarrow m_i$;

25   **else**

26   ***neRecord_list*** $\leftarrow m_i$;

27 ***Record_List*** $\leftarrow$ ***neRecord_list*** ;

28 **return** ***Record_List***, E_j ;

---

2. *Reputation Calculation:* For the prediction of V_i's behavior, beta distribution [16] can be used to gain the probability distribution of its reputation C_i:

$$C_i \sim Beta(a_i + 1, b_i + 1). \tag{5}$$

Let R_i be the statistical expectation of the reputation distribution, so V_i's reputation value is calculated as:

$$R_i = E(Beta(a_i + 1, b_i + 1)) = \frac{a_i + 1}{a_i + b_i + 2}. \tag{6}$$

Step 4: Reputation Dissemination. Because of the unique nature of IoV, we set a time-to-live (denoted as T_i) for the reputation value R_i. If a normal behavior occurs, R_i increases and T_i becomes longer; whereas if an abnormal behavior occurs, R_i decreases and T_i becomes shorter. T_i is changed as follows:

$$
\begin{aligned}
t &= \begin{cases} 1, & R_i^{\text{new}} - R_i^{\text{old}} > 0 \\ -1, & R_i^{\text{new}} - R_i^{\text{old}} \leq 0 \end{cases}, \\
T_i &= \begin{cases} t + T_i^{\text{old}}, & t > 0 \\ \mu \cdot t + T_i^{\text{old}}, & t < 0 \end{cases}.
\end{aligned}
\tag{7}
$$

The vehicle may intentionally conceal messages, that is, it does not report any events until T_i is up, so we introduce a time decay factor $\lambda = \frac{1}{T_i}$ to prevent this behavior, and R_i will be reduced as follows:

$$
R_i^{new} = R_i^{old} \cdot e^{-\lambda}.
\tag{8}
$$

Steps 3 and 4 aforementioned are summarized in Algorithm 2.

Algorithm 2: Vehicle's Reputation Value Calculation and Updating

---

   Input: Record messages list **Record_List**

1 **foreach** *record in* **Record_List do**

2   Update ledgers according to Eq. (3) and Eq. (4);

3 **foreach** V_i *in* **CreditLedger do**

4   Query a, b, R_i^{old} of V_i;

5   Calculate R_i according to Eq. (6);

6   **if** $R_i^{new} == R_i^{old}$ **then**

7   Update R_i^{new} according to Eq. (8);

8   Update T_i^{new} according to Eq. (7);

4.2 R-TRM

R-TRM refers to the collaborative filtering technique applied in vehicles. Although RSUs have joined the blockchain, it is also necessary to evaluate RSUs for vehicles, in order to improve the QoS and further help vehicles to choose higher-quality services. A vehicle aggregates its direct reputation value and the neighbor's indirect reputation value to obtain a comprehensive reputation value of RSU. The process of R-TRM is summarized in Fig. 4, which is also summarized in Algorithm 3.

Step 1: Feedback Collection. For black hole attack, if V_i sends a request to RSU_k and does not receive a response for a while, it will regarded that RSU_k behaves abnormally. As for duplicate attack, if the number of the same packets

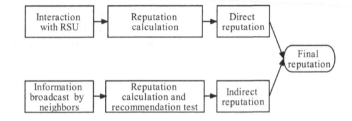

Fig. 4. The Process of R-TRM

sent by RSU_k passes the threshold, it is considered abnormal. As for energy depletion attack, if the number of packets sent by RSU_k passes the threshold, it is regarded abnormal. Then V_i updates its records in the local cache according to Eq. (4). In addition, V_i needs to share its current experience with RSUs every once in a while and collect the messages about RSUs broadcast by its neighbors.

Step 2: Reputation Calculation

1. *Direct Reputation:* Direct reputation is gained by direct interaction of V_i. The calculation method of direct reputation R_{ik}^d of V_i to RSU_k is shown below:

$$R_{ik}^d = E(Beta(a_{ik}^d + 1, b_{ik}^d + 1)) = \frac{a_{ik}^d + 1}{a_{ik}^d + b_{ik}^d + 2}, \tag{9}$$

   where a_{ik}^d and b_{ik}^d are the sum of normal and abnormal behaviors of RSU_k observed by V_i, respectively.

2. *Indirect Reputation:* Indirect reputation come from neighbors. However, the recommendation credibility of neighbors cannot be completely measured by the broadcast messages, so the credibility of the recommendation is tested as below:

$$Test = \left| R_{ik}^d - R_{uk}^d \right| < Thr_t, \tag{10}$$

   where R_{ik}^d and R_{uk}^d are the direct reputation values of V_i and its neighborhood V_u to RSU_k, respectively. If the test fails, the reputation recommendation from V_u is discarded; otherwise, it is accepted. Since the messages is not real-time, the credibility of indirect trust is reduced according to λ. Therefore, the indirect reputation R_{uk}^{id} is calculated as:

$$R_{uk}^{id} = E(Beta(a_{uk}^d + 1, b_{uk}^d + 1)) \cdot e^{-\lambda}$$

$$= \frac{a_{uk}^d + 1}{a_{uk}^d + b_{uk}^d + 2} \cdot e^{-\lambda},$$

$$T = T_{now} - T_{send}, \tag{11}$$

$$\lambda = \frac{1}{T},$$

where T_{send} represents the time when the broadcast message is sended, and T_{now} represents the current time.

Step 3: Reputation Aggregation. Because of the attacks, V_i should pay more attention to its own direct observations and partly take the advice of others. Therefore, aggregating direct and indirect reputation to obtain the final credibility of RSU_k is in the following way:

$$R_{ik} = \omega \cdot R_{ik}^d + \varphi \cdot \frac{\sum_{u=1}^n R_{uk}^{id}}{n}, \qquad (12)$$

where n denotes the number of trustworthy neighbors of V_i. ω and φ are the weight factors of direct and indirect reputation, respectively.

Algorithm 3: RSU's Reputation Value Calculation and Updating

Input: Messages list in V_i's cache ***Messages_List***
Output: RSU_k's Reputation value ***R_{ik}***
1   Create an empty list of trustworthy neighbors' recommendation
    recommend_list ;
2   Calculate R_{ik}^d according to Eq. (9) ;
3   **foreach** V_u *in* ***Messages_List*** **do**
4   Calculate R_{uk}^d according to Eq. (9) ;
5   Calculate $Test$ according to Eq. (10) ;
6   **if** $Test < Thr_t$ **then**
7   Calculate R_{uk}^{id} according to Eq. (11) ;
8   ***recommend_list*** $\leftarrow R_{uk}^{id}$;
9   **foreach** R_{uk}^d *in* ***recommend_list*** **do**
10   Calculate ***R_{ik}*** according to Eq. (12) ;
11   **return** ***R_{ik}*** ;

---

5   Security Analysis

In this section, we conduct security analysis from the following aspects.

5.1   Resist Malicious Vehicle Attacks

The vehicle is a semi-trusted entity in the system, and according to the previous elaboration, it may launch four kinds of attacks. Effects of these four attacks on the system are considered in the proposed scheme.

1. *Messages Spoofing Attack:* Duplicate and obsolete messages sent by the vehicle will be discarded by the V-TRM and therefore will not significantly affect system performance. If a vehicle sends a abnormal message, other honest vehicles will give their feedback about the event corresponding to the message,

and since most vehicles are honest, the vehicle's message will be judged to be wrong and the vehicle's behavior will be judged to be abnormal. As a result, the number of abnormal behaviors of the vehicle will increase, thereby reducing its reputation value. Moreover, abnormal behavior will make time-to-live for its reputation value become shorter.

2. *Collusion Attack:* Malicious vehicles collusion will increase the probability that abnormal messages will be judged correct, so the system does not limit the number of verified vehicles. If the majority of vehicles are honest, these colluding vehicles will not be able to fully control the result of the message. Moreover, the penalty factor set by the system will make the penalty brought by the abnormal behavior greater than the benefit brought by the normal behavior, and the behavior of vehicle collusion is still not worthy in the long run.

3. *Random Rating Attack:* Instead of providing accurate messages, vehicles submit randomly generated feedback to the system. This kind of attack is advantageous to the attacker in many systems that encourage feedback submission. Although this paper uses Time-to-live to encourage feedback submission, it also sets a penalty factor to punish abnormal behaviors. Therefore, even if more participation in feedback can improve the reputation value of the vehicle to a certain extent, the existence of the penalty factor will cause the vehicle to lose more reputation value.

4. *Harboring Attack:* The vehicle may not want to share and only want to obtain system services for free, in which case the vehicle will remain accepting messages without sharing or verifying messages for a long time. Moreover, vehicles that receive malicious attacks may also exhibit this characteristic. To address this attack, we set the time-to-live of reputation value to encourage vehicles to actively share news, otherwise the reputation value will decrease over time.

5.2 Resist Compromised RSU Attacks

A malicious RSU may also launch four types of attacks, but we will treat Duplicate Attack and Energy Depletion Attack together when discussing the resistance of the proposed scheme to these four types of attacks.

1. *Black Hole Attack:* When the vehicle communicates with the RSU, the vehicle sends the request packet to the RSU, and if it does not receive a reply from the RSU for a while, the vehicle retransmits the packet. When retransmission exceeds a certain threshold, the vehicle will change RSU for service, and at the same time, the vehicle adds a abnormal behavior to the RSU, which will reduce the reputation of the RSU, and the reputation can be recommended to other vehicles, other vehicles will take this advice, and eventually the abnormal RSU can be found due to low reputation.

2. *Duplicate Attack and Energy Depletion Attack:* After receiving valid packets from the same RSU for more than a threshold, the vehicle considers the RSU to be abnormal. Therefore, the vehicle discards packets from the RSU, increases the number of abnormal behaviors of the RSU, and recommends the new reputation value of the RSU to other vehicles.

3. *Collusion Attack:* If malicious vehicles help malicious RSU launch attacks, giving the malicious RSU an untrue recommendation reputation values may cause other vehicles to choose a low-quality RSU for service. However, when vehicle collects recommendation values of other vehicles, it adopts a collaborative filtering method to remove some abnormal recommendation reputation values according to the direct reputation value, and reduce the malicious recommendation from other vehicles.

6   Performance Evaluation

To evaluate the feasibility and efficiency of the proposed system, we perform the system evaluation based on the Hyperledger Fabric platform [1] and MATLAB_R2020a. The Hyperledger Fabric provides a blockchain development platform, and the settings of parameters are listed in Table 2.

Table 2. Key Parameters

Parameter	Value
Number of vehicles	50
γ	0.015
Δd	[0, 300]
μ	2
Thr_m	222
Trustworthy neighbors	(0, 50)
Signature algorithm	ECDSA [27]

6.1   Event Occurrence Probability

All messages are aggregated to get the accuracy of the probability of the event through MSC. Among all vehicles reporting accident, the proportion of malicious vehicles varies from 0% to 100% by a step of 10%. Ten experiments are conducted for each ratio of malicious vehicles. The locations of malicious vehicles and the types of messages spoofing attacks that occur are both randomly selected. We compare the proposed BPTRM with BTM (blockchain-trust management) proposed in [31]. As can be observed from Fig. 5, the lower proportion of malicious vehicles get higher probability of the eventual event. BPTRM proposed in this paper considers more factors in reality than BTM. For example, BTM only considers the false messages in the messages spoofing attack, but does not consider the effect of outdated and duplicate messages on the results. Therefore, as the proportion of malicious vehicles improves, the probability of occurrence of events derived by BTM will be higher, so BPTRM can effectively improve the judgment accuracy of events.

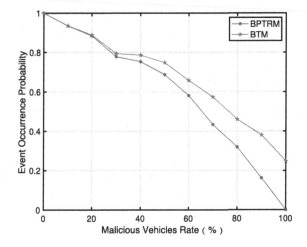

Fig. 5. Event Occurrence Probability

6.2   Reputation Value

To demonstrate the correctness and sensitivity of BPTRM, we simulate the tendency of reputation value influenced by normal and abnormal behavior. To illustrate more clearly, we also introduced BTM as a benchmark. The total number of normal behaviors of the initial vehicle is 3, the total number of abnormal behaviors is 3, the survival time of the reputation value is 24, and the initial reputation value is calculated by the given initial conditions. BTM formalizes an inverse trigonometric function to calculate reputation value by using weighted aggregation and considering that the tendency of reputation value becomes slower over

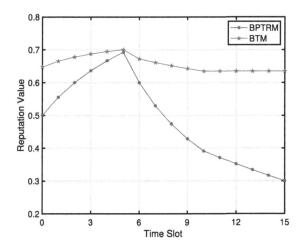

Fig. 6. Reputation Value Changes over Time

a long period of time. The simulation results are shown in Fig. 6. Due to the different methods used to calculate reputation, the initial reputation value is not the same for the three normal behaviors and the three abnormal behaviors. In particular, BTM vehicles have an initial reputation of 0.65 and BPTRM is 0.5 During time slots 0–5, the vehicle behaves honestly and well. During time slots 6–10, the vehicle begins to attack. As the punishment intensity of BPTRM is higher than BTM, and the reputation value decreases faster. During slots 11–15, the vehicle becomes inactive. Then the reputation value of BPTRM decreases more rapidly, which can effectively detect whether the vehicle has a harboring attack. In addition, Fig. 6 can also verify the correctness of choosing the beta distribution, that is, the reputation value will not grow and decline slowly like BTM when the number of vehicle behaviors is large, which is more in line with the reality.

6.3   Time-to-Live of Reputation

In order to prevent vehicles from concealing selfish behavior, such as harboring attack, we set a time-to-live for the reputation value of each vehicle. The relationship between reputation value and the time-to-live (TTL) are shown in Table 3. At the beginning, the reputation value is 0.5, and the initial TTL is

Table 3. Time-to-live of Reputation Value Change Trend.

Update Rounds	Reputation Value	TTL
1–8	0.6667	25
	0.7500	26
	0.8000	27
	0.8333	28
	0.8571	28
	0.888	28
	0.9	28
9–19	0.75	26
	0.6429	24
	0.5625	22
	0.5	20
	0.45	18
	0.4091	16
	0.375	14
	0.3462	12
	0.3214	10
	0.3	8
19–20	null	null

24. During rounds 1–8, the vehicle behaves honestly and well, and the time-to-live increases. In order to prevent the vehicle from deliberately increasing the time-to-live of the reputation value, when the reputation value of the vehicle is greater than 0.85, the time-to-live will no longer increase. During rounds 9–19, the vehicle behaves aggressively, and in order to punish the vehicle, the time-to-live decreases faster than it increases. When the reputation value of the vehicle is less than 0.3, we will remove the relevant messages of the vehicle from the *CreditLedger*, and all of its information will be empty.

6.4   Impact of Neighbor Recommendation

We analyze the influence of the vehicle's trusted neighbor on the total indirect reputation of neighbor recommendation. In the absence of interaction between vehicles, the RSU's reputation is entirely derived from a vehicle's own past experience, and here we set the initial reputation value is 0.5. Figure 7 shows the relationship between the percentage of trustworthy neighbors and the total recommended reputation value. Here we compare three cases where the recommendation confidence threshold Thr_t is *0.1, 0.2* and *0.3*.

Because of the existence of recommendation credibility test, untrusted neighbors have little influence on the average value of total recommended reputation value, so the curve moves smoothly. Therefore, the reliability test of recommendation must be carried out. In the case of the same proportion of trusted neighbors, when the threshold is smaller, the recommended indirect reputation average will be closer to the benchmark (0.5).

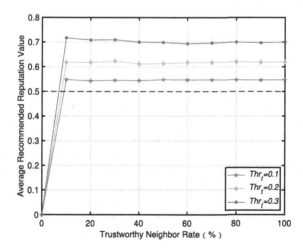

Fig. 7. Relationship Between Percentage of Trustworthy Neighbor and the Average Recommended Reputation value.

6.5   Performance of Blockchain

In this subsection, we evaluate the performance of blockchain.

Delay. The first is the delay. In our scheme, the time delay contains two cases: 1) vehicle queries the reputation value of other vehicles; 2) RSU informs the vehicle of road conditions. These two cases are implemented by QSC and MSC, respectively. As shown in Fig. 8, the average latency increases gradually as the transaction arrival rate increases. In addition, the smaller the batch size, the shorter the average transaction latency and the shorter the average transaction processing time. This is because using smaller batch sizes reduces memory usage without having transactions be hanged, in other words, making the program more responsive.

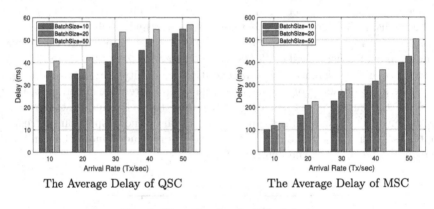

Fig. 8. Time Overhead of Blockchain

Transaction Throughput. We use the performance testing tool Tape to evaluate the performance of the BPTRM implemented in this paper, and explore the impact of different batchSize and different transaction arrival rate (TAR) on the transaction throughput. TAR indicate rate at which transactions reach the blockchain, that is, the number of concurrent calls of the smart contract. It can be observed from Fig. 9 that as the batchSize increasing, transaction throughput firstly increases and then becomes stable. Moreover, due to the excessive number of transactions arriving at the same time, the processing rate of the system is exceeded. There is little difference in transaction throughput for different TAR and batchSize.

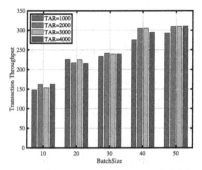
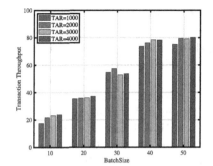

The Average Throughout of QSC   The Average Throughout of MSC

Fig. 9. Transaction Throughput of Blockchain

6.6   Memory Cost of Ledgers

In this subsection, we discuss the storage overhead of ledger data in the blockchain file system. As a result of that BPTRM can realize the functions of vehicles reporting the same event only once and canceling the vehicles with reputation below the threshold, only the reputation-related messages and behavior records of the vehicle are stored, which make great memory extensibility to blockchain. To show that BPTRM has better memory scalability, we compare the memory cost with BTM. As can be seen from Fig. 10, the storage of BTM increases linearly, and since BTM requires the storage of message signature data, it takes up more memory than BPTRM.

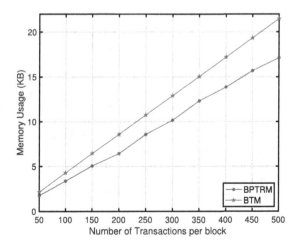

Fig. 10. Memory Occupied by Ledger Data

7 Conclusion

In this paper, we propose a blockchain-based privacy-preserving trust and reputation management system for IoV. The system writes the vehicle's behavior analysis, reputation calculation update, and query algorithms into smart contracts using the blockchain file system, ensuring the accuracy and validity of the vehicle reputation value. Meanwhile, in order to improve the communication efficiency with RSUs, vehicles employ collaborative filtering to evaluate RSUs thoroughly. Furthermore, the system defines reputation survival time, which plays a more effective role in limiting malicious vehicles. In order to verify the feasibility of the system, we carried out extensive experiments. The robustness of the reputation scheme is demonstrated by adjusting the number of malicious vehicles in different proportions, and the superiority of credit calculation is demonstrated by comparing with other schemes. By simulating the influence of different attack behaviors on vehicle reputation, the effect of reputation scheme against attack is demonstrated. By deploying smart contracts to the blockchain, the performance of the blockchain under different parameters is measured, proving the availability of the system. On the whole, the results indicate that the proposed system perform effectively in recognition of malicious nodes and reputation management.

Acknowledgments. This research was supported in part by the National Natural Science Foundation of China (No. 61971131), in part by "Zhishan" Scholars Programs of Southeast University, and in part by the Ministry of Educations Key Lab for Computer Network and Information Integration, Southeast University, Nanjing, China.

References

1. Hyperledger fabric. https://www.hyperledger.org/. Accessed 13 Sept 2022
2. Bellini, E., Iraqi, Y., Damiani, E.: Blockchain-based distributed trust and reputation management systems: a survey. IEEE Access **8**, 21127–21151 (2020). https://doi.org/10.1109/ACCESS.2020.2969820
3. Bhargava, A., Verma, S., Chaurasia, B.K., Tomar, G.S.: Computational trust model for Internet of Vehicles. In: Conference on Information and Communication Technology (CICT), pp. 1–5 (2017). https://doi.org/10.1109/INFOCOMTECH.2017.8340600
4. Dahiya, R., Jiang, F., Doss, R.R.: A feedback-driven lightweight reputation scheme for IoV. In: IEEE International Conference on Trust, Security and Privacy in Computing and Communications (TrustCom), pp. 1060–1068 (2020). https://doi.org/10.1109/TrustCom50675.2020.00141
5. Dias, J.A.F.F., Rodrigues, J.J.P.C., Shu, L., Ullah, S.: Performance evaluation of a cooperative reputation system for vehicular delay-tolerant networks. EURASIP J. Wirel. Commun. Networking (2014). https://doi.org/10.1186/1687-1499-2014-88
6. Firdaus, M., Rahmadika, S., Rhee, K.H.: Decentralized trusted data sharing management on Internet of Vehicle Edge Computing (IoVEC) networks using consortium blockchain. Sensors **21**(7), 2410 (2021)

7. Gong, C., Xu, C., Zhou, Z., Zhang, T., Yang, S.: A reputation management scheme for identifying malicious nodes in VANET. In: IEEE International Conference on High Performance Switching and Routing (HPSR), pp. 1–6 (2019). https://doi.org/10.1109/HPSR.2019.8808102

8. Gyawali, S., Qian, Y., Hu, R.Q.: Resource allocation in vehicular communications using graph and deep reinforcement learning. In: IEEE Global Communications Conference (GLOBECOM), pp. 1–6 (2019). https://doi.org/10.1109/GLOBECOM38437.2019.9013594

9. Halabi, T., Zulkernine, M.: Trust-based cooperative game model for secure collaboration in the Internet of Vehicles. In: IEEE International Conference on Communications (ICC), pp. 1–6 (2019). https://doi.org/10.1109/ICC.2019.8762069

10. Hasan, O., Brunie, L., Bertino, E.: Privacy-preserving reputation systems based on blockchain and other cryptographic building blocks: a survey. ACM Comput. Surv. 55(2), 1–37 (2023). https://doi.org/10.1145/3490236

11. Hildebrand, B., Baza, M., Salman, T., Amsaad, F., Razaqu, A., Alourani, A.: A comprehensive review on blockchains for Internet of Vehicles: challenges and directions (2022)

12. Junejo, M.H., et al.: A privacy-preserving attack-resistant trust model for Internet of Vehicles ad hoc networks. Sci. Program. 2020, 1–21 (2020). https://doi.org/10.1155/2020/8831611

13. Kamel, J., Wolf, M., van der Hei, R.W., Kaiser, A., Urien, P., Kargl, F.: VeReMi extension: a dataset for comparable evaluation of misbehavior detection in VANETs. In: IEEE International Conference on Communications (ICC), pp. 1–6 (2020). https://doi.org/10.1109/ICC40277.2020.9149132

14. Kang, J., Xiong, Z., Niyato, D., Ye, D., Kim, D.I., Zhao, J.: Toward secure blockchain-enabled Internet of Vehicles: optimizing consensus management using reputation and contract theory. IEEE Trans. Veh. Technol. 68(3), 2906–2920 (2019). https://doi.org/10.1109/TVT.2019.2894944

15. Kang, J., et al.: Blockchain for secure and efficient data sharing in vehicular edge computing and networks. IEEE Internet Things J. 6(3), 4660–4670 (2019). https://doi.org/10.1109/JIOT.2018.2875542

16. Kerman, J.: Neutral noninformative and informative conjugate beta and gamma prior distributions. Electron. J. Stat. 5, 1450–1470 (2011)

17. Kumar, S., Velliangiri, S., Karthikeyan, P., Kumari, S., Kumar, S., Khan, M.K.: A survey on the blockchain techniques for the Internet of Vehicles security. Trans. Emerg. Telecommun. Technol. 35, e4317 (2024). https://doi.org/10.1002/ett.4317

18. Li, Q., Malip, A., Martin, K.M., Ng, S.L., Zhang, J.: A reputation-based announcement scheme for VANETs. IEEE Trans. Veh. Technol. 61(9), 4095–4108 (2012). https://doi.org/10.1109/TVT.2012.2209903

19. Li, W., Song, H.: ART: an attack-resistant trust management scheme for securing vehicular ad hoc networks. IEEE Trans. Intell. Transp. Syst. 17(4), 960–969 (2016). https://doi.org/10.1109/TITS.2015.2494017

20. Liu, X., Huang, H., Xiao, F., Ma, Z.: A blockchain-based trust management with conditional privacy-preserving announcement scheme for VANETs. IEEE Internet Things J. 7(5), 4101–4112 (2020). https://doi.org/10.1109/JIOT.2019.2957421

21. Monir, M., Abdel-Hamid, A., Abd El Aziz, M.: A categorized trust-based message reporting scheme for VANETs. In: Awad, A., Hassanien, A., Baba, K. (eds.) Advances in Security of Information and Communication Networks. Communications in Computer and Information Science, vol. 381, pp. 65–83. Springer, Cham (2013). https://doi.org/10.1007/978-3-642-40597-6_6

22. Najafi, M., Khoukhi, L., Lemercier, M.: Decentralized reputation model based on Bayes' theorem in vehicular networks. In: IEEE International Conference on Communications, pp. 1–6 (2021). https://doi.org/10.1109/ICC42927.2021.9500491
23. Ning, J., Wang, J., Liu, J., Kato, N.: Attacker identification and intrusion detection for in-vehicle networks. IEEE Commun. Lett. **23**(11), 1927–1930 (2019). https://doi.org/10.1109/LCOMM.2019.2937097
24. Schaub, A., Bazin, R., Hasan, O., Brunie, L.: A trustless privacy-preserving reputation system. In: ICT Systems Security and Privacy Protection, SEC 2016. IFIP Advances in Information and Communication Technology, vol. 471, pp. 398–411 (2016). https://doi.org/10.1007/978-3-319-33630-5_27
25. Sun, L., Yang, Q., Chen, X., Chen, Z.: RC-chain: reputation-based crowdsourcing blockchain for vehicular networks. J. Netw. Comput. Appl. **176**, 102956 (2020)
26. Whitby, A., Jøsang, A., Indulska, J.: Filtering out unfair ratings in Bayesian reputation systems. In: Autonomous Agents & Multi Agent Systems (2004)
27. Yang, X., Liu, M., Au, M.H., Luo, X., Ye, Q.: Efficient verifiably encrypted ECDSA-like signatures and their applications. IEEE Trans. Inf. Forensics Secur. **17**, 1573–1582 (2022). https://doi.org/10.1109/TIFS.2022.3165978
28. Yang, Z., Yang, K., Lei, L., Zheng, K., Leung, V.C.M.: Blockchain-based decentralized trust management in vehicular networks. IEEE Internet Things J. **6**(2), 1495–1505 (2019). https://doi.org/10.1109/JIOT.2018.2836144
29. Yang, Z., Zheng, K., Yang, K., Leung, V.C.M.: A blockchain-based reputation system for data credibility assessment in vehicular networks. In: IEEE Annual International Symposium on Personal, Indoor, and Mobile Radio Communications (PIMRC), pp. 1–5 (2017). https://doi.org/10.1109/PIMRC.2017.8292724
30. Yu, Y., Guo, L., Liu, Y., Zheng, J., Zong, Y.: An efficient SDN-based DDoS attack detection and rapid response platform in vehicular networks. IEEE Access **6**, 44570–44579 (2018). https://doi.org/10.1109/ACCESS.2018.2854567
31. Zhang, H., Liu, J., Zhao, H., Wang, P., Kato, N.: Blockchain-based trust management for Internet of Vehicles. IEEE Trans. Emerg. Top. Comput. **9**(3), 1397–1409 (2021). https://doi.org/10.1109/TETC.2020.3033532

Blockchain Privacy Protection

An Efficient Consortium Blockchain Dual Privacy Protection Scheme

Haipeng Yang[1](✉), Peng Han[2], Lili Xiong[3], and Yuanyuan Li[1]

[1] College of Computer Science and Technology, Chongqing University of Posts and Telecommunications, Chongqing, China
s220201116@stu.cqupt.edu.cn
[2] Chongqing Research Center for Information and Automation Technology, Chongqing, China
[3] Chongqing Academy of Science and Technology, Chongqing, China

Abstract. The ledger on the blockchain is public, so that the transactions on the chain can be verified and traced by other nodes, but it will also lead to the privacy of blockchain users being leaked or analyzed by some malicious users to learn their true identities. Therefore, this paper suggests a privacy preserving scheme based on verifiability certificateless ring signatures and homomorphic encryption to solve privacy concerns in consortium blockchain. Firstly, the certificateless ring signature based on elliptic curve is improved to increase the verifiability to prevent malicious users from using the unconditional anonymity of ring signature to perform some malicious acts. In the meantime, the certificateless cryptosystem has the advantages of keyless escrow and high security, which can make our entire solution more secure. Secondly, the transaction amount is encrypted with homomorphic encryption where the data is available but not visible, which protects the privacy of the transaction amount while facilitating subsequent verification. Finally, it is analyzed and compared with other schemes, which proves that the scheme has certain advantages in terms of efficiency while protecting double privacy.

Keywords: Certificateless ring signature · Homomorphic encryption · Consortium chain · Privacy protection

1 Introduction

Blockchain technology is a new computer paradigm proposed by the Bitcoin white paper [1], which is decentralized, untamperable and traceable. A consortium chain is a cooperative participation between multiple organizations to jointly manage a blockchain network. The data on the consortium chain can only be viewed by organizations and authorized users within the consortium, and the framework can be applied in various applications in healthcare [2], finance [3] and other industries. Among them, Hyperledger Fabric [4] is the outstanding representative of the consortium chain.

J. Zhu et al. (Eds.): CBCS 2023, CCIS 2098, pp. 225–241, 2024.
https://doi.org/10.1007/978-981-97-3203-6_12

Blockchain ensures the authenticity and reliability of the ledger by making the public ledger available to participants to view all transaction data and verify its validity. Similarly, transactions in a consortium chain are usually visible, at least to authorized participants. This openness will publicize the details of the transaction as well as the identity of the trader to other participants. Some illegal elements can contact the user's network address through the payment circulation information thus obtaining the user's real identity [5], resulting in the leakage of the transaction privacy of the members of the consortium chain. In 2017 and 2018 [6], the virtual addresses of users in the blockchain network were analyzed to discover the relationship between users' real information and their addresses. In 2020, Bitcoin's hardware wallet was also attacked, resulting in the privacy of hundreds of thousands of users being compromised. Therefore, protecting users' privacy becomes particularly important in blockchain. The ring signature algorithm, proposed by Rivest et al. [7] in 2001, is anonymous, unforgeable and spontaneous. In the application of blockchain, ring signature can hide the transaction address of the members in the consortium chain, thus providing protection for the privacy of the user's identity. Some existing privacy protection schemes based on ring signatures have three problems, first, unconditional anonymity, the governing body can not track down the malicious participants. Second, the scheme exists a large number of computations and is less efficient. Third, it does not achieve double protection of user privacy.

Based on the above analysis, this paper suggests a privacy preserving scheme with verifiability certificateless ring signature and homomorphic encryption for the privacy problems in the consortium chain. Firstly, the certificateless ring signature of scheme [8] is improved to increase the signer identity verifiability. The scheme utilizes the verifiability certificateless ring signature to protect the user's identity privacy. When a transaction dispute occurs, the authoritative node utilizes the identity information of the signer in the block to trace his real identity in order to prevent malicious users from doing evil. Secondly, homomorphic encryption is used to protect the traders' payment amounts and account balance, forming a dual protection strategy. Finally, a transaction protocol is developed for the protection strategy of this scheme to ensure the legitimacy of the transaction.

2   Related Works

Numerous technologies have been suggested to tackle the privacy challenges associated with blockchain. For example, Chaum [9] proposed the idea of coin mixing in 1981, which achieves the confusion of multiple input and output addresses by mixing the transaction records of multiple digital currencies together, making the origin and destination of individual transactions more difficult to trace, thus achieving the privacy of users' identity. CoinJoin [10] is a typical coin mixing technique, but this protocol requires that the transaction amounts involved in the mixing service are the same, and it is not possible to encrypt these transaction amounts. The Zerocoin protocol [11], based on zero-knowledge proofs, can hide a trader's trading address so that the transaction cannot be connected. To some extent, the ledger can be protected from analysis by attackers, but it requires additional storage and is computationally inefficient. Lightning Network [12] proposes an off-chain payment scheme in which the two sides of the transaction outside the chain can make multiple transactions, but the global ledger will only record the beginning of the transaction and the last transaction. Off-chain payments hide some transaction details to a certain degree, but the user's identity privacy is not protected.

Ring signatures offer unconditional anonymity and non-forgeability compared to general digital signatures, making them widely applied in protecting the sharing economy [13], electronic payments [14], and electronic voting [15], among others. Li et al. [16] proposed an elliptic curve ring signature scheme and used the anonymity of this scheme to construct a private data storage protocol to protect the identity information of the members of the blockchain, making the signer unconditionally anonymous. However, unconditional anonymity can lead to malicious activities, so Zhang et al. [17] proposed a conditional anonymous ring signature method to cope with the problem. This approach ensures user anonymity while allowing authorized nodes to detect and address undesirable behavior. When detecting such behavior, the authorized nodes can initiate a confirmation protocol to verify the identity of the transaction user. Chen et al. [18] utilized certificateless ring signature to protect the identity information of the members of the consortium chain, and part of the member's private key is produced by multiple generation centers, which has some fault tolerance when some nodes are down. The aforementioned solution primarily focuses on privacy protection of user identities within the blockchain network, without addressing data protection. Wang et al. [19] employed homomorphic encryption to protect the transaction amount of a trader in the blockchain from being obtained by other participants, but did not achieve user identity privacy protection. Scheme [20] combines aggregated signatures and the concept of coin mixing to propose a fully anonymous scheme for protecting user identity and transaction amount privacy. However, it is not applicable to consortium blockchain scenarios.

3   Preliminaries

3.1   Homomorphic Encryption

The algorithm mechanism [21] supports the operation of numbers in an encrypted state, and the result of the operation is also in an encrypted state, which can be well applied to protect data privacy. In this paper, the Paillier algorithm [22] with additive homomorphism is used, and the following is the specific process:

1. **Key generation**: There exist two primes p and q, where p and q need to satisfy the existence of a greatest common divisor between $(p-1)(q-1)$ and pq. The public key (N, g) and the private key (λ, μ) of Paillier's algorithm can be computed from p and q, respectively, where g is an integer.

2. **Encryption**: For the data to be encrypted m, choose a random integer r and compute $en = E(m) = g^m r^N \mod N^2$.
3. **Decryption**: Decrypt the ciphertext en to get $m = \mu \times L(en^\lambda \mod N^2) \mod N^2$.

3.2   Proof of Interval Range

Since this paper utilizes the Paillier algorithm to encrypt the transaction amount and account balance, the verification node cannot directly verify whether the transaction is legitimate or not. Therefore, this paper uses interval range proof [23] for transaction legitimacy verification.

Assume that there are public safety parameters t, l, s. n is a large composite number whose factor is decomposed, g is an element in a multiplicative group, and h is an element in a cyclic group generated by g. $E(x, r) = g^x h^{r_0} \mod n$ is a FO commitment, the prover send this commitment to the verifier to ensure $x \in [a, b]$, where $r_0 \in \{-2^s n + 1, \ldots, 2^s n - 1\}$. The following briefly summarizes the proof:

1. The prover calculates $E_0 = g^{x-a+1} h^{r_0}$, where let $y = x - (a - 1)$.
2. The prover randomly selects an integer $\alpha \neq 0, 0 \leq \omega \leq 2^{s+T}$, so that it satisfies $u = \alpha^2 y + \omega > 2^{l+t+s+T}$. Then selects three random numbers $r_1, r_2, r_3 \in \{-2^s n + 1, \ldots, 2^s n - 1\}$, so that it satisfies $-r_0 \alpha^2 - r_1 \alpha - r_2 \in [-2^s n + 1, 2^s n - 1]$, and calculates $E_i = E_{i-1}^\alpha g^{r_i}$, where i=1, 2. $F = g^\omega h^{r_3} \mod n$, $U = g^u / E_2$. The prover sends (u, E_1, E_2, F) to the verifier, and Compute PK_i and expose:

$$PK_1\{\alpha, r_1, r_2 : E_1 = E_0^\alpha h^{r_1} \mod n \wedge E_2 = E_1^\alpha \mod n\}$$
$$PK_2\{\omega, r_3, -r_0\alpha^2 - r_1\alpha - r_2 : F = g^\omega h^{r_3} \mod n \wedge U = g^\omega$$
$$h^{-r_0\alpha^2 - r_1\alpha - r_2} \mod n\}$$
$$PK_3\{\omega, r_3 : F = g^\omega h^{r_3} \mod n \wedge -2^{t+l+s+T} \leq \omega \leq 2^{t+l+s+T}\}$$

3. After receiving the information, the verifier calculates $E_0 = E/g^a$, $U = g^u / E_2$, and then uses the known information to verify whether PK_i is equal and whether $u = \alpha^2 y + \omega > 2^{l+t+s+T}$ is true through the above formula. If both are true, the verifier is sure of $x \geq a$.

When verifying $x \leq b$, the verifier can make $y = (b + 1) - x$, and substituting y into the above process can prove $x \leq b$, and finally it can be obtained that $x \in [a, b]$ is established. In the above process, $y = x - (a - 1)$ is employed to validate the authenticity of the account balance, that is, to validate whether the balance is greater than or equal to 0, and is not suitable for verifying the transaction amount. The transaction amount is generally greater than 0, so it is necessary to change the value of y in the process, so that $y = x - a$ can verify whether $x > a$ is established, and when verifying $x < b$, let $y = b - x$.

4   Scheme Design

This chapter mainly describes the consortium chain privacy protection scheme of certificateless ring signature and homomorphic encryption. Certificateless ring signatures are used to protect the identity of traders, and the privacy of the transaction amount is protected by homomorphic encryption, thus forming a double protection. The scheme model is shown in Fig. 1. The nodes in the consortium chain are categorized into three parts: Authoritative Node (AN), Verification Node (VN), and Normal Node (NN). The specific description is as follows.

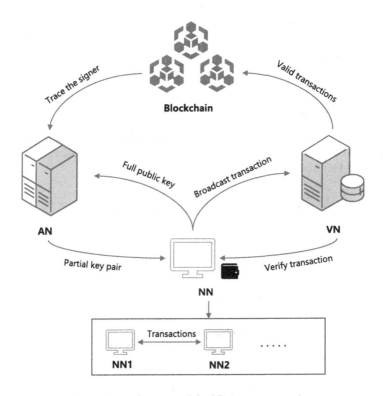

Fig. 1. The scheme model of Privacy protection.

4.1   Role Classification

This paper combines the characteristics of the certificateless ring signature and the consortium chain, and divides the nodes in the consortium chain into three parts. Among them, only normal nodes conduct transactions, so the anonymity of both parties in the scheme is aimed at normal nodes other than the transaction party. There is a common pair of public and private keys between verification nodes, and normal nodes can use their public keys to encrypt transaction information to prevent other normal nodes from stealing information.

1. **Authoritative Node** (AN): The administrator of the consortium chain, responsible for the generation of the system key and Paillier algorithm key in the consortium chain. When a user registers to join the network, AN generates a partial key for them and add authentication for it. When there is a transaction dispute or malicious behavior, the authoritative node can track the signer of the transaction.
2. **Verification Node** (VN): Maintain the global ledger. When the ordinary node makes a transaction, it is necessary to judge the legality of the transaction, and if it is legal, then update the account balances of both parties, otherwise the transaction is rejected.
3. **Normal Node** (NN): Traders, authoritative nodes and verification nodes in the alliance chain do not trade, only ordinary nodes trade between each other. After the transaction between ordinary nodes, the transaction needs to be broadcast to the verification node to verify the legitimacy of the transaction.

4.2 Certificateless Ring Signature Model

In the context of a consortium blockchain, this solution divides the process of verifiable anonymous ring signatures into five stages. The detailed flow is shown below (Table 1):

Table 1. Symbols explanation of model.

Symbol	Description
q	Orders of G and Z_q^*
G	A multiplicative group
P	A generator of G
ID_i	Ring member i
$pk_i = (X_i, Y_i)$	The public key of user i
y_i	The partial key of user i generated by AN
x_i	The partial key of user i generated by user
$H_i()$	Secure hash function
P_{pub}	The public key of AN
$Rsign_i$	Ring signature of user i
$Sign_i$	Signature of user i
Enc_p	Encryption using homomorphic encryption
Enc_{pub}	Encryption using system public key
Enc_i	Encryption using user i's public key
$account_i$	Account balance of user i
$address_i$	Address of user i

1. **System**: The authoritative node selects a $q-order$ group G based on the security parameters and selects a generator element P of G. Afterwards, a random integer s is selected as the system key in the Z_q^* and the corresponding system master public key $P_{pub} = sP$ is computed. $H_1 : \{0,1\}^*-> Z_q^*$, $H_2 : \{0,1\}^* \times G-> Z_q^*$, $H_3 : \{0,1\}^* \times G \times Z_q^*-> Z_q^*$, $H_4 : G-> Z_q^*$, $H_5 : G \times Z_q^*-> Z_q^*$ is the created secure hash function. Finally, expose the public parameter $\{G,q,P_{pub},P,H_i\}$.

2. **Registration**: The new user sends a registration information to the authoritative node, AN authenticates the user, and after the verification is passed, AN calculates $y_i = sH_1(ID_i)$ and $Y_i = y_iP$ for the registered user to obtain part of the key. AN then sends (Y_i, y_i) to the user. After the registered user receives the partial key, verify $Y_i = P_{pub} * H_1(ID_i)$, and after the verification passes, the partial key generated by AN is valid.

   The user selects the random integer x_i as another part of his private key, where $x_i \in Z_q^*$, and then calculates $X_i = x_iP$, which allows user to obtain the complete public key $pk_i = (X_i, Y_i)$ and the complete private key $sk_i = (x_i, y_i)$. Then, the user chooses an integer $u_i \in Z_q^*$, and calculates $U_i = u_iP$ and $h_2 = H_2(ID_i, pk_i)$ to generate the signature information $\sigma_i = u_i + (x_i + y_i)h_2$. Then the user encrypts (σ, U_i) using the public key P_{pub} and sends $\{ID_i, pk_i, Enc_{pub}(\sigma, U_i)\}$ to the AN. After the AN receives the message, it decrypts it with its own private key, obtains the signed message, and then verifies whether the $\sigma P = U_i + (X_i + P_0H_1(ID_i))h_2$ equation is equal, if it is equal, it means that the user's public key pk_i is correct, and then the administrator generates authentication for the user $\{ID_i, pk_i\}$.

3. **Signature**: Assuming that the signer is user t. When signer ID_t signs message m, they need to select other ring members including his own public key form set $L = ((X_1, Y_1), (X_2, Y_2), ..., (X_n, Y_n))$, and the signature generation process include the following:
   - The user ID_t selects a random number $a \in Z_q^*$, calculates $w = a + y_i$, $U = aP$, $R = wP$, $t = H_4(R, X_s, Y_s, w, a)$, and the signer keeps the secret value w, a.
   - The user ID_t selects $n-1$ random numbers $S_i \in Z_q^*$, $i \neq t$. And then computes $h_i = H_3(m, S_i, pk_i)$, where $0 \leq i \leq n-1$, but $i \neq t$.
   - The user ID_t selects a random number $k \in Z_q^*$ and calculates $S_t = H_4(kP + \sum_{i=0,i\neq t}^{n-1} h_i(X_i + Y_i)) - \sum_{i=0,i\neq t}^{n-1} S_i$. After obtaining S_t, the signer calculates $h_t = H_3(M, S_t, pk_t)$ and $T = k - h_t(x_t + y_t)$.
   - Generate the ring signature message $\sigma = (S_0, S_1, ..., S_n, M, T, t)$.

4. **Verification**: When verifying a signature, the verifier first computes the corresponding $h_i = H_3(m, S_i, pk_i)$ values for each user, where $i = 0, 1, ..., n-1$. After computing these values, the verifier examines if the subsequent equation is true. If it does, it indicates that the signature is correctly generated by a member of the ring; otherwise, it signifies that the signature is invalid.

$$\sum_{i=0}^{n-1} S_i = H_4(\sum_{i=0}^{n-1} h_iX_i + \sum_{i=0}^{n-1} h_iY_i + TP) \tag{1}$$

5. **Confirmation**: When the verifier verifies the true identity of the signer, the signer reveals the identity information (R, U, pk_s, w, a). The verifier calculates $t' = H_1(R, X_t, Y_t, w, a)$, and then verifies whether the equations $t' = t$ and $R = U + Y_i$ are true. If both equations are true, the actual identification of the signer can be determined. $R = U + Y_i$ can verify the relationship between the identity information leaked by the user and the public key associated with the user, so as to determine the validity of the identity information.

4.3   Transaction Process

In the part, the transaction process of users after using certificateless ring signature and homomorphic encryption is described. Since the essence of transaction verification is to prevent malicious behavior by the transaction initiator, the transaction initiator needs to encrypt their identity information using the system secret key P_{pub} and include it in the transaction. In case of disputes, the AN can trace the actual identification of the signer. Firstly, the two parties involved in the transaction communicate to verify that neither party has altered the transaction amount. The confirmed transaction is then sent to the verification node, which first verifies whether the signature of the transaction is valid, then verifies whether the identity information of the transaction initiator is valid, and finally verifies whether the amount is legal. When all is valid, the VN updates the account balance of the user involved in the transaction to the post-transaction amount.

The existing transaction is Alice and Bob, Alice is the initiator of the transaction, Bob is the receiver of the transaction, and the amount to be paid by Alice to Bob is m. The following is the transaction process of this scheme:

1. Receiver B encrypts the determined transaction amount m using homomorphic encryption, then signs it with a ring signature, and forms an information $Rsig_B(Enc_p(m))\|sig_B(address_B)$ with its own address, and finally encrypts the information with A's public key and sends it to A, the content is:

$$Enc_A(Rsig_B(Enc_p(m))\|sig_B(address_B)) \tag{2}$$

2. When A receives the message, A decrypts it with private key, and uses B's public key to verify the address of B in the message. After confirmation, A signs its identity information and its own identity using a ring signature, in the form:

$$Rsig_A(Rsig_B(Enc_p(m)), Enc_{pub}(w, a, pk_A)) \tag{3}$$

At the same time, in order to prove that his account balance can meet the execution of this transaction, A needs to verify to the VN that the balance $account'_A$ after executing the transaction is greater than or equal to 0. Therefore, A needs to encrypt its address, identity information, account balance and other information after the transaction with the public key of the VN, and then broadcast it to the VN, and the information content is:

$$Enc_v(Rsig_A(Rsig_B(Enc_p(m)), Enc_{pub}(w, a, pk_A))\|sig_B($$
$$address_B)\|sig_A(address_A)\|Enc_p(account'_A)\|R\|U) \tag{4}$$

3. When the VN receives the transaction information of the NN, it decrypts the information using its private key. After decryption, first verify whether the signature of the transaction comes from the ring member, and then verify whether R, U and part of the public key of the initiator A in the transaction information satisfy Equation $R = U + Y_A$, if it is true, it means that the signer's identity information is valid, otherwise the transaction is rejected.
4. The VN determines that the address in the transaction information comes from receiver B according to B's signature. This is done to prevent the transaction initiator from changing the recipient's address during the process. Furthermore, the legitimacy of the amount to be paid and the balance of the initiator A's account after the completion of the transaction need to be verified. This is done here by verifying $m > 0$ and $account'_A \geq 0$, if the inequality holds then the transaction is legitimate, otherwise this transaction is rejected. When verifying the amount m to be paid for A, A utilizes an interval range proof to prove to the VN that $m > 0$. By substituting $y = x$ into the proof, it can be verified if the condition holds true. Similarly, when verifying the account balance $account'_A$ for A after the transaction, A also utilizes an interval range proof to prove to the validation node that $account'_A \geq 0$. By substituting $y = account'_A + 1$ into the proof, it can be verified if the condition holds true. Once both interval proofs have been successfully verified, the following equation is checked for its validity:

$$Enc_p(account_A) = Enc_p(account'_A) + Enc_p(m) \tag{5}$$

where $account_A$ represents the current balance of user A in the ledger, i.e. the balance of the account when the amount m has not been paid. When the verification is equal, it indicates that the transaction is legitimate. Finally, the balance $Enc_p(account'_B)$ after B's transaction is calculated, where $Enc_p(account'_B) = Enc_p(account_B) - Enc_p(m)$, and the balance after the transaction is updated to the global ledger.
5. After passing the above transaction verification, the VN writes the transaction information $Rsig_A(Rsig_B(Enc_p(m)), Enc_{pub}(w, a, pk_A))$ and the information $Enc_{pub}(R)$ encrypted with the system public key into the block together, in the form of:

$$Rsig_A(Rsig_B(Enc_p(m)), Enc_{pub}(w, a, pk_A))\|Enc_{pub}(R)) \tag{6}$$

Figure 2 illustrates the specific flow of the transaction protocol for the scheme. When a transaction dispute occurs, the AN decrypts the identity information in the transactions within the block using its private key. It then calculates $R' = wP$ and verifies whether $R' = R$ holds true. After verifying it, the AN computes $t' = H_1(R, X_t, Y_t, w, a)$ based on the identity information and checks if $t' = t$ holds true. If it holds true, it confirms the true identity of the signer.

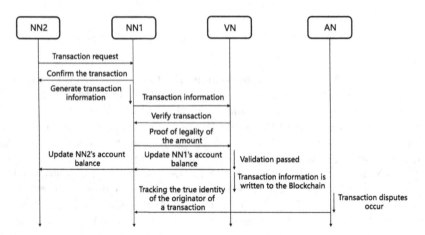

Fig. 2. Specific transaction process.

5   Scheme Analysis

5.1   Correctness Analysis

When the verifier receives the signature information $\sigma = (S_0, S_1, ..., S_n, M, T, t)$, it first calculates the corresponding hash value h_i for each random number S_i corresponding to each ring member in the signature information. Then, it uses the ring member public key and known condition $X_i = x_i P, Y_i = y_i P$ for effective verification to make the below proving:

$$\sum_{i=0}^{n-1} S_i = H_4\left(\sum_{i=0}^{n-1} h_i X_i + \sum_{i=0}^{n-1} h_i Y_i + TP\right)$$

$$= H_4\left(kP - h_s(x_t + y_t)P + \sum_{i=0}^{n-1} h_i(X_i + Y_i)\right)$$

$$= H_4\left(kP + \sum_{i=0, i \neq t}^{n-1} h_i(X_i + Y_i)\right)$$

In this scheme, In the process of verifying that the transaction is legitimate, the equation $Enc_p(account_A) = Enc_p(account'_A) + Enc_p(m)$ represents the relationship between the account balance of the payer A and the amount to be disbursed, through which the transaction amount can be prevented from being tampered with by the recipient B. Verifying whether the equation is true requires verification according to additive homomorphism, that is, legitimacy verification through Equation $Enc_p(x)Enc_p(y) = Enc_p(x + y)$, as follows:

$$Enc_p(account_A) = g^{account_A}r^N \quad \mod N^2$$

$$Enc_p(account_A') = g^{account_A'}r_1^N \quad \mod N^2$$

$$Enc_p(m) = g^m r_2^N \quad \mod N^2$$

$$Enc_p(account_A')Enc_p(m) = g^{account_A'+m}(r_1 r_2)^N \quad \mod N^2$$

$$= Enc_P(account_A)$$

where $account_A = account_A' + m$, $r = r_1 r_2$, so VN can verify through the above equation whether the pre-transaction amount of the transaction payer A is the same as the post-transaction amount plus the payment amount.

5.2   Anonymity Analysis

In the ring signature $\sigma = (S_0, S_1, ..., S_n, M, T, t)$, except for S_t, the rest of S_i are randomly selected in Z_q^*. Now suppose that an attacker wants to directly obtain the signature of the real signer, the attacker has $N = \prod_{i=1}^{n-1}(q - (i - 1))$ possible ways to choose $n - 1$ random numbers. Since S_i is random and each random value is selected with equal probability, the probability that the attacker can correctly choose $n - 1$ random numbers is:

$$Pro(S_0, \ldots, S_{n-1}) = \frac{1}{q} \cdot \frac{1}{q-1} \cdots \frac{1}{q-(n-2)} = \frac{1}{N}$$

From the equation, we can see that the probability of the attacker correctly obtaining n-1 random numbers is dependent on the order q. Therefore, as the order q increases, the probability of a successful attack by the attacker decreases. In the given scheme, the order of the group q is a large prime number, which means the probability of the attacker correctly obtaining n-1 random numbers can be considered negligible. In both the calculation of $S_t = H_4(TP + \sum_{i=0,i\neq t}^{n-1} h_i(X_i + Y_i) - \sum_{i=0,i\neq t}^{n-1} S_i)$ and $T = k - h_s(x_s + y_s)$, the value of k is randomly chosen, which ensures that S_t and T in Z_q^* are uniformly distributed. As a result, the attacker cannot gain anything about the signer's address information from the signature. The identity information (R, w, a, pk_t) of the initiating party in the transaction is encrypted using the system key P_{pub}, and only the private key of the AN can decrypt it. Furthermore, the properties of the hash function ensure that an attacker cannot push out any information from t in σ. Therefore, the probability of the attacker knowing the true identity of the signer is not higher than $1/n$. Even if the members within the ring make guesses, the likelihood of accurately deducing the genuine signer's identity is no greater than $1/(n-1)$. And, this probability tends to zero as the number of ring members increases.

5.3   Security Analysis

1. **Unforgeability**: If an adversary A can successfully forge a verifiable, certificateless ring signature σ that can be verified, then there exists an algorithm that can output two valid certificateless verifiable ring signatures σ and σ', where $S_i = S'_i, i \neq t$. Additionally, there is the equation $T = k - h_t(y_t + x_t), T' = k - h'_t(y_t + x_t)$, as derived from the previous equation $(x_t + y_t)P = (T - T')(h_t - h'_t)^{-1}P$. Each user's keys in the ring are produced based on the discrete logarithm problem, and the adversary cannot compute a member's private key in a probabilistic polynomial time. Therefore, the value $(x_t + y_t)$ in the equation is unknown. If the adversary successfully forges a signature, then $ECDLP$ difficulty is solved, which is currently infeasible to solve within a reasonable time frame. Hence, the signature $\sigma = (S_0, S_1, \ldots, S_{n-1}, M, T, t)$ possesses unforgeability.

2. **linkability attacks**: When a member in the network wants to generate a certificateless ring signature, he chooses other ring members including his own public key as well as his own private keys to generate the signature. The randomness element in the signature ensures that the signature of the same user for the same information also has randomness. The obfuscation of public keys and the introduction of randomness in signatures increase the difficulty for attackers to trace the signatory, thereby effectively preventing linkability attacks.

3. **Tampering attacks**: When the transaction is carried out in this scheme, the transaction amount is encrypted using homomorphic encryption, and the attacker cannot steal the plaintext information of the amount. And the transaction amount is signed and certified by both parties to the transaction, and it is not feasible for either party to change the transaction amount because one of the parties or the attacker cannot forge the signature of the other party.

5.4   Efficiency Analysis

To ensure the confidentiality of the member's identity, the scheme uses a verifiable certificateless ring signature algorithm. Homomorphic encryption protect the privacy of transaction amounts and account balances, and interval range proofs verify the validity of transactions. Therefore, the time overhead of this scheme is related to three algorithms: ring signature, Paillier encryption, and zero-knowledge proofs. Let SM, SA, ME, MM, and H represent scalar multiplication, scalar addition, modular exponentiation, modular multiplication, and hash operation, respectively. Table 2 presents the computational time overhead for each phase of this scheme.

Table 2. Computational Efficiency of the Scheme

Operation	SM	SA	ME	MM	H
sign	n+2	n	0	0	n+1
Encrypt	0	0	2	1	0
Verify	n+1	n+1	14	7	n+1
Total	2n+3	2n+1	16	8	2(n+1)

From Table 2, it can be shown that the computational overhead of this scheme mainly consists of operations on points on elliptic curves. The time complexity for multiplication, addition, and hash operations is denoted as $O(n)$, while the time complexity for modular exponentiation and modular multiplication is denoted as $O(1)$. The computational overhead in this scheme is lower compared to the use of bilinear pairings, so the efficiency of this scheme is reasonable.

Table 3. Comparison with others.

Scheme	Sign	Verify	Identity anonymity	Data protection
Li et al. [16]	$(4n-2)T_m + 2(n-1)T_a$	$2nT_m + (4n-2)T_a$	Yes	No
Zeng et al. [24]	$3T_e + (2n-1)T_m + 3nT_a$	$2T_e + nT_m + (2n-1)T_a$	Yes	No
Wang et al. [20]	nT_m	$(n+1)T_P + (n-1)T_m + 6T_e$	Yes	Yes
Zhao et al. [25]	$(n+2)T_m + 2(n-1)T_a$	$nT_m + (2n-1)T_a + 2T_p$	Yes	No
Yang et al. [26]	$T_p + 2T_m$	$2T_p + 3T_m + T_a$	Yes	No
ours	$(n+2)T_m + nT_a$	$(n+1)(T_m + T_a) + 14ME + 7MM$	Yes	Yes

In order to demonstrate the comprehensiveness as well as the advantages of this scheme compared to other schemes, Table 3 is compared with some existing privacy-preserving schemes. In the table, T_a represents scalar addition, T_m represents scalar multiplication, and T_p represents pairing operations. In Table 3, The scheme of Li et al. [16] have enhanced user anonymity, but the users are completely anonymous. Therefore, in the event of disputes or malicious behavior, the administrator is unable to find the true identity of the signer. The scheme of Zhao et al. [25] utilizes an elliptic curve-based certificateless ring signature anonymous scheme, which achieves higher efficiency compared to traditional certificateless ring signature schemes. However, it only provides unconditional anonymity for the users. The scheme of Yang et al. [26] combines the SM9 algorithm with group signature algorithm, achieving high efficiency in signature generation and verification. However, similar to the previous two schemes, it only provides identity anonymity and does not allow for the tracing of the true identity of the signer. The scheme of Zeng et al. [24] proposed a conditional ring signature algorithm to protect vehicle identity information in vehicular ad hoc networks. The scheme achieves both anonymity and traceability. However, the efficiency of this scheme is relatively low. The above protection scheme only protects the privacy of the member's identity, and does not protect the privacy of user data. Wang et al. [20]

achieved complete anonymity privacy protection using the BGL03 aggregate signature and BGN06 homomorphic encryption scheme. However, the verification process in this scheme requires a significant number of bilinear pairing operations, resulting in lower verification efficiency. From Table 3 and Fig. 3, it can be analyzed that our scheme also has certain advantages in efficiency under the dual protection of identity and transaction privacy.

5.5 Performance Evaluation

The environment of this experiment is configured as Windows 11 operating system, Intel(R) Core(TM), i5-10300H CPU, 2.5 GHz processor, 16 GB RAM. Programming language Java, cryptographic library JPBC to implement the scheme arithmetic operation.

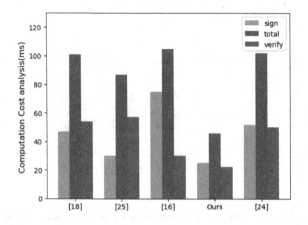

Fig. 3. Average time of encryption and decryption.

When using ring signatures to anonymize the identity of a trader in a consortium chain, both the payer and receiver of the transaction need to sign the transaction using the ring signature algorithm. In our scheme, not only do both parties of the transaction need to sign using the ring signature, but the receiver of the transaction also needs to invoke the Paillier algorithm to encrypt the transaction amount. Figure 4 simulates the time overhead for nodes of each scheme to initiate a transaction when there is no transaction dispute. From Fig. 4, it can be seen that the time overhead of scheme [25] and our scheme is similar, but scheme [25] primarily focuses on anonymizing the user's identity, neglecting to safeguard the member's transaction privacy.

Figure 5 simulates the time overhead required to verify the legitimacy of a transaction after the verification node receives a transaction from a regular node. Both schemes [25] and [18] require time-consuming bilinear mapping for verification, so their computational overhead for verification is higher than the other two schemes when the size of ring is low. Since the bilinear mapping

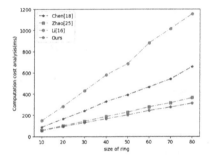
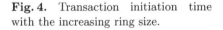
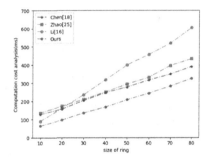

Fig. 4. Transaction initiation time with the increasing ring size.

Fig. 5. Transaction verification time with the increasing ring size.

computation of the above two schemes is independent of the size of ring, the verification time overhead of scheme [16] is higher than the remaining schemes as the size of ring increases. Therefore, our solution has certain advantages in the efficiency of initiating and verifying transactions while protecting the dual privacy of traders.

6 Conclusion

This paper addresses the issues of identity privacy and transaction amount privacy of users in a consortium blockchain. It proposes a privacy protection scheme based on certificateless ring signatures and homomorphic encryption. This scheme aims to protect user anonymity while also ensuring the privacy of transaction amounts between ordinary users. To prevent malicious behavior by transaction initiators, a protocol is established in the transaction process. The transaction initiator encrypts their identity information using the system's public key and writes it into the block along with the transaction information. However, it is possible for the transaction initiator to provide incorrect identity information. The verification nodes verify the identity information provided by the initiator, and if it is incorrect, the transaction is rejected. Therefore, the correct identity of the signer is written to the block. When a transaction dispute arises, the authoritative nodes have the ability to determine the true identity of the signer by utilizing the signer's identity information stored in the block. However, only the administrators have access to this information, establishing a form of conditional anonymity. Furthermore, this paper has conducted an analysis and comparison with other privacy protection schemes, demonstrating the advantages of this program.

References

1. Nakamoto, S.: Bitcoin: a peer-to-peer electronic cash system. Decentralized Bus. Rev. 21260 (2008)
2. Chen, Y., Ding, S., Xu, Z., et al.: Blockchain-based medical records secure storage and medical service framework. J. Med. Chem. **43**, 1–9 (2019)
3. Treleaven, P., Brown, R.G., Yang, D.: Blockchain technology in finance. Computer **50**(9), 14–17 (2017)
4. Androulaki, E., et al.: Hyperledger fabric: a distributed operating system for permissioned blockchains. In: Proceedings of the Thirteenth EuroSys Conference, pp. 1–15 (2018)
5. Goldfeder, S., Kalodner, H., Reisman, D., Narayanan, A.: When the cookie meets the blockchain: privacy risks of web payments via cryptocurrencies. arXiv preprint arXiv:1708.04748 (2017)
6. Möser, M., et al.: An empirical analysis of traceability in the Monero blockchain. arXiv preprint arXiv:1704.04299 (2017)
7. Rivest, R.L., Shamir, A., Tauman, Y.: How to leak a secret. In: Boyd, C. (ed.) ASIACRYPT 2001. LNCS, vol. 2248, pp. 552–565. Springer, Heidelberg (2001). https://doi.org/10.1007/3-540-45682-1_32
8. Deng, L., Li, S., Huang, H., Jiang, Y., Ning, B.: Efficient certificateless ring signature scheme based on elliptic curve. J. Internet Technol. **43**, 723–731 (2020)
9. Chaum, D.L.: Untraceable electronic mail, return addresses, and digital pseudonyms. Commun. ACM **24**(2), 84–90 (1981)
10. Maxwell, G.: CoinJoin: bitcoin privacy for the real world. In: Post on Bitcoin Forum, p. 110 (2013)
11. Miers, I., Garman, C., Green, M., Rubin, A.D.: ZeroCoin: anonymous distributed e-cash from bitcoin. In: IEEE S&P, pp. 397–411. IEEE (2013)
12. Decker, C., Wattenhofer, R.: A fast and scalable payment network with bitcoin duplex micropayment channels. In: Pelc, A., Schwarzmann, A.A. (eds.) SSS 2015. LNCS, vol. 9212, pp. 3–18. Springer, Cham (2015). https://doi.org/10.1007/978-3-319-21741-3_1
13. Zhang, M., Chen, X.: A post-quantum certificateless ring signature scheme for privacy-preserving of blockchain sharing economy. In: Sun, X., Zhang, X., Xia, Z., Bertino, E. (eds.) ICAIS 2021. LNCS, vol. 12737, pp. 265–278. Springer, Cham (2021). https://doi.org/10.1007/978-3-030-78612-0_22
14. Liu, Y., Liu, X., Tang, C., et al.: Unlinkable coin mixing scheme for transaction privacy enhancement of bitcoin. IEEE Access **6**, 23261–23270 (2018)
15. Wang, B., Sun, J., He, Y., et al.: Large-scale election based on blockchain. Procedia Comput. Sci **129**, 234–237 (2018)
16. Li, X., Mei, Y., Gong, J., Xiang, F., Sun, Z.: A blockchain privacy protection scheme based on ring signature. IEEE Access **8**, 76765–76772 (2020)
17. Zhang, X., Ye, C.: A novel privacy protection of permissioned blockchains with conditionally anonymous ring signature. Cluster Comput. **25**, 1221–1235 (2022)
18. Chen, S., Zhai, S., Wang, Y.: Blockchain privacy protection algorithm based on ring signature. J. Xidian Univ. 86–93 (2020)
19. Wang, Q., Qin, B., Hu, J., Xiao, F.: Preserving transaction privacy in bitcoin. Future Gener. Comput. Syst. **107**, 793–804 (2020)
20. Wang, Z., Liu, J., Zhang, Z., Yu, H.: Full anonymous blockchain based on aggregate signature and confidential transaction. J. Comput. Res. Dev. **55**, 2185–2198 (2018)

21. Rivest, R.L., Adleman, L., Dertouzos, M.L., et al.: On data banks and privacy homomorphisms. Found. Secure Comput. 4(11), 169–180 (1978)
22. Paillier, P.: Public-key cryptosystems based on composite degree residuosity classes. In: Stern, J. (ed.) EUROCRYPT 1999. LNCS, vol. 1592, pp. 223–238. Springer, Heidelberg (1999). https://doi.org/10.1007/3-540-48910-X_16
23. Wu, Q.H., Zhang, J.H., Wang, Y.M.: Simple proof that a committed number is in a specific interval. Sheng Tai Xue Bao, p. 1071 (2004)
24. Zeng, S., Huang, Y., Liu, X.: Privacy-preserving communication for VANETs with conditionally anonymous ring signature. Int. J. Netw. Secur. 17, 135–141 (2015)
25. Zhao, K., Sun, D., Ren, G., et al.: Public auditing scheme with identity privacy preserving based on certificateless ring signature for wireless body area networks. IEEE Access 8, 41975–41984 (2020)
26. Yang, C., Zhang, Y.: Privacy preserving scheme in block chain with provably secure based on SM9 algorithm. J. Softw. 30, 1692–1704 (2019)

Construction of a Sanitizable Signature and Its Application in Blockchain

Gang Di[1,2], Mingjun Liu[1,3,4(✉)], Pengcheng Zhang[1], Xinyu Zhao[1], Yi Lv[1,3], and Yi Sun[5]

[1] Institute of Digital Currency, the People's Bank of China, Beijing 100073, China
liumingjun@pbcdci.cn
[2] Department of Automation, Tsinghua University, Beijing 100084, China
[3] Shenzhen Financial Technology Research Institute, Shenzhen 518057, China
[4] Institute for Network Sciences and Cyberspace, Tsinghua University, Beijing 100084, China
[5] Institute of Computing Technology, Chinese Academy of Sciences, Beijing 100086, China

Abstract. A sanitizable signature allows the signer delegate partial signing rights to a trusted sanitizer, who can change certain fields of the original message, while the authenticity of other data in the message is still verifiable. In this paper, the core component of the chameleon hash of the sanitizable signature is improved based on elliptic curves, and a security proof is provided. The experimental results show that the proposed chameleon hash and the corresponding sanitizable signature have high computational efficiency under the same security strength. This paper also proposes a sanitizable signature scheme that can be applied to blockchain evaluation, which can protect sensitive information while verifying the authenticity of user data.

Keyword: Blockchain · Sanitizable Signature · Chameleon Hash

1 Introduction

Blockchain evaluation is an important means for standardizing the technical quality of blockchain products, promoting blockchain applications, and facilitating the healthy development of the blockchain industry. Blockchain evaluation typically involves three parties: blockchain users, blockchain operating organizations, and blockchain evaluation institutions. How to ensure the security of user privacy data during the evaluation process is an urgent issue to be addressed in blockchain evaluation. From the perspective of data security, there is a contradiction in blockchain evaluation: on the one hand, for the sake of authenticity of the evaluation, a blockchain evaluation institution needs a blockchain operating organization to provide the real data of users in the blockchain system being tested rather than some virtual data constructed by the institution being evaluated to pass the evaluation; on the other hand, the blockchain system being tested stores some key information or sensitive data, which are confidential or require privacy protection, and the blockchain operating organization is often not allowed or unwilling to provide these real data to the evaluation institution.

© The Author(s), under exclusive license to Springer Nature Singapore Pte Ltd. 2024
J. Zhu et al. (Eds.): CBCS 2023, CCIS 2098, pp. 242–256, 2024.
https://doi.org/10.1007/978-981-97-3203-6_13

In this paper, a sanitizable signature scheme i applied in the blockchain evaluation scenario to resolve the aforementioned contradiction. Sanitizable signatures were initially introduced in [1], allowing signer to delegate part of the signing rights to a sanitizer, who can change certain fields prespecified by the signer in the original message, while the integrity and authenticity of the parts of the original message that are not allowed to change remain verifiable. Verifiers can verify the authenticity of signatures but cannot know the information that was authorized by the signer for the sanitizer to change. Sanitizable signatures have many application scenarios, such as the anonymization of medical data, desensitization during the decryption of confidential documents, or secure routing [1]. Taking the scenario of medical data anonymization as an example, a patient's medical data can be saved in the hospital through a sanitizable signature. To solve the problem of patient privacy protection in medical research, the patient can designate the hospital as the sanitizer to modify certain private information specified by the patient. When a medical research institution needs the hospital's medical data, the hospital can desensitize the personal privacy of the patient's medical data before submitting it to the research institution. Since the sanitizable signature does not affect the verification of the signature, the research institution can verify the patient's signature to confirm that this is the patient's real medical data, and the data processed by the sanitizable signature will not leak the user's privacy. In the blockchain evaluation scenario, the real user of the blockchain system uses a sanitizable signature to sign the data to be put on the blockchain as the signer and designates the blockchain operating organization as the sanitizer and authorizes it to modify certain sensitive fields of the user data. When the blockchain evaluation institution (verifier) evaluates the blockchain system, the blockchain operating organization can replace the user to modify or desensitize certain sensitive fields specified by the user and send the modified message and the original signature to the evaluation institution. Through the above processing, the blockchain evaluation institution can verify the user's signature to confirm that the data are truly signed by the blockchain user; at the same time, the blockchain operating organization can modify sensitive data, making it impossible for the blockchain evaluation institution to obtain users' sensitive data during the evaluation process and reducing users' concerns about privacy leakage during blockchain evaluation.

The core of the sanitizable signature is the design of the chameleon hash, which is usually constructed based on the discrete logarithm problem (DLP) over the subgroup of quadratic residues modulo p. This paper improves the core component of the sanitizable signature, the chameleon hash, based on the elliptic curve discrete logarithm problem (ECDLP), while the security proof of the improved chameleon hash and sanitizable signature is also given. The advantages of chameleon hashes constructed based on the ECDLP are shorter operation data length and higher computational efficiency. The experimental results show that under the same security strength, the improved sanitizable signature proposed in this paper is significantly more efficient than previous schemes.

The remainder of this paper is organized as follows. Section 2 introduces preliminary knowledge of sanitizable signatures. Section 3 describes the design of a chameleon hash based on the ECDLP and describes the corresponding sanitizable signature scheme.

Section 4 analyses the privacy protection needs of users on the blockchain and presents a sanitizable signature scheme applied to blockchain evaluation. Section 5 provides the conclusion.

2 Preliminary Knowledge

2.1 Sanitizable Signature

Integrity is one of the important attributes of digital signatures, and usually any modification will make the signature invalid after the message was signed. But in certain scenarios where the original signer cannot sign again or the cost for the original signer to sign again is too high, people may wish for a partially trusted third party to make partial modifications to the signed message without altering its core content (for example, anonymizing a document). Besides introduced the sanitizable signatures in [1], five basic security properties of sanitizable signatures were identified: unforgeability, privacy, immutability, accountability, and transparency ([2] formalized these properties):

Unforgeability: No one can forge the signature of the signer or the sanitizer.

Privacy: No one can recover the original message from the sanitized message.

Immutability: The sanitizer can only modify parts of the message that have been authorized by the signer and cannot arbitrarily modify other parts of the message.

Accountability: If there is a dispute between the signer and the sanitizer over whether a valid message-signature pair (m, σ) comes from the signer or the sanitizer, the Judge algorithm can correctly resolve this dispute.

Transparency: Apart from the signer and the sanitizer, no one can distinguish whether the signature comes from the signer or the sanitizer.

Subsequently, an increasing number of scholars have focused on sanitizable signatures, and several new security properties have been proposed. [3] proposed unlinkability, and [4] proposed invisibility:

Unlinkability: It is not possible to associate different sanitizable signatures with the original message, i.e., linking two sanitized versions of the same message is infeasible.

Unlinkability means that attackers cannot link two sanitized signatures back to the original message. Taking the medical data application scenario as an example, suppose there are two different sanitizable signatures for a specific patient's medical records: one sanitizable signature desensitizes this patient's health record and thus only contains the patient's personal information; the other signature desensitizes the patient's personal information and thus is this patient's anonymous health record. If an attacker can link these two sanitized messages, the attacker can recover the patient's complete medical record.

Invisibility: Without knowing any private key, the verifier cannot know which message blocks allowed by the signer to modify.

Invisibility ensures that an unrelated person neither knows which block can be modified by the sanitizer nor knows how many blocks can be modified.

The constructions that satisfy these novel sanitizable signature schemes include [3] constructing a sanitizable signature with unlinkable properties based on group signatures, [5] constructing a sanitizable signature with unlinkable properties based on Re-Randomizable Keys technology, [6] constructing a sanitizable signature with invisible and unlinkable properties based on a class of weak sanitizable signatures and verifiable ring signatures, and [7] constructing a sanitizable signature with invisible and unlinkable properties based on zero-knowledge proofing technology. However, to achieve signature unlinkability and invisibility, it is necessary to introduce more complex and time-consuming cryptographic tools, such as group signatures, key rerandomization, and zero-knowledge proofs, resulting in lower efficiency of these sanitizable signature algorithms. Therefore, in specific scenarios where these two new security properties are not considered, the original sanitizable signature schemes that satisfy only the five basic properties are more efficient. Table 1 lists the performance of existing sanitizable signatures, showing a clear advantage in performance for the sanitizable signature scheme provided in [1] that satisfies only the five basic properties. In fact, under the same computational environment, this advantage would be even greater. Section 3.3 lists the simulation results of the sanitizable signature from [1] in the current general computing environment: the sanitization algorithm only requires 352.683 microseconds, the signature algorithm of the sanitizable signature only requires 576.950 microseconds, and the verification algorithm of the sanitizable signature only requires 433.090 microseconds.

Table 1. Performance of sanitizable signatures.

	[1]	[6]
Sanit	28.196 ms	2002 ms
Sign	44.518 ms	8367 ms
Verify	34.497 ms	764 ms

The Sanitizable Signature Scheme, *SanSig* (the description is mainly from [2]), consists of seven algorithms: $KGen_{sig}$, $KGen_{san}$, *Sign*, *Sanit*, *Verify*, *Proof*, and *Judge*:

Key Generation. There are two key generation algorithms in the sanitizable signature scheme: $KGen_{sig}$ and $KGen_{san}$. $KGen_{sig}$ is used by the signer to generate the signer's public-private key pairs (sk_{sig}, pk_{sig}); $KGen_{san}$ is used by the sanitizer to generate the sanitizer's public-private key pairs (sk_{san}, pk_{san}). That is,

$$(pk_{sig}, \ sk_{sig}) \ \leftarrow \ KGen_{sig}(1^n),$$
$$(pk_{san}, \ sk_{san}) \ \leftarrow \ KGen_{san}(1^n).$$

Sign. The *Sign* algorithm takes a message $m \in \{0, 1\}^*$, the signer's private key sk_{sig}, the sanitizer's public key pk_{san}, and the description ADM as input, where ADM indicates the message blocks within message m that the sanitizer is allowed to modify. The algorithm outputs a signature:

$$\sigma \ \leftarrow \ Sign(m, sk_{sig}, pk_{san}, ADM).$$

Sanit. The algorithm takes the message m, signature σ, signer's public key pk_{sig}, and sanitizer's private key sk_{san} as inputs. This algorithm modifies message m to m' according to the modification instructions MOD (requiring that MOD instructions can only modify message blocks specified by ADM) and gets signature σ' corresponding to m'.

$$(m', \sigma') \leftarrow Sanit(m, MOD, \sigma, pk_{sig}, sk_{san}).$$

Verify. The algorithm verifies the correctness of the signature σ of message m under the public keys pk_{sig} and pk_{san} and outputs $d \in \{true, false\}$.

$$d \leftarrow Verify(m, \sigma, pk_{sig}, pk_{san}).$$

Proof. The algorithm takes the private key sk_{sig}, message m, signature σ, and the sanitizer's public key pk_{san} as inputs and outputs a proof $\pi \in \{0, 1\}^*$:

$$\pi \leftarrow Proof(sk_{sig}, m, \sigma, pk_{san}).$$

Judge. The *Judge* algorithm takes the message m and signature σ, both parties' public keys (pk_{sign} and pk_{san}), and the proof π. The algorithm outputs a decision $d \in \{Sig, San\}$, judging whether the message-signature pair's creator is the signer ($d = Sig$) or the sanitizer ($d = San$).

$$d \leftarrow Judge(m, \sigma, pk_{sig}, pk_{san}, \pi).$$

Constructing a sanitizable signature scheme requires two basic components:

- A digital signature scheme. The signature algorithm $S(\cdot)$ and the verification algorithm $V(\cdot)$ are included. Here, the underlying signature and verification algorithms are represented by $S(\cdot)$ and $V(\cdot)$, respectively, to distinguish them from the higher-level sanitizable signature algorithm $Sign(\cdot)$ and verification algorithm $Verify(\cdot)$.
- A chameleon hash scheme. The chameleon hash computes the hash value of message m with random number r under public key pk, denoted as $CH_{pk}(m, r)$. The chameleon hash has the same security properties as any hash function, with the difference being that the owner of the private key sk corresponding to pk may construct collisions, meaning that they can construct m' and r' such that $CH_{pk}(m, r) = CH_{pk}(m', r')$.

Based on the above two basic components, the sanitizable signature scheme given in [1] is as follows: To achieve a sanitizable signature for message $m = (m_1, ..., m_t)$, the signer (whose private key is sk_{sign}) first needs to select a unique identifier ID_m (mainly to prevent replay) for message m, confirm the sanitizer and its public key pk_{san}, and determine which blocks $(m_{i_1}, \cdots, m_{i_t})$ can be modified by the sanitizer. At this point, the signer can construct the signature

$$\sigma = Sign(m, r; sk_{sign}, pk_{san}) = S_{sk_{sign}}(ID_m||t||pk_{san}||\overline{m}_i|| \cdots ||\overline{m}_t)$$

where

$$\overline{m}_i = \begin{cases} CH_{pk_{san}}(ID_m||i||m_i, r_i), & i \in \{i_1, i_2, \cdots i_t\} \\ m_i||i, & otherwize \end{cases}$$

The sanitizer knows the private key sk_{san}, so for those message blocks that can be modified by the sanitizer, the sanitizer can construct a chameleon hash collision while replacing the original message with any message, i.e., for $i \in \{i_1, i_2, ..., i_t\}$, the sanitizer can generate (m_i', r_i') such that $CH_{pk_{san}}(ID_m||i||m_i, r_i) = CH_{pk_{san}}(ID_m||i||m_i', r_i')$.

Therefore, the sanitizer can modify $m_i, i \in \{i_1, i_2, ..., i_t\}$ into any message without affecting the verification of the signature σ.

By disclosing the original message, the signer can prove to a trusted third party that a sanitized message must not be generated by himself. Since only the sanitizer can find collisions (the signer cannot construct collisions), it can be inferred from the fact that a chameleon hash collision occurs when the sanitizer has modified the original message, thereby achieving the auditability of the sanitizable signature.

2.2 Chameleon Hash

As seen from Sect. 2.1, the core of the sanitizable signature is the design of the chameleon hash. A chameleon hash is a trapdoor collision-resistant hash function: without trapdoor information, a chameleon hash has the same properties as a cryptographic hash, such as resistance to preimages and collisions; but with the trapdoor known, collisions can be easily constructed. Since [8] introduced the concept of chameleon hashes, various chameleon hash schemes have been proposed [9–11], and chameleon hashes have been widely applied in various signature schemes, such as sanitizable signatures [1, 2], chameleon signatures [8], online/offline signatures [11], and proxy signatures [12, 13].

However, not all chameleon hashes are suitable for constructing sanitizable signatures. For example, in [8], the chameleon hash is defined by

$$CH_y(m, r) = g^m y^r \tag{1}$$

where g is a generator of a prime order cyclic group, x is private key, $y = g^x$ is public key. For the sanitized message (m', r'), since $CH_y(m, r) = CH_y(m', r')$, i.e., $g^m y^r = g^{m'} y^{r'}$, private key x can be calculated by $x = \frac{m-m'}{r'-r}$, which is known as the key exposure problem. [9] presented a class of chameleon hash schemes that are resistant to key exposure and suitable for sanitizable signatures, and [1, 2] used this scheme to construct sanitizable signatures. This chameleon hash scheme is as follows:

Initial Setup: Let p be a security prime of bit length κ, where $p = 2q + 1$ is a prime and q is also a prime. g is a generator of the subgroup of quadratic residues Q_p of Z_p^*, i.e., the order of g is q. The sanitizer randomly selects x from $[1, q - 1]$ as private key; then, the corresponding public key $y = g^x$. Let $\mathcal{H}$ be a collision-resistant hash function that can map bit strings of arbitrary length to fixed-length bit strings of length τ, i.e., $\mathcal{H}$: $\{0, 1\}^* \rightarrow \{0, 1\}^\tau$.

Chameleon Hash Scheme: Select random numbers $(r, s) \in Z_q \times Z_q$; then, the chameleon hash $CH_y(m, r, s)$ of message m under public key y can be calculated by the following formula:

$$\begin{cases} e = \mathcal{H}(m, r) \\ CH_y(m, r, s) = r - (y^e g^s \bmod p) \bmod q \end{cases} \tag{2}$$

Find Collisions: Let $C = CH_y(m, r, s)$; constructing a collision means finding (m', r', s') such that.

$$e' = \mathcal{H}(m', r'),\ CH_y(m', r', s') = r' - \left(y^{e'}g^{s'}\bmod p\right)\bmod q = C$$

The sanitizer can choose any message m', generate a random number $k' \in [1, q-1]$, and calculate $r' = C + \left(g^{k'}\bmod p\right)\bmod q$, $e' = \mathcal{H}(m', r')$ and $s' = k' - e'x\bmod q$. Then, $r' - \left(y^{e'}g^{s'}\bmod p\right)\bmod q = C + (g^{k'}\bmod p) - (g^{xe'}g^{s'}\bmod p)\bmod q = C$. That is, $CH_y(m', r', s') = CH_y(m, r, s)$.

[9] proposed the following security requirements for chameleon hashes:

Semantic Security: The output value C of a chameleon hash does not reveal any information about the message m. Let H[X] represent the entropy of the random variable X, and H[$X|Y$] represent the entropy of X given the random variable Y (also known as conditional entropy). Semantic security means that H[$m|C$] of the message m given the chameleon hash C is equal to H[m] of m in the entire message space.

Collision Resistance: Given only the public key y and m, r, s, there is no efficient algorithm that can find m', r', s' with a nonnegligible probability that satisfies $CH_y(m', r', s') = CH_y(m, r, s)$.

Key Exposure Freeness: Given the public key y and m, r, s, m', r', s' that satisfy $CH_y(m', r', s') = CH_y(m, r, s)$, there is no polynomial-time algorithm that can find the private key x with a nonnegligible probability.

For the sanitizable signature scheme *SanSig* defined in Sect. 2.1, [2] proves that if the underlying components, chameleon hash and digital signature are secure, then this sanitizable signature scheme is secure under five basic security properties:

Lemma 1 ([2]): Assuming that the underlying chameleon hash is semantically secure, collision resistant, and resistant to key exposure and that the underlying signature algorithm is unforgeable under chosen message attacks, then the higher-level sanitizable signature scheme is secure, i.e., it satisfies unforgeability, privacy, immutability, auditability, and transparency.

3 Construction of Chameleon Hash and Sanitizable Signatures Based on an Elliptical Curve

3.1 Chameleon Hash

The chameleon hash scheme listed in Sect. 2.2 is a foundational component in sanitizable signatures constructed based on DLP over the subgroup of quadratic residues modulo p. This paper constructs a chameleon hash scheme based on ECDLP, offering advantages of shorter data processing length and higher computational efficiency. The process of the improved chameleon hash scheme is as follows:

Initial Setup: Let E be an elliptic curve over the finite field F_p, $\mathcal{G}$ be an n-order cyclic subgroup of E, and G be the generator (base point) of $\mathcal{G}$. The sanitizer can randomly choose x from $[1, n-1]$ as private key, so public key is $Y = x \cdot G$.

Chameleon Hash Scheme: Choose a random point $R \in \mathcal{G}$ and a random number $s \in [1, n-1]$; then, the chameleon hash $CH_Y(m, R, s)$ of message m under public key Y can be calculated by the following formula:

$$\begin{cases} e = \mathcal{H}(m, R), \\ CH_Y(m, R, s) = R + e \cdot Y + s \cdot G \end{cases} \tag{3}$$

The sanitizer who possesses private key x can easily find a collision:

Find Collision: Let $C = CH_Y(m, R, s)$; constructing a collision means finding (m', R', s') satisfying:

$$e' = \mathcal{H}(m', R'), CH_Y(m', R', s') = R' + e' \cdot G + s' \cdot G = C$$

Since sanitizer holds private key x, he may choose any message m', generate random number $k' \in [1, n-1]$, then calculate $R' = C + k' \cdot G$, $e' = \mathcal{H}(m', R')$, $s' = (-k' - e' \cdot x) \bmod n$. Then, $R' + e' \cdot Y + s' \cdot G = C + k' \cdot G + (e' \cdot x) \cdot G + s' \cdot G = C + [k' + (e' \cdot x) + s'] \cdot G = C$. That is, $CH_Y(m', R', s') = CH_Y(m, R, s)$.

For (3), it is required that $R' \neq R$; otherwise, the scheme would degenerate into scheme (1) in Sect. 2.2, which has a key leakage problem.

Replacing the chameleon hash in the sanitizable signature scheme from Sect. 2.1 with the aforementioned new chameleon hash (3) results in the corresponding sanitizable signature algorithm.

3.2 Security Analysis

It can be proven that chameleon hash (3) satisfies the security requirements for chameleon hashes.

Theorem 1: The chameleon hash scheme (3) satisfies semantic security, collision resistance, and key exposure resistance.

Proof: (i) Semantic Security.
When calculating the chameleon hash C according to formula (3), the choice of s is completely independent of m and R. Therefore, $s \cdot G$ uniformly covers the group $\mathcal{G}$ and is independent of R and $\mathcal{H}(m, R) \cdot Y$, which means that for each pair of R and m, there is a one-to-one correspondence between hash value C and s, implying that conditional probability $p(m, R|C) = p(m, R|s)$. Since s is independent of m and R, it follows that $p(m, R|C) = p(m, R|s) = p(m, R)$. Therefore, for H($m, R|C$), we have:

$$\begin{aligned} & H(m, R|C) \\ = & -\sum_{m \in \{0,1\}^*, R \in \mathcal{G}} \sum_{C \in \mathcal{G}} p(m, R, C) \log(p(m, R|C)) \\ = & -\sum_{m \in \{0,1\}^*, R \in \mathcal{G}} \sum_{C \in \mathcal{G}} p(m, R, C) \log(p(m, R, C)) \\ = & -\sum_{m \in \{0,1\}^*, R \in \mathcal{G}} p(m, R) \log(p(m, R)) \\ & H(m, R) \end{aligned}$$

(ii) Collision Resistance and Key Exposure Resistance

The Nyberg-Rueppel variant signature scheme is presented in [14]:

Let p be a safe prime, that is, $p = 2q + 1$, and q is also prime. Let $g \in Zq$ with order q. The signer's private key is $x \in Z_q$, so public key is $y = g^x \mod p$. For the message to be signed m, then signature (r, s) can be calculated by ($k \in Z_q$ is a random number):

$$r = m \cdot g^{-k} \mod p$$

$$s = k - \bar{r} \cdot x \mod q$$

The corresponding signature verification checks whether $r \cdot y^{\bar{r}} \cdot g^s \mod p$ equals m. Formally, the chameleon hash scheme $CH_Y(m, R, s) = R + e \cdot G + s \cdot G$ in this paper is consistent with the verification of the Nyberg-Rueppel variant signature, with the difference being that our chameleon hash scheme is represented using an additive group, while the Nyberg-Rueppel variant's verification uses a multiplicative group, and we replace the coefficient of Y in our scheme with $e = \mathcal{H}(m, r)$ instead of the $\bar{r}$ used in the Nyberg-Rueppel variant. Therefore,

- The collision resistance of chameleon hash (3) (given public key Y, m, R, s, there is no efficient algorithm that can find m', R', s' such that $R + e \cdot Y + s \cdot G = R' + e' \cdot Y + s' \cdot G$) is equivalent to the resistance to signature forgery attacks of the Nyberg-Rueppel variant signature scheme (given public key y, m, r, s, there is no efficient algorithm that can find m', r', s' such that $r \cdot y^{\bar{r}} \cdot g^s \mod p = r' \cdot y^{\bar{r}'} \cdot g^{s'} \mod p$).
- The key exposure resistance of chameleon hash (3) (given public key Y, m, R, s, m', R', s' satisfying $R + e \cdot Y + s \cdot G = R' + e' \cdot Y + s' \cdot G$, there is no efficient algorithm that can find the private key x) is equivalent to the resistance to key recovery attacks of the Nyberg-Rueppel variant signature scheme (given public key y, m, r, s, m', r', s' satisfying $r \cdot y^{\bar{r}} \cdot g^s \mod p = r' \cdot y^{\bar{r}'} \cdot g^{s'} \mod p$, there is no efficient algorithm that can find the private key x).

[14] has proven that the aforementioned Nyberg-Rueppel variant signature scheme is resistant to signature forgery and key recovery attacks; therefore, if $\mathcal{H}$ is collision resistant, the chameleon hash (3) is resistant to both collision and key exposure. □

For the sanitizable signature scheme *SanSig* defined in Sect. 2.1, by Theorem 1 and Lemma 1, the following can be proven:

Theorem 2: Assuming that the underlying signature algorithm is unforgeable under adaptive chosen-message attacks, the sanitizable signature scheme constructed based on the chameleon hash scheme (3) is secure, i.e., it satisfies the five basic security properties of unforgeability, immutability, privacy, transparency, and auditability.

3.3 Performance

In the Thinkbook X1 Carbon Gen8 environment (Memory: 16G, CPU: i7-10710U), the chameleon hash scheme and the corresponding sanitizable signature scheme described in Sect. 3.1 were implemented in the C language based on the OPENSSL 3.0.0 library. These results were compared with the scheme of [1].

Table 2. Choice of cryptographic algorithm

	[1]		This paper
	Original Implementation	Simulated Implementation	
Signature algorithm S(·)	DSA	DSA	ECDSA
	RSA1024-SHA1	RSA1024-SHA256	Sep256r1-SHA256
Chameleon Hash	Constructed based on the subgroup of quadratic residues modulo p(1024bit)		Constructed based on the elliptic curve secp256r1

The sanitizable signature scheme in [1] is currently the most efficient scheme available. This paper lists the implementation results given in the original text, and for fairness in comparison, it also lists the simulated implementation results of the scheme from [1] under the same experimental conditions for comparison with our scheme. The algorithms used in the underlying digital signature and chameleon hash are shown in Table 2. The underlying digital signature algorithm in [1] chooses the DSA signature algorithm based on RSA1024-SHA1, the simulation scheme uses the DSA signature algorithm based on RSA1024-SHA256, and our scheme chooses the ECDSA signature algorithm based on secp256r1-SHA256; for the chameleon hash, both [1] and the simulation scheme are constructed based on the subgroup of quadratic residues modulo p (1024 bits), while our chameleon hash scheme is constructed based on the elliptic curve secp256r1. The cryptographic algorithms SHA256, RSA1024 and secp256r1 are all implemented by calling the OPENSSL library.

Table 3. Performance comparison

	[1]		This paper
	Original Implementation	Simulated Implementation	
$S(·)$	10.653 ms	116.080 μs	32.056 μs
$V(·)$	0.609 ms	15.770 μs	82.553 μs
Chameleon Hash	33.863 ms	424.245 μs	89.075 μs
Find collision	28.196 ms	352.683 μs	76.365 μs
$Sign(·)$	44.518 ms	576.950 μs	127.389 μs
$Verify(·)$	34.497 ms	433.090 μs	177.736 μs

The experimental results are shown in Table 3. The performance of our scheme (Chameleon Hash, 89.075 microseconds; *Sanit,* 76.365 microseconds; *Sign,* 127.389 microseconds; *Verify,* 77.736 microseconds) is significantly better than that of the scheme from [1] (Chameleon Hash, 424.245 microseconds; *Sanit,* 352.683 microseconds; *Sign,* 576.950 microseconds; *Verify,* 433.090 microseconds). It is important to emphasize that the security strength of a 1024-bit RSA signature is roughly equivalent to that of a 160-bit ECDSA algorithm [15] (while secp256r1 is a 256-bit elliptic curve); therefore, at the same level of security strength, our chameleon hash and the corresponding sanitizable signature algorithm have a performance advantage over the previous scheme.

4   Application of Sanitizable Signatures in Blockchain Evaluation

With the increase in blockchain application scenarios, the issue of users' privacy leakage is becoming increasingly diverse. Some privacy protection issues currently have effective solutions, while others do not yet have mature solutions. According to the different scopes of knowledge, user data in blockchain systems can be divided into three types:

(1) Content that is completely public;
(2) Content that is known only to the transaction parties and does not need to be known by the blockchain operating organization or other users;
(3) User data for sharing and processing on the blockchain, but during the process of sharing with third parties by the blockchain operating organization, it is desirable that private or sensitive data not be known to the third parties.

For (1), content that does not involve privacy and confidentiality protection can be directly put on the blockchain in plaintext without encryption; for (2), data encryption on the blockchain and authorized decryption can be used to solve the issue.

For (3), there is not yet a good solution. We use a sanitizable signature to solve this type of privacy protection issue in scenarios such as blockchain evaluation. Real users sign the data on the blockchain using sanitizable signatures, designating the blockchain operating organization as the sanitizer and authorizing the operating organization to modify certain sensitive fields of the data. When a blockchain evaluation institution (verifier) needs to evaluate the blockchain system, the blockchain operating organization can modify or desensitize certain sensitive fields in the original message on behalf of the user and provide the modified message along with the original signature of the signer to the evaluation institution. On the one hand, the blockchain evaluation institution can verify that the data are authentic data signed by the blockchain user through verifying the user's signature; on the other hand, users authorize the blockchain operating organization to desensitize some sensitive data, preventing the blockchain evaluation institution from obtaining some of the original data of users during the evaluation process and reducing concerns about privacy leakage during the evaluation process.

This paper uses sanitizable signatures to address privacy protection issues in blockchain evaluation scenarios, as shown in Fig. 1. The scheme contains four steps: initial setup, transaction recorded on the blockchain, message sanitization and evaluation.

Initial Setup: Blockchain users generate public–private key pairs using the signer's key generation algorithm $KGen_{sig}$; for example, user A's key pair is (pk_{UserA}, sk_{UserA}); blockchain operating organizations generate public–private key pairs (pk_{san}, sk_{san}) using the sanitizer's key generation algorithm $KGen_{san}$.

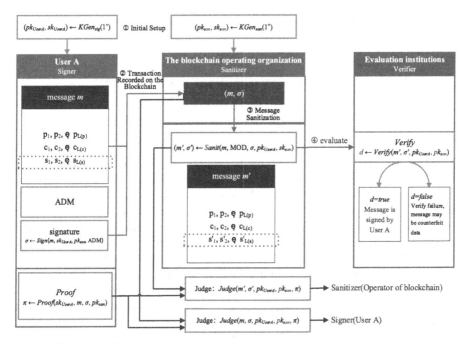

Fig. 1. Application scheme of sanitizable signatures in blockchain evaluation

Transaction Recorded on the Blockchain: Suppose blockchain user A wants to upload a transaction message m to the blockchain system, including the following content:

$$m = \{$$
$$(p_1, p_2, \cdots, p_{L_p}) // L_p \text{ plaintext messages}$$
$$(c_1, c_2, \cdots, c_{L_c}) // L_c \text{ ciphertext messages}$$
$$(s_1, s_2, \cdots, s_{L_s}) // L_s \text{ messages that can be sanitized}$$
$$\}$$

Then, the signature corresponding to message m is $\sigma \leftarrow Sign(m, sk_{UserA}, pk_{san}, ADM)$. $(p_1, p_2, \cdots, p_{L_p})$ is publicly available information, so users do not need to encrypt or desensitize it when putting it on the blockchain, and there is no need to hide its content from the blockchain evaluation institution; $(c_1, c_2, \cdots, c_{L_c})$ involves the core sensitive information of user A, so users encrypt/desensitize it directly when putting it on the blockchain, and the blockchain operating organization cannot know its specific content; although $(s_1, s_2, \cdots, s_{L_s})$ stored in plaintext on the blockchain, user A or the blockchain operating organization does not want the blockchain evaluation institution to know this content. Before signing, user A needs to determine ADM = $\{s_1, s_2, \cdots, s_{L_s}\}$, and the messages in ADM can be modified by the sanitizer (i.e., the blockchain operating organization), authorizing the blockchain operating organization to desensitize these messages during the evaluation process.

Message Sanitization: Before submitting data to the evaluation institution, the blockchain operating organization can sanitize user A's on-chain information (m, σ)

to obtain (m', σ') using the *Sanit* algorithm defined in Sect. 2.1 with user A's public key pk_{UserA} and the sanitor's private key sk_{san}.

$$m' = \{$$
$$(p_1, p_2, \cdots, p_{L_p})//L_p \text{ plaintext messages}$$
$$(c_1, c_2, \cdots, c_{L_c})//L_c \text{ ciphertext messages}$$
$$(s_1', s_2', \cdots, s_{L_s}')//(s_1, s_2, \cdots, s_{L_s}) \text{ is desensitized}$$
$$\}$$

Evaluate: The information provided by the blockchain operating organization to the blockchain evaluation institution is (m', σ'). The evaluation institution can verify the message using the algorithm *Verify*: $d \leftarrow Verify(m, \sigma, pk_{UserA}, pk_{san})$. When $d = true$, the verification is successful, and the evaluation institution can confirm that the message is user A's authentic data; when $d = false$, the verification fails, indicating that the message was not signed by user A, and this transaction message might be fictitiously constructed. Since the blockchain evaluation institution receives the desensitized message, it cannot obtain the original information from the message (m', σ'), ensuring the protection of user privacy data and the rights of the blockchain operating organization.

Notably, in the blockchain evaluation process, for the following two reasons, it is not necessary to consider unlinkability and invisibility when using sanitizable signatures for privacy protection in blockchain evaluation scenarios. The advantage is that only five basic security properties need to be considered in our sanitizable signature scheme, allowing for efficient implementation, as in [1].

(1) The data to be tested in the blockchain evaluation process are often one-time, and even if users may use sanitizable signatures on other occasions, the sensitive message that needs to be sanitized often highly overlaps, so attacks targeting unlinkability usually do not meet the conditions for an attack;

(2) The blockchain operating organization needs to first clarify with the blockchain evaluation institution which entries are the original data to be evaluated and which entries have been desensitized. Since the data to be evaluated will not be provided to other third parties, invisibility does not need to be considered in the blockchain evaluation scenario.

In the third-party evaluation process of the underlying blockchain for Project mBridge [16], we have tested the sanitizable signature scheme to protect users' privacy data: the central bank, as the sanitizer, can desensitize certain privacy data authorized by users, preventing the evaluation institution from obtaining users' privacy data during the blockchain evaluation process.

To realize user privacy protection, the cost is to reduce the efficiency of the signature. As shown in Table 3, for the original ECDSA signature algorithm without privacy protection, one signature $S(\cdot)$ takes 32.056 microseconds and one verification $V(\cdot)$ takes 82.553 microseconds, while for our sanitizable signature, one signature $Sign(\cdot)$ takes 127.389 microseconds and one verification $Verify(\cdot)$ takes 177.736 microseconds, approximately 2 to 4 times the original signature. Therefore, if the evaluation does not need to verify the real data or the user can desensitize sensitive data at any time, this scheme will reduce the signature efficiency in the application scenarios. Therefore, this scheme is applicable to scenes where the evaluation organization needs to verify the real data, and the user cannot or cannot facilitate signing at any time.

5 Conclusion

This paper reviewed the demands for user privacy protection in blockchain evaluation scenarios and proposed the application of sanitizable signature technology to address privacy protection issues for users during the blockchain evaluation process. This approach was piloted in the third-party evaluation process of the underlying blockchain for the multiple-central bank digital currency common platform mBridge.

In terms of the construction of the sanitizable signature scheme, this paper has improved the key component, the chameleon hash, of the sanitizable signature and provided a proof of its security. The experimental results show that the sanitizable signature scheme based on our chameleon hash proposed in this paper significantly outperforms previous schemes in terms of implementation efficiency at the same level of security strength, making it more practical. Future research could consider two directions: one is to apply this efficient sanitizable signature scheme to a wider range of scenarios, and the other is to consider more efficient construction methods for sanitizable signatures that meet all security requirements.

Acknowledgments. This work was supported by the National Key R&D Program of China (2021YFB2700400).

References

1. Ateniese, G., Chou, D.H., de Medeiros, B., Tsudik, G.: Sanitizable signatures. In: di Vimercati, S.d.C., Syverson, P., Gollmann, D. (eds.) ESORICS 2005. LNCS, vol. 3679, pp. 159–177. Springer, Heidelberg (2005). https://doi.org/10.1007/11555827_10
2. Brzuska, C., et al.: Security of sanitizable signatures revisited. In: Jarecki, S., Tsudik, G. (eds.) PKC 2009. LNCS, vol. 5443, pp. 317–336. Springer, Heidelberg (2009). https://doi.org/10.1007/978-3-642-00468-1_18
3. Brzuska, C., Fischlin, M., Lehmann, A., Schröder, D.: Unlinkability of sanitizable signatures. In: Nguyen, P.Q., Pointcheval, D. (eds.) PKC 2010. LNCS, vol. 6056, pp. 444–461. Springer, Heidelberg (2010). https://doi.org/10.1007/978-3-642-13013-7_26
4. Camenisch, J., Derler, D., Krenn, S., Pöhls, H.C., Samelin, K., Slamanig, D.: Chameleon-hashes with ephemeral trapdoors. In: Fehr, S. (ed.) PKC 2017. LNCS, vol. 10175, pp. 152–182. Springer, Heidelberg (2017). https://doi.org/10.1007/978-3-662-54388-7_6
5. Fleischhacker, N., Krupp, J., Malavolta, G., Schneider, J., Schröder, D., Simkin, M.: Efficient unlinkable sanitizable signatures from signatures with re-randomizable keys. In: Cheng, CM., Chung, K.M., Persiano, G., Yang, BY. (eds.) Public-Key Cryptography – PKC 2016. LNCS, vol. 9614, pp. 301–330. Springer, Heidelberg (2016). https://doi.org/10.1007/978-3-662-49384-7_12
6. Beck, M.T., et al.: Practical strongly invisible and strongly accountable sanitizable signatures. In: Pieprzyk, J., Suriadi, S. (eds.) ACISP 2017. LNCS, vol. 10342, pp. 437–452. Springer, Cham (2017). https://doi.org/10.1007/978-3-319-60055-0_23

7. Bossuat, A., Bultel, X.: Unlinkable and invisible γ -sanitizable signatures. In: Sako, K., Tippenhauer, N.O. (eds.) ACNS 2021. LNCS, vol. 12726, pp. 251–283. Springer, Cham (2021). https://doi.org/10.1007/978-3-030-78372-3_10

8. Krawczyk, H., Rabin, T.: Chameleon signatures. In: Proceedings of the Network and Distributed Systems Security Symposium - NDSS 2000, pp. 143–154 (2000)

9. Ateniese, G., de Medeiros, B.: On the key exposure problem in chameleon hashes. In: Blundo, C., Cimato, S. (eds.) SCN 2004. LNCS, vol. 3352, pp. 165–179. Springer, Heidelberg (2005). https://doi.org/10.1007/978-3-540-30598-9_12

10. Bellare, M., Ristov, T.: A characterization of chameleon hash functions and new, efficient designs. J. Cryptol. **27**(4), 799–823 (2014)

11. Shamir, A., Tauman, Y.: Improved online/offline signature schemes. In: Kilian, J. (eds.) CRYPTO 2001. LNCS, vol. 2139, pp. 355–367. Springer, Heidelberg (2001). https://doi.org/10.1007/3-540-44647-8_21

12. Mehta, M., Harn, L.: Efficient one-time proxy signatures. In: IEE Proceedings – Communications, vol. 152, no. 2, pp. 129–133 (2005)

13. Chandrasekhar, S., Chakrabarti, S., Singhal, M., Calvert, K.L.: Efficient proxy signatures based on trapdoor hash functions. IET Inf. Secur. **4**(4), 322–332 (2010)

14. Nyberg, K., Rueppel, R.A.: Message recovery for signature schemes based on the discrete logarithm problem. In: De Santis, A. (eds.) EUROCRYPT 1994. LNCS, vol. 950, pp. 182–193. Springer, Heidelberg (1995). https://doi.org/10.1007/BFb0053434

15. Barker, E.: Recommendation for key management - part 1: general, NIST Special Publication (SP) 800-57, Part1, Rev. 5, May 2020. https://csrc.nist.gov/pubs/sp/800/57/pt1/r5/final

16. BIS Innovation Hub: Project mBridge: experimenting with a multi-CBDC platform for cross-border payments. https://www.bis.org/about/bisih/topics/cbdc/mcbdc_bridge.htm

Author Index

Printed in the United States
by Baker & Taylor Publisher Services